# OPTIMISATION METHODS
## IN
# PASCAL

**Brian D. Bunday,**
B.Sc., Ph.D., F.S.S., F.I.M.A.

*School of Mathematical Sciences, University of Bradford*


**Gerald R. Garside,**
B.Sc., M.Sc., A.F.I.M.A., M.B.C.S.

*School of Computing, University of Bradford*

*Cheeney*
*1987 October.*

Edward Arnold

© B. D. Bunday and G. R. Garside, 1987

First published 1987 by
Edward Arnold (Publishers) Ltd
41 Bedford Square, London WC1B 3DQ

Edward Arnold
3 East Read Street, Baltimore,
Maryland 21202, USA

Edward Arnold (Australia) Pty Ltd
80 Waverley Road, Caulfield East,
Victoria 3145, Australia

**British Library Cataloguing in Publication Data**

Bunday, B. D
    Optimisation methods in PASCAL.
    1. Mathematical optimization—Data
    processing   2. PASCAL (Computer program
    language)
    I. Title   II. Garside, Gerald R.
    515      QA402.5

ISBN 0-7131-3615-4

Text set in 10/12pt Times Compugraphic
by Mathematical Composition Setters Ltd, Salisbury.
Printed and bound in Great Britain
by J. W. Arrowsmith, Bristol

# Preface

This book provides a first course in optimisation which should be suitable for undergraduate and postgraduate students who have a sound knowledge of $n$ variable calculus and who are also conversant with the computer language Pascal. The emphasis is placed on the thinking that transforms a theoretical idea into a practical computational procedure. Although all the methods have been made plausible, mathematical rigour has been made secondary to the main aim of producing algorithms capable of implementation on a computer.

It is hoped that the reader will make a real effort to get involved with the programs. It is not claimed that they could not be improved. In this way he or she will gain a deeper insight into the ideas underlying the methods and the practical problems that have to be solved when one tries to apply them in a real situation.

Not all methods that are available have been discussed. However, it is hoped that those that have been selected cover the more important ideas underlying optimisation procedures. Much still remains to be done and we hope that some readers will be stimulated into making their own contributions towards improving the methodology of the subject.

A few remarks about Pascal and the way in which it is used in this book are appropriate. The programs have been written in Level 0 ISO Pascal. The modular and data structuring facilities of Pascal have been used in implementing the algorithms and these, together with the comments in the code should make the programs reasonably easy to follow.

Since Pascal is a compiled language, each optimisation problem will require some modification to the code and recompilation before the problem can be solved. The parts of each program that may require such modification are indicated by the symbols {**} on the right hand side of the appropriate lines.

All the programs given in this book have been compiled and run successfully on a mainframe (CDC 180-830 using the University of Minnesota Pascal-6000 V4.0 compiler running under NOS 2.3), a minicomputer (Vax 11/750 using the Berkeley Pascal compiler running under UNIX 4.2BSD) and a microcomputer (an IBM-compatible Ericsson PC using Turbo Pascal running under DOS 2.11). The output shown in the text is that from the CDC machine.

It may be necessary or desirable to make slight alterations to the input/output instructions in the program code dependent on the host machine and whether interactive features are favoured or data and output files used. For example, on Turbo Pascal using files it will be necessary to assign file names, reset and rewrite files, include file names in read/write instructions and close files. The manner in which the programs have been written should make the points of required alteration easy to identify.

Different machines store numbers to different accuracies and will not precisely reproduce the results given here although the differences should only occur in the least significant digits.

Finally it is a pleasure to thank Mrs Valerie Hunter who transformed a rather messy manuscript into a neat and tidy typescript.

BRIAN BUNDAY AND GERALD GARSIDE
1986

# Contents

# Introduction

This book is concerned with methods for finding the optimum value (maximum or minimum) of a function $f(x_1, x_2, \ldots x_n)$ of $n$ real variables. If the function refers to the profit obtained by producing quantities $x_i$ of products $P_i$ it may well be that our desire is to maximise the function. If on the other hand it refers to costs involved in an operation we should probably want to minimise the function. From the mathematical point of view there is little point in considering both maximisation and minimisation, since maximising $f$ is equivalent to minimising $-f$. We shall normally confine ourselves to minimisation.

The values of the variables may be constrained or unconstrained. If, for example, they do indeed refer to the quantities of particular products that we can produce, there will be limits on our production capacity and the quantities that the market can absorb. Thus any solution to our optimisation problem must take account of these constraints. For convenience Part I deals with problems in which the variables are not constrained; Part II considers problems where the variables are constrained.

In any practical optimisation problem there are many overlapping phases. Modelling the physical situation under consideration so as to derive the mathematical function to be minimised, along with the constraints, if any, on the variables, is vital. Then an appropriate procedure for carrying out the minimisation has to be chosen. This procedure has to be implemented in practice and in many real situations this will involve programming a computer to carry out extensive calculations. Finally, the mathematical result has to be interpreted back in terms of the physical context of the problem.

Although it is not intended to neglect totally any of these phases, the main thrust of this book is to emphasise the procedures which are available to carry out the minimisation process, and to discuss the ways in which such procedures can be transformed into organised calculations capable of being carried out by a computer.

It is no accident that many of the important methods have developed over the last three decades, a period that has witnessed the advent of the digital computer. The methods are computer methods. It is difficult to envisage them being of any real practical value without an extremely fast and efficient calculator being available. Many main-frame computers will have optimisation packages which implement these methods. These can be very efficient and allow a wide range of problems to be solved. They can, however, be a little remote, and can be used without an appreciation of what is really going on.

The advent of the microcomputer into the home and classroom, and the increasing availability of minicomputers and mainframe machines to students, has meant that the user can get more intimately involved with the computer program.

From the student's point of view this involvement can lead to a keener appreciation of the methodology and its computer implementation. For most of the methods discussed in this book (it is not claimed that the list of such methods is exhaustive) computer programs in the language Pascal have been included. A full explanation of the derivation and coding for these programs is given and they should give the student a new insight into the real application of optimisation methods.

The programs will run on any machine for which a compiler including the Level 0 ISO Pascal features is available. The authors do not claim that the programs are the ultimate in elegance and efficiency, although they have been written using the modular and data structuring facilities of Pascal in an attempt to make them easy to follow and readable. In particular, points and their attributes in $n$ dimensions are represented as variables with the appropriate record structure to incorporate those attributes. An attempt has been made to achieve a homogeneity in style and it is hoped that this will aid the reader in program comprehension as he or she progresses through the material in this book.

# Part 1
# Unconstrained Optimisation

# 1
# Classical Methods

## 1.1 Functions of One Variable

A function $f(x)$ has a local minimum at the value $x_0$ if there exists a positive value $\delta$ such that if $|x - x_0| < \delta$, $f(x) \geqslant f(x_0)$; i.e. if there exists a neighbourhood of $x_0$ such that for all values of $x$ in this neighbourhood, $f(x)$ is at least as large as $f(x_0)$.

$f(x)$ has a global minimum at $x^*$ if $f(x) \geqslant f(x^*)$ for all values of $x$.

Figure 1.1 shows a graphical representation of a function $f(x)$. It has a local minimum at $x_0$ and a global minimum at $x^*$.

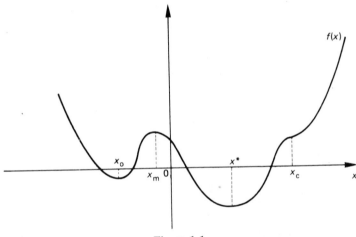

**Figure 1.1**

The classical approach to the problem of finding the values $x_0$ and $x^*$ is to find equations which must be satisfied by $x_0$ and $x^*$. The function and its derivatives represented in Fig. 1.1 are continuous, and we see that at both $x_0$ and $x^*$ the derivative $f'(x)$, the gradient of the function, is zero. Thus $x_0$ and $x^*$ will be solutions of the equation

$$f'(x) = 0. \tag{1.1}$$

The values $x_m$, at which there is a local maximum, and $x_c$, at which there is a horizontal point of inflexion also satisfy this equation. Thus equation 1.1 is only a *necessary* condition for a minimum. It is not *sufficient* for a minimum.

However, we notice that at $x_0$ and $x^*$, $f'(x)$ changes sign from negative to positive. At $x_m$ the change is from positive to negative whilst at $x_c$ the derivative does not change sign as $x$ passes through the value $x_c$. Thus at a minimum the derivative is an increasing function and since the rate of increase of $f'(x)$ is measured by the second derivative we shall expect

$$f''(x_0) > 0, \quad f''(x^*) > 0 \quad \text{while} \quad f''(x_m) < 0.$$

If, however, the second derivative is zero the situation remains ambiguous.

The intuitive results above can be put on a firmer footing by considering the Taylor series expansion of $f(x)$ about $x_0$ (or $x^*$ or $x_m$). This of course calls for continuity of $f(x)$ and its derivatives.

$$f(x_0 + h) - f(x_0) = hf'(x_0) + \frac{h^2}{2!} f''(x_0) + \cdots \tag{1.2}$$

If $x_0$ gives a minimum the left hand side is non-negative for all $h(|h| < \delta)$ however small. Thus $f'(x_0)$ must be zero and this is the necessary condition (equation 1.1). For if it were positive a sufficiently small negative $h$ value would make the right hand side negative, and if it were negative a sufficiently small positive $h$ value would make the right hand side negative.

Since the next term involves $h^2$ we see that if

$$f''(x_0) > 0 \tag{1.3}$$

we shall indeed have a minimum. If $f'(x_m) = 0$ and $f''(x_m) < 0$ then by similar arguments $x_m$ gives a maximum. We should have to compare $f(x_0)$ and $f(x^*)$ to distinguish between the local and the global minimum.

**Example 1**

Examine the nature of the turning points of the function $f(x) = x^3 - 2x^2 + x + 1$.

$$f'(x) = 3x^2 - 4x + 1 = 0$$

when

$$(3x - 1)(x - 1) = 0$$

$$\text{i.e.} \quad x = \tfrac{1}{3} \quad \text{or} \quad x = 1.$$

When $x = \tfrac{1}{3}$, $f'(x)$ changes sign from positive to negative. When $x = 1$, $f'(x)$ changes sign from negative to positive. Thus $x = \tfrac{1}{3}$ gives a maximum and $x = 1$ gives a minimum.

In this example it might be easier to resolve the situation by considering the second derivative

$$f''(x) = 6x - 4.$$

$$f''(\tfrac{1}{3}) = -2 \text{ is negative}; \quad x = \tfrac{1}{3} \text{ gives a maximum.}$$

$$f''(1) = 2 \text{ is positive}; \quad x = 1 \text{ gives a minimum.}$$

The ambiguous case where $f''(x) = 0$ can be settled when it arises by continuing the Taylor series expansion:

$$f(x_0 + h) - f(x_0) = hf'(x_0) + \frac{h^2}{2!} f''(x_0) + \frac{h^3}{3!} f'''(x_0) + \frac{h^4}{4!} f''''(x_0) + \cdots$$

We can then derive the rule:

if $f(x)$ and its derivatives are continuous then $x_0$ is an extreme point (maximum or minimum) if and only if $n$ is even, where $n$ is the order of the first non-vanishing derivative at $x_0$. If $f''(x_0) < 0$, $x_0$ gives a maximum; if $f''(x_0) > 0$, $x_0$ gives a minimum.

**Example 2**

Find the turning point of $f(x) = (x - 1)^6$.

$$f'(x) = 6(x - 1)^5 = 0 \quad \text{when } x = 1.$$

$f^6(1) = 6!$ is the first non-vanishing derivative at $x = 1$. Thus $f(x)$ has a minimum when $x = 1$.

## 1.2 Functions of $n$ Variables

We consider the function of $n$ real variables

$$f(x_1, x_2, x_3, ..., x_n) = f(\mathbf{x}).$$

The point with co-ordinates $(x_1, x_2, ..., x_n)$ in $n$ dimensional Euclidean space is denoted by the column vector $\mathbf{x}$. The gradient of the function, i.e. the vector with components $(\partial f/\partial x_1, \partial f/\partial x_2, ..., \partial f/\partial x_n)$ is denoted by $\nabla f(\mathbf{x})$ or sometimes $\mathbf{g}(\mathbf{x})$. The Hessian matrix of $f(\mathbf{x})$ is denoted by $\mathbf{G}(\mathbf{x})$ and is the symmetric $n \times n$ matrix with elements

$$G_{ij} = \frac{\partial^2 f}{\partial x_i \partial x_j}.$$

$f(\mathbf{x})$ has a local minimum at $\mathbf{x}_0$ if there exists a neighbourhood of $\mathbf{x}_0$ such that $f(\mathbf{x})$ is at least as large as $f(\mathbf{x}_0)$ for all points in the neighbourhood; i.e. there exists a positive $\delta$ such that for $|\mathbf{x} - \mathbf{x}_0| < \delta$, $f(\mathbf{x}) \geqslant f(\mathbf{x}_0)$.

For the global minimum $\mathbf{x}^*$, $f(\mathbf{x}) \geqslant f(\mathbf{x}^*)$ for all $\mathbf{x}$.

With these definitions and certain differentiability assumptions we can generalise equation 1.2 to give

$$f(\mathbf{x}_0 + \mathbf{h}) - f(\mathbf{x}_0) = \sum_{i=1}^{n} h_i \frac{\partial f}{\partial x_i}(\mathbf{x}_0) + \frac{1}{2!} \sum_{i=1}^{n} \sum_{j=1}^{n} h_i h_j \frac{\partial^2 f}{\partial x_i \partial x_j}(\mathbf{x}_0) + \cdots$$

$$= \mathbf{h}^T \nabla f(\mathbf{x}_0) + \tfrac{1}{2} \mathbf{h}^T \mathbf{G}(\mathbf{x}_0)\mathbf{h} + \cdots \tag{1.4}$$

Then if $\mathbf{x}_0$ gives a minimum for $f(\mathbf{x})$ each of the first partial derivatives $\partial f/\partial x_i$ $(i = 1, ..., n)$ must vanish at $\mathbf{x}_0$. For if not, by choosing $h_i$ appropriately we could make $f(\mathbf{x}_0 + \mathbf{h}) - f(\mathbf{x}_0)$ negative.

Thus a necessary condition for a minimum at $\mathbf{x}_0$ is

$$\nabla f(\mathbf{x}_0) = \mathbf{0} \tag{1.5}$$

$$\text{i.e.} \quad \frac{\partial f(\mathbf{x}_0)}{\partial x_i} = 0 \quad (i = 1, ..., n). \tag{1.6}$$

Then the sign of $f(\mathbf{x}_0 + \mathbf{h}) - f(\mathbf{x}_0)$ is determined by that of

$$\tfrac{1}{2}\mathbf{h}^T\mathbf{G}(\mathbf{x}_0)\mathbf{h}. \tag{1.7}$$

If $\mathbf{G}(\mathbf{x}_0)$ is positive definite this is positive for all $\mathbf{h}$. Thus sufficient conditions for a minimum are

$$\nabla f(\mathbf{x}_0) = \mathbf{0}, \quad \mathbf{G}(\mathbf{x}_0) \text{ positive definite.} \tag{1.8}$$

For a maximum we require

$$\nabla f(\mathbf{x}_m) = \mathbf{0}, \quad \mathbf{G}(\mathbf{x}_m) \text{ negative definite.} \tag{1.9}$$

**Example 1**

Examine the extreme point(s) of

$$f(\mathbf{x}) = x_1^2 + x_2^2 + x_3^2 - 4x_1 - 8x_2 - 12x_3 + 100.$$

$$\nabla f(\mathbf{x}) = \begin{pmatrix} 2x_1 - 4 \\ 2x_2 - 8 \\ 2x_3 - 12 \end{pmatrix} = \mathbf{0} \quad \text{when } x_1 = 2, \ x_2 = 4, \ x_3 = 6.$$

$$\mathbf{G}(\mathbf{x}) = \begin{pmatrix} 2 & 0 & 0 \\ 0 & 2 & 0 \\ 0 & 0 & 2 \end{pmatrix} \quad \begin{array}{l} \text{is positive definite. All the} \\ \text{eigenvalues are positive at 2.} \end{array}$$

Thus (2, 4, 6) is a minimum of $f(\mathbf{x})$.

## 1.3 Newton's Method

For functions of one variable the classical approach finds the values of $x$ at the turning points of $f(x)$ as the solutions of the equation

$$f'(x) = 0.$$

This equation may not be easy to solve. We therefore consider briefly a numerical method for its solution. A rough sketch of the curve $y = f'(x)$ may allow us to obtain an approximate solution. If we can find two values $a$ and $b$ such that $f'(a)$

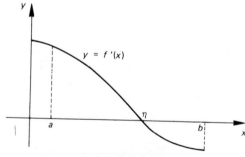

**Figure 1.2**

and $f'(b)$ have opposite signs, then, subject to certain continuity assumptions, there will be a root $\eta$ of the equation, with $a < \eta < b$ (see Fig. 1.2).

Newton's method enables us to improve on a relatively crude approximation to a root of the equation $\phi(x) = 0$. [$\phi(x) \equiv f'(x)$ in the context of our problems.] In Fig. 1.3, $x_0$, the $x$ co-ordinate of P, is an approximation to the root of $\phi(x) = 0$. Let PT be the tangent at P on the curve and T the point where the tangent meets the $x$- axis. Then in general OT will be a better approximation to the root which is at K.

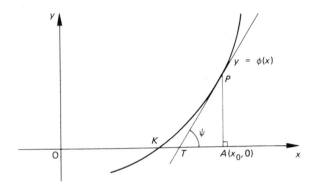

**Figure 1.3**

Now $OT = OA - TA = x_0 - TA$. Also

$$\frac{PA}{TA} = \tan \psi = \phi'(x_0).$$

$$\therefore \quad TA = \frac{PA}{\phi'(x_0)} = \frac{\phi(x_0)}{\phi'(x_0)}$$

$$\therefore \quad x_1 = x_0 - \frac{\phi(x_0)}{\phi'(x_0)}$$

We can similarly improve upon $x_1$,

$$x_2 = x_1 - \frac{\phi(x_1)}{\phi'(x_1)}$$

and in general

$$x_{r+1} = x_r - \frac{\phi(x_r)}{\phi'(x_r)}. \tag{1.10}$$

The recalculations can be continued until two successive approximations agree to the required accuracy. The program given carries out this algorithm. It is general in the sense that $\phi(x)$ and $\phi'(x)$ are evaluated by the FUNCTION *phi* and the FUNCTION *phidash* respectively. The accuracy of the solution can be set by giving *epsilon* a sufficiently small value. $f(x)$ [$f'(x) = \phi(x)$] is evaluated by the FUNCTION *f*.

```
PROGRAM Turningpoint (input,output);
{ To find a turning point of the function f(x) }
{ using Newton's Method.                       }
CONST
  fw=8 ; dp=2;  { Output format constants }                      {**}

VAR
  epsilon : real;  { Required accuracy of solution }
  z, x : real;     { Previous and current iterated values }
  r : integer;     { Iteration counter }

FUNCTION f (x:real): real;
BEGIN  f := x*x/2.0 - sin(x)  END;                               {**}

FUNCTION phi (x:real): real;
BEGIN  phi := x - cos(x)  END;                                   {**}

FUNCTION phidash (x:real): real;
BEGIN  phidash := 1 + sin(x)  END;                              {**}

BEGIN  { Main Program }
  writeln('PROGRAM TO FIND A TURNING POINT OF F(X)');
  writeln; write('ACCURACY REQUIRED =');
  read(epsilon); writeln(epsilon:fw:dp);
  write('INITIAL VALUE =');
  read(z); writeln(z:fw:dp); writeln;
  writeln('SUCCESSIVE APPROXIMATIONS'); writeln;
  writeln('   R  ', '  ':fw-4, 'X[R]', '  ':fw-4, 'X[R+1]');
  r:=0;
  { Commence iterative process }
  REPEAT
    x:=z; z := x - phi(x)/phidash(x);
    writeln(r:4, '  ', x:fw:dp, '  ', z:fw:dp);
    r:=r+1
  UNTIL abs(z-x)<epsilon;
  writeln; writeln('FINAL SOLUTION');
  IF phidash(z)>0.0 THEN write('MINIMUM') ELSE write('MAXIMUM');
  writeln(' =', f(x):fw:dp,'    AT',z:fw:dp)
END.
```

## Example 1

Find the minimum of $y = \frac{1}{2} x^2 - \sin x$.

The FUNCTIONs as listed are appropriate.

$$f(x) = \frac{1}{2} x^2 - \sin x$$

$$\phi(x) = f'(x) = x - \cos x = 0 \quad \text{when } x = 0 \cdot 7391$$

from the output below.

$$\phi'(x) = 1 + \sin x \quad \text{which is positive when } x = 0 \cdot 7391.$$

Thus the minimum of $y$ is $-0 \cdot 4005$ when $x = 0 \cdot 7391$ to 4 decimal places.

```
PROGRAM TO FIND A TURNING POINT OF F(X)

ACCURACY REQUIRED =    0.000010000
INITIAL VALUE =   0.500000000

SUCCESSIVE APPROXIMATIONS

    R         X[R]            X[R+1]
    0     0.500000000     0.755222417
    1     0.755222417     0.739141666
    2     0.739141666     0.739085134
    3     0.739085134     0.739085133


FINAL SOLUTION
MINIMUM =   -0.400488612     AT    0.739085133
```

Newton's method will fail if the first approximation to the root is such that the value of $\phi(x_0)/\phi'(x_0)$ is not small enough (see Fig. 1.4). The usual remedy is to improve the initial approximation to the root when the iterations will generally converge.

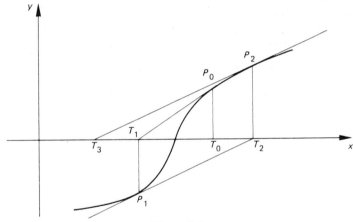

**Figure 1.4**

## Exercises 1

**1**   Find the maximum and minimum values of $f(x) = x(x-1)^2$.

**2**   Find the maximum and minimum values of $f(x) = x/(x^2+1)$.

**3**   Show that the minimum value of $a \cos \theta + b \sin \theta$ is $-\sqrt{(a^2+b^2)}$. Can you do this without involving the derivative?

**4**   An isosceles triangle of vertical angle $2\theta$ is inscribed in a circle of radius $r$. Find an expression for the area of the triangle as a function of $\theta$ and show that this is a maximum when the triangle is equilateral.

**5**   Consider the function $f(x) = x^{2/3} - 1$. Sketch its graph. Show that $f(x)$ has a minimum when $x = 0$. What is the value of $f'(x)$ when $x = 0$? Does $f'(x)$ change sign as $x$ increases through the value 0?

**6** Consider the function $f(x) = |x|$. Find its minimum value. What can you say about $f'(x)$ at this value?

**7** Find the minimum value of $-e^{-x} \sinh(x/2)$.

**8** When a production run is made to produce a quantity of a certain commodity there is a set up cost of £$K$. The commodity is held in stock until it is used and the cost of holding 1 unit in stock is £$S$ per unit time. The commodity is used at a uniform rate $R$ per unit time. Show that if it is produced regularly in lots of size $x$ at time intervals $x/R$ then the cost per unit time of running this system is

$$C = \frac{KR}{x} + \frac{Sx}{2}.$$

Show that $C$ is minimised by choosing $x = \sqrt{2KR/S}$.

**9** Examine the turning values of $f(x) = x^4 - 14x^3 + 60x^2 - 70x$. [This simple looking example illustrates one of the problems with the classical approach. We have to solve the equation $f'(x) = 0$. In this case it is a cubic which does not easily factorise. Paradoxically one way to proceed might be to use one of the numerical methods of the next chapter to minimise the function $\phi(x) = [f'(x)]^2$. When $\phi(x)$ is minimised, its minimum will be zero and we will have a solution to $f'(x) = 0$.]

**10** Examine the turning points of $f(\mathbf{x}) = x_1^2 + 4x_1x_2 + 5x_2^2$.

**11** Examine the turning points of $-x_1^2 - 6x_2^2 - 23x_3^2 - 4x_1x_2 + 6x_1x_3 + 20x_2x_3$.

**12** $f(\mathbf{x})$ is the quadratic function

$$f(\mathbf{x}) = a + \mathbf{b}^T\mathbf{x} + \tfrac{1}{2}\mathbf{x}^T\mathbf{G}\mathbf{x}$$

where $a$ is a constant, $\mathbf{b}$ is a vector independent of $\mathbf{x}$, and $\mathbf{G}$ is a positive definite symmetric matrix independent of $\mathbf{x}$.
Show that

$$\mathbf{x}^* = -\mathbf{G}^{-1}\mathbf{b}.$$

**13** Show that the function $f(\mathbf{x}) = (x_1 - a)^2 + (x_2 - b)^2 + (x_3 - c)^2$ has a minimum at $(a, b, c)$.

**14** $f(\mathbf{x}) = f(x_1, x_2)$ has a minimum at $(x_1^*, x_2^*)$. Show that the conditions 1.8 become

$$\frac{\partial f}{\partial x_1}(x_1^*, x_2^*) = 0; \quad \frac{\partial f}{\partial x_2}(x_1^*, x_2^*) = 0,$$

$$\frac{\partial^2 f}{\partial x_1^2}(x_1^*, x_2^*) > 0,$$

$$\frac{\partial^2 f}{\partial x_1^2}(x_1^*, x_2^*) \frac{\partial^2 f}{\partial x_2^2}(x_1^*, x_2^*) - \left[\frac{\partial^2 f}{\partial x_1 x_2}(x_1^*, x_2^*)\right]^2 > 0.$$

**15**  A firm manufactures two similar products I and II. The costs of production are $c_i q_i$ ($i = 1, 2$) where $c_i$ are constants and the $q_i$ are the sales quantities of the two products. The latter are dependent on the prices ($p_1$ and $p_2$) of the two products. Analysis of past sales data has yielded the empirical formulae

$$q_1 = a_1 p_2 - b_1 p_1$$
$$q_2 = a_2 p_1 - b_2 p_2$$

where $a_1$, $a_2$, $b_1$, $b_2$ are positive constants. It is required to find the values of the prices $p_1$ and $p_2$ which maximise the total profits.

Find equations for $p_1$ and $p_2$ which maximise the profit and solve them. Show that if the solutions to these equations are positive and $4b_1 b_2 > (a_1 + a_2)^2$ these equations yield optimal prices.

**16**  Find the minimum of $e^{-x} - \cos x$.

# 2
# Search Methods—Functions of One Variable

## 2.1 Introduction

Question 9 in Exercises 1 illustrates a common problem that arises with the classical approach. We cannot easily solve the equation $f'(x) = 0$, and have to resort to numerical methods. In this chapter we consider some simple numerical procedures which directly locate the minimum of a function $f(x)$.

With such methods we literally search for the minimum of $f(x)$ in some range $a < x < b$ in which we suspect the minimum lies, by evaluating the function at chosen points in the interval. This strategy may be the only one available. For instance the cost of running a chemical process may depend on the operating temperature. The plant engineer knows that cost is a function of $T$ although he may not have an explicit function. He can, however, experiment and run the process at various temperatures, and hence find the cost at these temperatures and hope in this way to locate the minimum of the cost function, and the temperature at which to run the process for least cost.

We may try to find the position of the minimum by a point approximating it with sufficient accuracy, or we may determine a (short) interval in which the minimum is located. We try to achieve our objective as efficiently as possible, i.e., with as few function evaluations as possible. In the example cited it may not be possible to control the temperature precisely and an accuracy of $1°C$ or even $10°C$ may be quite acceptable. However, since it costs money to do an experiment the plant engineer will want to obtain this accuracy with as few experiments as possible.

We assume that we have two values $a$ and $b$ which specify an interval, maybe a very crude one, in which the true minimum point lies, and that within this interval the function is unimodal, i.e. has one minimum at $x^*$. Thus our function has a form similar to that shown in Fig 2.1. For such a function, if we know its value at three points

$$x_1, x_2, x_3 \quad \text{with} \quad a < x_1 < x_2 < x_3 < b$$

and $f(x_2) < f(x_1)$ and $f(x_2) < f(x_3)$ then

$$x_1 < x^* < x_3.$$

Thus we would have reduced the interval of uncertainty for the position of $x^*$ from $(a, b)$ to $(x_1, x_3)$.

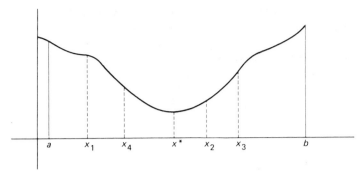

**Figure 2.1**

## 2.2 Fibonacci Search

Suppose that we want to locate the minimum as accurately as possible, i.e. with the shortest possible interval of uncertainty, but can only afford $n$ function evaluations. How should we choose the $n$ values at which we evaluate the function? In the first place it would seem clear that we should not make the decision for all the points at the outset of the exercise. Rather, we should let the function values we obtain from the early experiments determine the position of subsequent points. In effect as we obtain function values, we obtain information about the function and the position of its minimum. We use this information to guide us in our search.

Thus suppose, as in Fig. 2.1, that we have an interval of uncertainty $(x_1, x_3)$ and have a function value $f(x_2)$ within this interval. If we could carry out just one further experiment at the point $x_4$, where should we place $x_4$ so as to obtain the smallest possible interval of uncertainty?

Suppose $x_2 - x_1 = L$ and $x_3 - x_2 = R$ with $L > R$ (as in Fig. 2.1) and these will be fixed if $x_1$, $x_2$ and $x_3$ are known. If $x_4$ is placed in $(x_1, x_2)$ then

(i) if $f(x_4) < f(x_2)$ the new uncertainty interval will be $(x_1, x_2)$ of length $x_2 - x_1 = L$.

(ii) if $f(x_4) > f(x_2)$ the new uncertainty interval will be $(x_4, x_3)$ of length $x_3 - x_4$.

Since we do not know which of these outcomes will occur we choose $x_4$ so as to minimise the larger of $x_3 - x_4$ and $x_2 - x_1$. We achieve this by making $x_3 - x_4$ and $x_2 - x_1$ equal, i.e., by placing $x_4$ symmetrically in the interval with respect to $x_2$, the point already in the interval. Any other position for $x_4$ *could* result in an interval longer than $L$. Placing $x_4$ in this position means that we are not gambling on getting a particular outcome.

If we then found that we were allowed one more evaluation we should apply the same strategy to the interval $(x_1, x_2)$ in which we already have the value at $x_4$, (i), or $(x_4, x_3)$ in which we already have the value at $x_2$, (ii). Thus the strategy is clear once we have started. We place the next point within the interval being searched symmetrically with respect to the point already there. Paradoxically, to see how we should start we have to consider how we will finish.

At the $n$th evaluation we place the $n$th point symmetrically with respect to the $(n-1)$th point. The position of this latter point is in principle under our control.

In order to get the greatest interval reduction at this stage it should bisect the penultimate interval. Then $x_n$ would coincide with $x_{n-1}$. We appear to have a problem here since no new information is being obtained. In practice $x_{n-1}$ and $x_n$ are separated just sufficiently to enable us to decide which half, left or right, is the final uncertainty interval. They are placed at a distance $\varepsilon/2$ either side of the middle of $L_{n-1}$; $\varepsilon$ may be our choice or it may be the minimum separation of two points that is possible. (Our plant engineer could only control temperature to the nearest degree perhaps, then $\varepsilon = 1$.)

The interval of uncertainty will be of length $L_n$ and

$$L_{n-1} = 2L_n - \varepsilon. \quad \text{(See Fig. 2.2, bottom layer.)}$$

At this preceding stage $x_{n-1}$ and $x_{n-2}$ must be symmetrically placed within $L_{n-2}$ and distant $L_{n-1}$ from the ends of that interval. Thus

$$L_{n-2} = L_{n-1} + L_n. \quad \text{(See Fig. 2.2, middle layer.)}$$

N.B. As drawn it is evidently $x_{n-2}$ which remains as the included point at the penultimate stage.

Similarly at the previous stage

$$L_{n-3} = L_{n-2} + L_{n-1}. \quad \text{(See Fig. 2.2, top layer.)}$$

In general

$$L_{j-1} = L_j + L_{j+1} \quad \text{for } 1 < j < n. \tag{2.1}$$

Thus

$$L_{n-1} = 2L_n - \varepsilon$$
$$L_{n-2} = L_{n-1} + L_n = 3L_n - \varepsilon$$

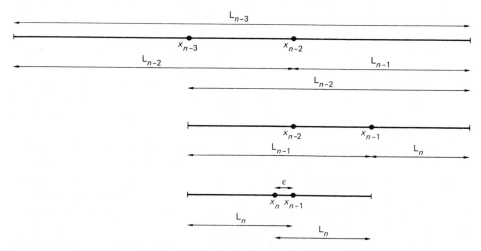

**Figure 2.2**

$$L_{n-3} = L_{n-2} + L_{n-1} = 5L_n - 2\varepsilon$$
$$L_{n-4} = L_{n-3} + L_{n-2} = 8L_n - 3\varepsilon \quad \text{etc.}$$

If we define the Fibonacci sequence of numbers by $F_0 = 1$, $F_1 = 1$ and $F_k = F_{k-1} + F_{k-2}$ for $k = 2, 3, \ldots$ then

$$L_{n-j} = F_{j+1}L_n - F_{j-1}\varepsilon, \quad j = 1, 2, \ldots, n-1. \tag{2.2}$$

If the original interval $(a, b)$ is of length $L_1(= b - a)$

$$L_1 = F_n L_n - \varepsilon F_{n-2}$$

$$\text{i.e.} \quad L_n = \frac{L_1}{F_n} + \varepsilon \frac{F_{n-2}}{F_n}. \tag{2.3}$$

Thus with $n$ function evaluations we reduce the original uncertainty interval to a fraction $1/F_n$ of its value (neglecting $\varepsilon$), and this is the best that can be done.

(i)   $x_4 < x_2$
      $f_4 < f_2$
      New interval $(x_1, x_2)$ with $x_4$ included.

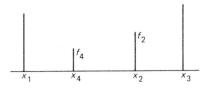

(ii)   $x_4 > x_2$
       $f_4 < f_2$
       New interval $(x_2, x_3)$ with $x_4$ included.

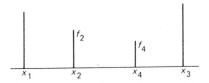

(iii)   $x_4 < x_2$
        $f_4 > f_2$
        New interval $(x_4, x_3)$ with $x_2$ included.

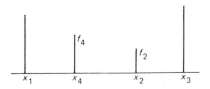

(iv)   $x_4 > x_2$
       $f_4 > f_2$
       New interval $(x_1, x_4)$ with $x_2$ included.

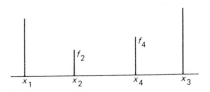

N.B.   The handling of cases (i)–(iv) is explicitly indicated by comments in the following program.

**Figure 2.3**

Once the search has begun it is easy to continue using our symmetry rule. Thus we need to find the position of the first point which is placed $L_2$ units from one end of the original interval. It does not matter which end because the second point is placed $L_2$ units from the other end by our rule.

$$L_2 = F_{n-1}L_n - \varepsilon F_{n-3}$$

$$= F_{n-1}\frac{L_1}{F_n} + \varepsilon \frac{(F_{n-1}F_{n-2} - F_n F_{n-3})}{F_n} \quad \text{by (2.3)}$$

$$= \frac{F_{n-1}}{F_n}L_1 + \frac{(-1)^n \varepsilon}{F_n}. \tag{2.4}$$

(See Question 2 in Exercises 2).

Once this first point is located we have no further use for the Fibonacci numbers. The $\varepsilon$ we use may be dictated by practical considerations or it may be arbitrary. It needs to be less than $L_1/F_{n+1}$ or else we are wasting function evaluations. (See Question 3 in Exercises 2.)

Thus the Fibonacci search, so called because of the natural occurrence of the Fibonacci numbers, is an iterative search routine. When we search the interval $(x_1, x_3)$ with $x_2$ already in this interval we always choose our next point $x_4$ so that $x_3 - x_4 = x_2 - x_1$ or $x_4 - x_1 = x_3 - x_2$, i.e.,

$$x_4 = x_1 - x_2 + x_3. \tag{2.5}$$

If $f(x_2) = f_2$ and $f(x_4) = f_4$ there are four cases to consider (see Fig. 2.3).

The program given incorporates the steps indicated. The function being considered is evidently $f(x) = x^4 - 14x^3 + 60x^2 - 70x$ (see FUNCTION $f$).

```
PROGRAM FibonacciSearch (input,output);
CONST
  fwx=14; dpx=8;  { Output format constants for x-values }        {**}
  fwf=14; dpf=8;  { Output format constants for function values } {**}
  fwn=4;          { Output field width for n }                    {**}
VAR
  n : integer;              { Number of function evaluations allowed }
  epsilon : real;           { Distance between final pair of x-values }
  a, b : real;              { End points of initial interval (a,b) }
  fib0, fib1,               { Used in the computation }
  fib2 : integer;           { of Fibonacci numbers      }
  x1, x2, x3, x4 : real;    { x-values for the current interval }
  f2, f4 : real;            { Function values at x2 and x4 }
  k : integer;

FUNCTION f (x:real): real;
BEGIN
  f := (((x - 14.0)*x + 60.0)*x - 70.0)*x                         {**}
END; { f }

PROCEDURE inputdata;
```

```
BEGIN  write(´     NUMBER OF FUNCTION EVALUATIONS, N =´);
  read(n); writeln(n:fwn);
  write(´     EPSILON =´); read(epsilon); writeln(epsilon:fwx:dpx);
  write(´     INTERVAL LIMITS (A, B) =´);
  read(a,b); writeln(´   ( ´, a:fwx:dpx, ´   , ´, b:fwx:dpx, ´ )´)
END; { inputdata }

BEGIN   { Main Program }
  writeln;  writeln(´     FIBONACCI SEARCH´);   writeln;
  inputdata; writeln; writeln(´ ´:fwx-8, ´CURRENT INTERVAL´);
  { Compute the (n-1)th and nth Fibonacci numbers }
  fib0:=1; fib1:=1;
  FOR k:=2 TO n DO
  BEGIN fib2:=fib1+fib0; fib0:=fib1; fib1:=fib2 END;
  { Compute initial values of x1, x2, x3 and f2 }
  x1:=a; x3:=b;
  IF odd(n) THEN epsilon:=-epsilon;
  x2 := a + ((b-a)*fib0 + epsilon)/fib1;   f2:=f(x2);
  FOR k:=2 TO n DO
  BEGIN  writeln(x1:fwx:dpx, x3:fwx:dpx);
    x4:=x1-x2+x3; f4:=f(x4);
    IF f4<f2 THEN
    BEGIN { Cases (i) and (ii) of Fig. 2.3 }
      IF x4<x2 THEN x3:=x2   { Case (i) }
              ELSE x1:=x2; { Case (ii) }
      x2:=x4; f2:=f4
    END
    ELSE   { Cases (iii) and (iv) of Fig. 2.3 }
      IF x4<x2 THEN x1:=x4 { Case (iii) }
              ELSE x3:=x4 { Case (iv) }
  END;
  writeln; writeln(´ ´:fwx-8, ´FINAL INTERVAL´);
  writeln(x1:fwx:dpx, x3:fwx:dpx); writeln;
  writeln(´   MINIMUM FUNCTION VALUE´, f2:fwf:dpf)
END.  { FibonacciSearch }
```

**Example 1**

Use Fibonacci search with 10 function evaluations to find the minimum of
$f(x) = 2x^2 - e^x$ in the range $(0, 1)$.

With $\varepsilon$ chosen as $10^{-8}$ the computer output appears below.

Note that the final interval of uncertainty has length

$$0 \cdot 359\,550\,56 - 0 \cdot 348\,314\,61 = 0 \cdot 011\,235\,95 \approx \tfrac{1}{89} = \frac{1}{F_{10}}.$$

With six figure accuracy the minimum is at $x^* = 0 \cdot 357\,403$ with $f(x^*) = -1 \cdot 174\,138$.

```
FIBONACCI SEARCH

NUMBER OF FUNCTION EVALUATIONS, N =  10
EPSILON =     0.00000001
INTERVAL LIMITS (A, B) = (     0.00000000  ,      1.00000000 )
```

```
    CURRENT INTERVAL
0.00000000    1.00000000
0.00000000    0.61797753
0.23595506    0.61797753
0.23595506    0.47191011
0.32584270    0.47191011
0.32584270    0.41573034
0.32584270    0.38202247
0.34831461    0.38202247
0.34831461    0.37078651

    FINAL INTERVAL
0.34831461    0.35955056

MINIMUM FUNCTION VALUE    −1.17413215
```

### Example 2

Find the minimum of $f(x) = x^4 - 14x^3 + 60x^2 - 70x$ in the range $(0, 2)$. Use 20 function evaluations. See Question 9 of Exercises 1.

With $n = 20$, $\varepsilon = 10^{-8}$, the output is given below.

```
FIBONACCI SEARCH

NUMBER OF FUNCTION EVALUATIONS, N =   20
EPSILON =    0.00000001
INTERVAL LIMITS (A, B) = (     0.00000000   ,    2.00000000 )

    CURRENT INTERVAL
0.00000000    2.00000000
0.00000000    1.23606797
0.47213594    1.23606797
0.47213594    0.94427188
0.65247579    0.94427188
0.65247579    0.83281564
0.72135940    0.83281564
0.76393203    0.83281564
0.76393203    0.80650466
0.76393203    0.79024301
0.77398136    0.79024301
0.77398136    0.78403070
0.77781838    0.78403070
0.77781838    0.78165540
0.77928010    0.78165540
0.78019368    0.78165540
0.78019368    0.78110725
0.78055911    0.78110725
0.78074182    0.78110725

    FINAL INTERVAL
0.78074182    0.78092454

MINIMUM FUNCTION VALUE    −24.36960152
```

## 2.3  Golden Section Search

It is not always possible to specify in advance how many function evaluations will be made. We need this number in Fibonacci search in order to determine $L_2$, the position of the first experiment (see equation 2.4).

The Golden Section search is nearly as efficient as the Fibonacci search but does not require $n$, the number of function evaluations, to be specified at the outset. When we have made $j$ evaluations, then, by the same reasoning as before we have that

$$L_{j-1} = L_j + L_{j+1} \quad \text{(see equation 2.1).} \tag{2.6}$$

However, if $n$ is not known we cannot use the condition $L_{n-1} = 2L_n - \varepsilon$. If we keep the ratio of successive intervals constant,

$$\frac{L_{j-1}}{L_j} = \frac{L_j}{L_{j+1}} = \frac{L_{j+1}}{L_{j+2}} \text{ etc.} = \tau, \tag{2.7}$$

then

$$\frac{L_{j-1}}{L_j} = 1 + \frac{L_{j+1}}{L_j},$$

i.e., $\tau = 1 + 1/\tau$.

$$\therefore \quad \tau^2 - \tau - 1 = 0 \quad \text{whence} \quad \tau = \frac{1 + \sqrt{5}}{2} \approx 1 \cdot 618\ 033\ 989.$$

Then

$$\frac{L_{j-1}}{L_{j+1}} = \tau^2, \quad \frac{L_{j-2}}{L_{j+1}} = \tau^3 \text{ etc.}$$

$$\therefore \quad \frac{L_1}{L_n} = \tau^{n-1}.$$

$$\therefore \quad L_n = \frac{L_1}{\tau^{n-1}}. \tag{2.8}$$

The results of the two function evaluations being considered will determine which interval is to be investigated further. This interval will contain one of the previous points and the next point is placed symmetrically with respect to this. The first point is placed at a distance $L_1/\tau$ from one end, the second the same distance from the other end. Since

$$\underset{n \to \infty}{\text{Limit}} \ \frac{F_{n-1}}{F_n} = \frac{1}{\tau}, \quad \text{(see Question 2, Exercises 2),}$$

we see from equation 2.4 that Golden Section search is a limiting form of Fibonacci search. The name Golden Section comes from the ratio in equation 2.7. We see that $L_{j-1}$ is divided into two parts such that the ratio of the whole to the greater part is equal to the ratio of the greater part to the smaller part, the so called Golden Ratio.

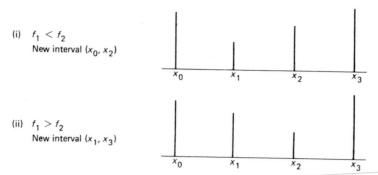

(i)  $f_1 < f_2$
New interval $(x_0, x_2)$

(ii)  $f_1 > f_2$
New interval $(x_1, x_3)$

N.B.   The handling of cases (i) and (ii) is explicitly indicated by comments in the following program.

**Figure 2.4**

Thus if we search the interval $(x_0, x_3)$ and have two function values $f_1$ and $f_2$ at $x_1$ and $x_2$ we have two cases to consider (see Fig. 2.4).

The following program implements the Golden Section search. The accuracy given can of course be varied by the choice of *epsilon* read by the PROCEDURE *inputdata*. When applied to the function $f(x) = -e^{-x} \ln(x)$ the output is given below. The interval searched is $(0, 2)$.

The true minimum is at $1 \cdot 763\,222\,11$ with function value $-0 \cdot 097\,260\,131\,3$.

```
PROGRAM GoldenSectionSearch (input,output);
CONST
   fwx=14; dpx=8;   { Output format constants for x-values }        {**}
   fwf=14; dpf=8;   { Output format constants for function values } {**}

VAR
   a, b : real;              { End points of initial interval (a,b) }
   epsilon : real;           { Maximum width of final interval }
   x0, x1, x2, x3 : real;    { x-values for current interval }
   f1, f2 : real;            { Function values at x1 and x2 }
   dx : real;                { Width of current interval }
   t,                        { Interval ratio (1.0+sqrt(5.0))/2.0 }
   t1, t2 : real;

FUNCTION f (x:real): real;
BEGIN
   f := -exp(-x)*ln(x)                                               {**}
END; { f }

PROCEDURE inputdata;
BEGIN  write('     INTERVAL LIMITS (A, B) =');
   read(a,b); writeln(' ( ', a:fwx:dpx, '   , ', b:fwx:dpx, ' )');
   write('    MAXIMUM WIDTH OF FINAL INTERVAL =');
   read(epsilon); writeln(epsilon:fwx:dpx)
END; { inputdata }
```

```
BEGIN  { Main Program }
  writeln;  writeln('    GOLDEN SECTION SEARCH');  writeln;
  inputdata; writeln; writeln(' ':fwx-8, 'CURRENT INTERVAL');
  { Compute Golden Ratio and initial values of x0, x1, x2, x3 }
  { and f1, f2                                                 }
  t := (1.0+sqrt(5.0))/2.0;  t2:=1/t;  t1:=1.0-t2;  dx:=b-a;
  x0:=a;  x1:=a+t1*dx;  x2:=a+t2*dx;  x3:=b;  f1:=f(x1);  f2:=f(x2);
  REPEAT  { Until interval is small enough }
    writeln(x0:fwx:dpx, x3:fwx:dpx);
    IF f2>f1 THEN  { Case (i) of Fig. 2.4 }
    BEGIN  dx:=x2-x0;  x3:=x2;  x2:=x1;
      x1 := x0+t1*dx;  f2:=f1;  f1:=f(x1)
    END
    ELSE  { Case (ii) of Fig. 2.4 }
    BEGIN  dx:=x3-x1;  x0:=x1;  x1:=x2;
      x2 := x0+t2*dx;  f1:=f2;  f2:=f(x2)
    END
  UNTIL  dx<epsilon;
  writeln; writeln(' ':fwx-8, 'FINAL INTERVAL');
  writeln(x0:fwx:dpx, x3:fwx:dpx); writeln;
  writeln('   MINIMUM FUNCTION VALUE', f2:fwf:dpf)
END. { GoldenSectionSearch }
```

```
GOLDEN SECTION SEARCH

INTERVAL LIMITS (A, B) = (       0.00000000  ,      2.00000000 )
MAXIMUM WIDTH OF FINAL INTERVAL =      0.00005000

    CURRENT INTERVAL
0.00000000     2.00000000
0.76393202     2.00000000
1.23606798     2.00000000
1.52786405     2.00000000
1.70820393     2.00000000
1.70820393     1.88854382
1.70820393     1.81966011
1.70820393     1.77708764
1.73451517     1.77708764
1.75077641     1.77708764
1.75077641     1.76703764
1.75698765     1.76703764
1.76082640     1.76703764
1.76082640     1.76466516
1.76229268     1.76466516
1.76229268     1.76375895
1.76285274     1.76375895
1.76285274     1.76341281
1.76306667     1.76341281
1.76306667     1.76328060
1.76314838     1.76328060
1.76319889     1.76328060
1.76319889     1.76324939
```

```
FINAL INTERVAL
1.76319889     1.76323010

MINIMUM FUNCTION VALUE    -0.09726013
```

## 2.4  The Curve Fitting Approach

In the previous two sections, we tried to determine a *small* interval in which the minimum of the function was located. In the next two sections a different approach is adopted. We use a few function values, at particular points, in order to approximate the function by a simple polynomial, at least over a limited range of values. We then approximate the position of the function minimum by the position of the polynomial's minimum. The latter is easy to calculate.

## 2.5  Quadratic Interpolation

If we know the values of a function $f(x)$ at three distinct points $\alpha$, $\beta$, $\gamma$ to be $f_\alpha$, $f_\beta$, $f_\gamma$ respectively, then we can approximate $f(x)$ by the quadratic function

$$\phi(x) = Ax^2 + Bx + C \tag{2.9}$$

where $A$, $B$ and $C$ are determined by the equations

$$\begin{aligned} A\alpha^2 + B\alpha + C &= f_\alpha \\ A\beta^2 + B\beta + C &= f_\beta. \\ A\gamma^2 + B\gamma + C &= f_\gamma \end{aligned} \tag{2.10}$$

The equations give

$$\begin{aligned} A &= [(\gamma - \beta)f_\alpha + (\alpha - \gamma)f_\beta + (\beta - \alpha)f_\gamma]/\Delta \\ B &= [(\beta^2 - \gamma^2)f_\alpha + (\gamma^2 - \alpha^2)f_\beta + (\alpha^2 - \beta^2)f_\gamma]/\Delta \\ C &= [\beta\gamma(\gamma - \beta)f_\alpha + \gamma\alpha(\alpha - \gamma)f_\beta + \alpha\beta(\beta - \alpha)f_\gamma]/\Delta \end{aligned} \tag{2.11}$$

where $\Delta = (\alpha - \beta)(\beta - \gamma)(\gamma - \alpha)$. Clearly $\phi(x)$ will have a minimum at $x = -B/2A$ if $A > 0$. Thus we approximate the position of the minimum of $f(x)$ by

$$\delta = \frac{1}{2} \left[ \frac{(\beta^2 - \gamma^2)f_\alpha + (\gamma^2 - \alpha^2)f_\beta + (\alpha^2 - \beta^2)f_\gamma}{(\beta - \gamma)f_\alpha + (\gamma - \alpha)f_\beta + (\alpha - \beta)f_\gamma} \right] \tag{2.12}$$

The method can be used in its own right for a function of one variable. It can be very useful for carrying out the linear search required in the procedures of Chapter 4. In these cases we wish to find the minimum of $f(\mathbf{x})$ at points on the line $\mathbf{x}_0 + \lambda\mathbf{d}$, where $\mathbf{x}_0$ is a given point, and $\mathbf{d}$ specifies a given direction. The values of $f(\mathbf{x}_0 + \lambda\mathbf{d})$ on this line are functions of the one variable $\lambda$,

$$\phi(\lambda) = f(\mathbf{x}_0 + \lambda\mathbf{d}). \tag{2.13}$$

The ideas and results above are transformed into a computational procedure as

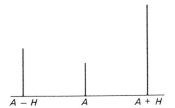 

**Figure 2.5**

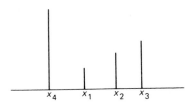

**Figure 2.6**

follows. We assume that we have a unimodal function $f(x)$ of one variable, an initial approximation to the position of its minimum, and a step length $H$, which is the same order of magnitude as the true minimum $x^*$ is from $A$ (not always easy conditions to satisfy). The steps in the procedure are as follows:

(i) Calculate $f(A)$ and $f(A + H)$.
(ii) If $f(A) < f(A + H)$ take the third point as $A - H$ and find $f(A - H)$. Otherwise take the third point as $A + 2H$ and find $f(A + 2H)$ (see Fig. 2.5).
(iii) Use the three points to find $\delta$ from equation 2.12 and evaluate $f(\delta)$.
(iv) If the difference between the positions of the lowest function value and the next lowest function value is less than the required accuracy terminate the process.
(v) If we do not terminate at stage (iv) we would normally discard the point with the highest function value and then return to step (iii). If however by retaining the point with the highest function value we put a definite bracket on the location of the minimum, then we should indeed retain this value and then return to step (iii). See Figure 2.6 in which we would retain $x_1$, $x_2$ and $x_4$ rather than $x_1$, $x_2$, $x_3$.

The program listed implements this procedure. Note that if the accuracy $E$ is set too small $\alpha$, $\beta$, $\gamma$ and $f_\alpha$, $f_\beta$, $f_\gamma$ will be very close together and $\delta$ (equation 2.12) may well become totally unreliable. To overcome this problem equation 2.12 is rewritten as

$$\delta = \tfrac{1}{2}(\alpha + \beta) + \frac{\tfrac{1}{2}(f_\alpha - f_\beta)(\beta - \gamma)(\gamma - \alpha)}{(\beta - \gamma)f_\alpha + (\gamma - \alpha)f_\beta + (\alpha - \beta)f_\gamma}. \tag{2.14}$$

```pascal
PROGRAM QuadraticInterpolation (input,output);
{ A program to implement Powell's quadratic interpolation method }
CONST
   fwx=14; dpx=8;   { Output format constants for x-values }
   fwf=14; dpf=8;   { Output format constants for function values }        {**}
TYPE                                                                        {**}
   point = RECORD          { To represent a single point (x,f(x)) }
             x, f : real
           END;
VAR
   A,                           { Initial estimate of position of minimum }
   H, E : real;                 { Step length and required accuracy }
   p1, p2, p3, p4 : point;      { The four points in the interpolation process }
   temp1, temp2, temp3, numerator, denominator : real;

FUNCTION f (x:real): real;
BEGIN
   f := 2.0*sqr(x) - exp(x)                                                 {**}
END; { f }

PROCEDURE order (VAR p,q:point);
{ To put p, q in order based on their function values }
VAR  r : point;
BEGIN
   IF p.f>q.f THEN BEGIN r:=p; p:=q; q:=r END
END; { order }

PROCEDURE inputdata;
BEGIN  write('    INITIAL VALUE, A ='); read(A); writeln(A:fwx:dpx);
   write('    STEP LENGTH, H ='); read(H); writeln(H:fwx:dpx);
   write('    REQUIRED ACCURACY, E ='); read(E); writeln(E:fwx:dpx)
END; { inputdata }

BEGIN  { Main Program }
   writeln; writeln('    QUADRATIC INTERPOLATION'); writeln;
   inputdata; writeln; writeln(' ':fwx-7, 'CURRENT VALUES');
   writeln; writeln(' ':(fwx - dpx DIV 2), 'X', ' ':fwx-1, 'F(X)'); writeln;
   { Initialise point values }
   p1.x:=A; p1.f:=f(p1.x); p2.x:=A+H; p2.f:=f(p2.x);
   IF p1.f<p2.f THEN p3.x:=A-H ELSE p3.x:=A+2.0*H;  p3.f:=f(p3.x);
   REPEAT  { Until required accuracy attained }
      temp1 := p2.x-p3.x;  temp2 := p3.x-p1.x;  temp3 := p1.x-p2.x;
      numerator := 0.5*(p1.f-p2.f)*temp1*temp2;
      denominator := temp1*p1.f + temp2*p2.f + temp3*p3.f;
      p4.x := 0.5*(p1.x+p2.x) + numerator/denominator;  p4.f:=f(p4.x);
      { Perform a tournament sort to order p1, p2, p3 ,p4 }
      order(p1,p2); order(p3,p4); order(p1,p3); order(p2,p4); order(p2,p3);
      writeln(p1.x:fwx:dpx, p1.f:fwf:dpf); writeln(p2.x:fwx:dpx, p2.f:fwf:dpf);
      writeln(p3.x:fwx:dpx, p3.f:fwf:dpf); writeln(p4.x:fwx:dpx, p4.f:fwf:dpf);
      { Retain the best three points }  writeln;
      IF ((p2.x>p1.x)=(p3.x>p1.x)) AND ((p2.x>p1.x)=NOT(p4.x>p1.x)) THEN p3:=p4
   UNTIL abs(p1.x-p2.x) < E;
   writeln; writeln('    FINAL SOLUTION'); writeln;
   writeln('    X =', p1.x:fwx:dpx, '    F =', p1.f:fwf:dpf)
END.
```

**Example 1**

Use quadratic interpolation to find the position of the minimum of $z = 2x^2 - e^x$ to an accuracy of $0 \cdot 0001$. Use 1 as the initial value $A$ and take $H = 0 \cdot 5$.

The computer output appears below.

```
QUADRATIC INTERPOLATION

INITIAL VALUE, A  =     1.00000000
STEP LENGTH,  H   =    0.50000000
REQUIRED ACCURACY, E  =      0.00010000

    CURRENT VALUES

        X                 F(X)

0.50000000      -1.14872127
0.04701979      -1.04372103
1.00000000      -0.71828183
1.50000000       0.01831093


0.37459168      -1.17375958
0.50000000      -1.14872127
0.04701979      -1.04372103
1.00000000      -0.71828183


0.36150412      -1.17411648
0.37459168      -1.17375958
0.50000000      -1.14872127
0.04701979      -1.04372103


0.35794058      -1.17413771
0.36150412      -1.17411648
0.37459168      -1.17375958
0.04701979      -1.04372103


0.35752044      -1.17413806
0.35794058      -1.17413771
0.36150412      -1.17411648
0.04701979      -1.04372103


0.35741954      -1.17413808
0.35752044      -1.17413806
0.35794058      -1.17413771
0.04701979      -1.04372103


0.35740635      -1.17413808
0.35741954      -1.17413808
0.35752044      -1.17413806
0.04701979      -1.04372103



FINAL SOLUTION

X  =      0.35740635    F  =     -1.17413808
```

## 2.6  Cubic Interpolation

The quadratic interpolation of the previous section, often called Powell's method, approximated the function by a quadratic. Davidon's method of the present section is more accurate and approximates the function by a cubic polynomial. It uses the values of the function and its gradient at two points in order to fit the cubic. It is widely used in the context of linear searches in Chapter 4, and we shall treat it from this point of view.

Thus we consider the problem of minimising $f(\mathbf{x})$ at points on the line $\mathbf{x}_0 + h\mathbf{d}$, i.e. of minimising

$$\phi(h) = f(\mathbf{x}_0 + h\mathbf{d})$$

$$= f(x_{01} + hd_1, x_{02} + hd_2, \ldots, x_{0n} + hd_n). \tag{2.15}$$

$$\frac{d\phi}{dh} = \frac{\partial f}{\partial x_1}(\mathbf{x}_0 + h\mathbf{d})d_1 + \frac{\partial f}{\partial x_2}(\mathbf{x}_0 + h\mathbf{d})d_2 + \cdots + \frac{\partial f}{\partial x_n}(\mathbf{x}_0 + h\mathbf{d})d_n.$$

$$\therefore \quad \frac{d\phi}{dh} = \nabla f(\mathbf{x}_0 + h\mathbf{d})^T\mathbf{d} = \mathbf{g}(\mathbf{x}_0 + h\mathbf{d})^T\mathbf{d}. \tag{2.16}$$

We suppose that we know the values of

$$\phi(p) = \phi_p, \quad \phi(q) = \phi_q$$

$$\frac{d\phi}{dh}(p) = G_p, \quad \frac{d\phi}{dh}(q) = G_q. \tag{2.17}$$

We can use this information to fit a cubic polynomial

$$a + bh + ch^2 + dh^3 \tag{2.18}$$

which will approximate $\phi(h)$. If $p = 0$, the equations determining $a$, $b$, $c$, $d$ are

$$
\begin{aligned}
a &= \phi_p \\
a + bq + cq^2 + dq^3 &= \phi_q \\
b &= G_p \\
b + 2cq + 3dq^2 &= G_q
\end{aligned}
\tag{2.19}
$$

with solution

$$a = \phi_p, \ b = G_p, \quad c = -\frac{(G_p + z)}{q}, \quad d = \frac{G_p + G_q + 2z}{3q^2} \tag{2.20}$$

where

$$z = \frac{3(\phi_p - \phi_q)}{q} + G_p + G_q.$$

The turning points of the fitted cubic are the solutions of

$$G_p - 2(G_p + z)\frac{h}{q} + (G_p + G_q + 2z)\left(\frac{h}{q}\right)^2 = 0.$$

Thus if $r$ is the position of the minimum of the fitted cubic

$$\frac{r}{q} = \frac{(G_p + z) \pm [(G_p + z)^2 - G_p(G_p + G_q + 2z)]^{1/2}}{G_p + G_q + 2z} = \frac{G_p + z \pm w}{G_p + G_q + 2z}, \quad (2.21)$$

where

$$w = (z^2 - G_p G_q)^{1/2}. \quad (2.22)$$

One of these corresponds to the minimum. The second derivative is

$$2c + 6dh. \quad (2.23)$$

If we take the positive sign, with

$$\frac{h}{q} = \frac{G_p + z + w}{G_p + G_q + 2z}$$

the second derivative has the value

$$-\frac{2(G_p + z)}{q} + \frac{2(G_p + G_q + 2z)}{q^2} \cdot \frac{q(G_p + z + w)}{(G_p + G_q + 2z)}$$

$$= \frac{1}{q}(-2G_p - 2z + 2G_p + 2z + 2w) = \frac{2w}{q} > 0.$$

Thus

$$\frac{r}{q} = \frac{G_p + z + w}{G_p + G_q + 2z}. \quad (2.24)$$

Better numerical results are obtained from the equivalent formula

$$\frac{r}{q} = 1 - \frac{G_q + w - z}{G_q - G_p + 2w} = \frac{z + w - G_p}{G_q - G_p + 2w}. \quad (2.25)$$

It is left as an exercise to show that equations 2.24 and 2.25 are equivalent.

The choice of $q$ is at our discretion. If $G_p < 0$ we would take $q$ to be positive, i.e. take a step in the direction of decreasing $\phi(h)$, otherwise we would take $q$ to be negative. The magnitude of $q$ is such that the interval $(0, q)$ includes the minimum. This will be so if $\phi_q > \phi_p$ (Fig. 2.7(i)) or if $G_q > 0$ (Fig. 2.7(ii)).

When neither of these conditions is satisfied we double the value of $q$, repeatedly if necessary, until our interval does bracket a minimum.

The problem of finding an initial value for $q$ remains. There are real difficulties in finding a value that will be satisfactory for *all* problems. Davidon and Fletcher and Powell suggest

$$q = \min\{\eta, -2(\phi_p - \phi_m)/G_p\} \quad (2.26)$$

where $\phi_m$ is an estimate, preferably on the low side of the true minimum of $\phi(h)$, and $\eta$ is a constant, usually taken to be 2 or 1.

The steps in the iterative procedure are thus

(i) Find $\phi_p = f(\mathbf{x}_0)$ and $G_p = [\mathbf{g}(\mathbf{x}_0)]^T\mathbf{d}$.
(ii) Check that $G_p < 0$ and if not search along $-\mathbf{d}$. Choose $q$ from equation 2.26. We just have to 'guess' for $\phi_m$.

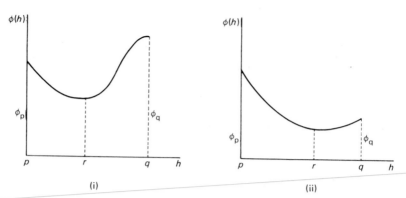

Figure 2.7

(iii) Evaluate $\phi_q = f(\mathbf{x}_0 + q\mathbf{d})$ and $G_q = [\mathbf{g}(\mathbf{x}_0 + q\mathbf{d})]^T\mathbf{d}$.

(iv) If $G_q > 0$ or $\phi_q > \phi_p$ we have bracketed the minimum. If not replace $q$ by $2q$ and return to step (iii).

(v) Use equation 2.25 to approximate the minimum by $r$ in $(0, q)$.

(vi) Stop if $|\,d\phi/dh\,| = |\,[\mathbf{g}(\mathbf{x}_0 + r\mathbf{d})]^T\mathbf{d}\,| = |\,G_r\,| < \varepsilon$ where $\varepsilon$ is some specified accuracy.

(vii) Return to step (v) using the interval $(0, r)$ if $G_r > 0$, or, the interval $(r, q)$ if $G_r \leqslant 0$.

The stopping condition at (vi) tests the derivative. Previous tests have stopped when the position of the minimum has shown no real movement. It might be noted that in general it is easier to find the minimum of the function than the position of the minimum. The latter is determined with less accuracy.

The algorithm just described is implemented in the following program.

```
PROGRAM CubicInterpolation (input,output);
{ A program to implement Davidon's cubic interpolation method }
CONST
  n=2;                 { Number of variables in function f }      {**}
  fwx=14; dpx=8;  { Output format constants for x-values }        {**}
  fwf=14; dpf=8;  { Output format constants for function values } {**}
TYPE
  vector = ARRAY [1..n] OF real;
  point = RECORD   { To represent values at a single point }
            x, g : vector;  { x-vector and gradient-vector }
            f : real;       { function value f(x) }
          END;
VAR
  d : vector;          { Direction of search }
  p, q, r : point;     { Search points }
  Gp, Gq, Gr : real;   { Gradient values in d-direction at p, q and r }
  phim : real;         { Initial estimate of position of minimum }
  E : real;            { Required accuracy of derivative }
  qx, rx : real;       { Distances between points in iterative process }
  it : integer;        { Iteration counter }
  i : integer;   z, w, qx0 : real;
```

```
FUNCTION f (x:vector): real;
{ The code here is dependent on the function being minimised }
BEGIN
  f := 100.0*sqr(x[2]-sqr(x[1])) + sqr(1.0-x[1])                    {**}
END; { f }


FUNCTION scalarmult (v1,v2:vector): real;
{ Performs the scalar multiplication of vectors v1 and v2 }
VAR i : integer;  sum : real;
BEGIN  sum:=0.0;
  FOR i:=1 TO n DO sum := sum + v1[i]*v2[i];
  scalarmult := sum
END; { scalarmult }


PROCEDURE gradients (VAR p:point);
{ Computes the partial derivatives of phi(h) at p.x }
{ The code here is dependent on the function being minimised}
VAR s : real;
BEGIN
  WITH p DO
  BEGIN  s:=sqr(x[1]);                                             {**}
    g[1] := -400.0*x[1]*(x[2]-s) - 2.0*(1.0-x[1]);               {**}
    g[2] := 200.0*(x[2]-s)                                        {**}
  END
END; { gradients }


PROCEDURE movepoint (VAR p1:point; p2:point; r:real);
{ p1 is made the point a distance r from p2 in the d-direction }
VAR i : integer;
BEGIN
  FOR i:=1 TO n DO p1.x[i] := p2.x[i] + r*d[i];
  p1.f := f(p1.x);  gradients(p1)
END; { movepoint }


PROCEDURE inputdata;
VAR i : integer;
BEGIN  writeln('    NUMBER OF VARIABLES =', n:3);
  writeln('    INITIAL POINT');
  FOR i:=1 TO n DO
  BEGIN write('    P[', i:2, ']'); read(p.x[i]); writeln(p.x[i]:fwx:dpx) END;
  writeln('    DIRECTION');
  FOR i:=1 TO n DO
  BEGIN write('    D[', i:2, ']'); read(d[i]); writeln(d[i]:fwx:dpx) END;
  write('    REQUIRED ACCURACY, E =');  read(E); writeln(E:fwx:dpx);
  write('    INITIAL ESTIMATE OF POSITION OF MINIMUM =');
  read(phim); writeln(phim:fwx:dpx)
END; { inputdata }


PROCEDURE outputline (it:integer; p:point);
VAR i : integer;
BEGIN  write(it:6, '    ', p.f:fwf:dpf);
  FOR i:=1 TO n DO write(p.x[i]:fwx:dpx); writeln
END; { outputline }
```

```
BEGIN   { Main Program }
  writeln; writeln('    CUBIC INTERPOLATION'); writeln;
  inputdata; writeln; write('ITERATION', '  ':fwf-4, 'F(X)');
  FOR i:=1 TO n DO write('  ':fwx-5, 'X[', i:2, ']'); writeln; writeln;
  it:=0; { Initialise iteration count }
  { Calculate function value and gradients at p }
  p.f := f(p.x); gradients(p); outputline(it,p);
  IF abs(scalarmult(p.g,d))<E THEN r:=p  { Minimum at initial point }
  ELSE
    REPEAT  { A search in the d-direction until gradient is negative }
      Gp := scalarmult(p.g,d);  qx := abs(2.0*(p.f-phim)/Gp);
      IF qx>1.0 THEN qx:=1.0;
      IF Gp>0.0 THEN BEGIN movepoint(p,p,-qx); writeln('INSTABILITY?') END
    UNTIL Gp<=0.0;
    { Find next point, q }
    qx0:=qx;
    REPEAT  { Until the minimum has been bracketed }
      movepoint(q,p,qx0);  Gq := scalarmult(q.g,d);  qx:=qx0;  qx0:=2.0*qx0
    UNTIL  (Gq>0.0) OR (q.f>p.f);
    { Iterate until minimum is found }
    REPEAT
      z := 3.0*(p.f-q.f)/qx + Gp + Gq;  w := sqr(z) - Gp*Gq;
      IF w<0.0 THEN w:=0.0;  w:=sqrt(w);  rx := qx*(z+w-Gp)/(Gq-Gp+2.0*w);
      movepoint(r,p,rx);  Gr := scalarmult(r.g,d);
      it:=it+1;  outputline(it,r);
      IF abs(Gr)>=E THEN
         IF Gr>0.0 THEN BEGIN  qx:=rx;  q:=r;  Gq:=Gr  END
         ELSE BEGIN  qx := qx-rx;  p:=r;  Gp:=Gr  END
    UNTIL abs(Gr)<E;
  writeln; writeln('    FUNCTION MINIMUM =', r.f:fwf:dpf);
  writeln('    NO. OF ITERATIONS =', it:4)
END. { CubicInterpolation }
```

## Example 1

Find the minimum of $f(x_1, x_2) = 100(x_2 - x_1^2)^2 + (1 - x_1)^2$ along the line through $(-1, 0)$ in the direction $(5, 1)$.

As listed FUNCTION $f$ and FUNCTION *gradients* are appropriate. The accuracy $E$ used was $0 \cdot 0001$ and $\phi_m$ was taken to be zero. With initial point $(-1, 0)$ the output given is listed. We have found the local minimum at A (Figure 2.8).

```
CUBIC INTERPOLATION

NUMBER OF VARIABLES =  2
INITIAL POINT
P[ 1]   -1.00000000
P[ 2]    0.00000000
DIRECTION
D[ 1]    5.00000000
D[ 2]    1.00000000
REQUIRED ACCURACY, E =     0.00010000
INITIAL ESTIMATE OF POSITION OF MINIMUM =     0.00000000
```

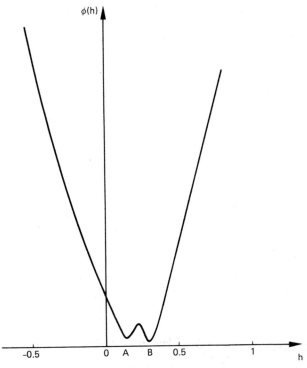

**Figure 2.8**

| ITERATION | F(X) | X[ 1] | X[ 2] |
|---|---|---|---|
| 0 | 104.00000000 | −1.00000000 | 0.00000000 |
| 1 | 2.11382292 | −0.39942471 | 0.12011506 |
| 2 | 1.82412327 | −0.33651145 | 0.13269771 |
| 3 | 1.82235478 | −0.34138633 | 0.13172273 |
| 4 | 1.82235475 | −0.34136650 | 0.13172670 |

```
FUNCTION MINIMUM =    1.82235475
NO. OF ITERATIONS =   4
```

With initial point (1·5, 0·5), also on the line, we obtain, after a somewhat hesitant start, the global minimum at B (Figure 2.8).

```
CUBIC INTERPOLATION

NUMBER OF VARIABLES =   2
INITIAL POINT
P[ 1]    1.50000000
P[ 2]    0.50000000
DIRECTION
D[ 1]    5.00000000
D[ 2]    1.00000000
REQUIRED ACCURACY, E =     0.00010000
INITIAL ESTIMATE OF POSITION OF MINIMUM =     0.00000000
```

```
ITERATION              F(X)              X[ 1]              X[ 2]

    0        306.50000000      1.50000000       0.50000000
INSTABILITY?
INSTABILITY?
INSTABILITY?
    1          0.19286814      0.56353216       0.31270643
    2          0.19286582      0.56336954       0.31267391
    3          0.19286582      0.56336969       0.31267394

    FUNCTION MINIMUM =      0.19286582
    NO. OF ITERATIONS =     3
```

The function being minimised is the quartic

$$\phi(h) = f(-1 + 5h, 0 + h)$$

$$= 100\{h - (1 - 5h)^2\}^2 + (2 - 5h)^2$$

Its graph is sketched in Fig. 2.8. May this example illustrate the difficulties and dangers involved in linear searches in the presence of multi-modality.

## 2.7  References

1  W. C. Davidon, 'Variable metric method for minimisation', *AEC R & D Report*, ANL-5990, Argonne National Laboratory, 1959.
2  R. Fletcher and M. J. D. Powell, 'A rapidly convergent descent method for minimisation', *The Comp Journal*, **6**, 163–168, 1963.
3  J. Kiefer, 'Sequential minimax search for a maximum', *Proc. Am. Math. Soc.*, **4**, 502–506, 1953.
4  M. J. D. Powell, 'An efficient method of finding the minimum of a function of several variables without calculating derivatives', *The Comp. Journal*, **7**, 155–162, 1964.

## Exercises 2

1  If $F_0 = 1$ and $F_1 = 1$ and $F_k = F_{k-1} + F_{k-2}$ for $k \geqslant 2$ show that

$$F_n = \frac{\tau^{n+1} - (-\tau)^{-(n+1)}}{\sqrt{5}} \quad \text{where } \tau = \frac{1 + \sqrt{5}}{2} \approx 1 \cdot 618\ 033\ 989.$$

Show by using the recurrence that $F_2 = 2$, $F_3 = 3$, $F_4 = 5$, $F_5 = 8$, $F_6 = 13, \ldots$, $F_{10} = 89, \ldots$etc. $\ldots$ $F_{19} = 6765$, $F_{20} = 10\ 946$.

2  Show that

(i) $F_{n-1}F_{n-2} - F_n F_{n-3} = (-1)^n$. [See equation 2.4.]
(ii) $F_n \approx \tau^{n+1}/\sqrt{5}$ for large $n$.
(iii) $F_{n-1}/F_n \approx 1/\tau$ for large $n$.

3  If we have to separate our points by at least $\varepsilon$, $2\varepsilon$ will be the smallest practical interval of uncertainty; thus $L_n \geqslant 2\varepsilon$ sets a bound on $n$, the number of useful

experiments. Show that this leads to

$$\varepsilon < L_1/F_{n+1}.$$

**4** Show that in order to reduce the interval of uncertainty to 1% of its original value, we need 11 function evaluations with Fibonacci search. If we choose the positions of all the points at the outset what is the minimum number of points needed? [Don't gamble on getting favourable outcomes.]

**5** Use Fibonacci search with 10 function evaluations to locate the minimum of $2x^2 + 3e^{-x}$ in the interval $(0, 1)$.

**6** Use Fibonacci search to locate the minimum of $x^4 - 14x^3 + 60x^2 - 70x$ within the interval $(5, 7)$ with an accuracy of $0 \cdot 01$. How many function evaluations are needed?

**7** Use Golden search to find the minimum of $2x^2 + 3e^{-x}$ correct to 2 decimal places. Use $(0, 1)$ as the original interval of uncertainty. How many function evaluations are needed? C.f. Question 5.

**8** If $\alpha = 0$, $\beta = t$, $\gamma = 2t$ show that $\delta$ (equation 2.12) is given by

$$\delta = \frac{4f_\beta - 3f_\alpha - f_\gamma}{4f_\beta - 2f_\alpha - 2f_\gamma} \cdot t$$

and that this gives a minimum if $f_\alpha + f_\gamma > 2f_\beta$.

**9** Use quadratic interpolation to find the position of the minimum of $-e^{-x} \ln(x)$ within the interval $(1, 3)$ to an accuracy of $0 \cdot 001$. [Make sure you don't use negative $x$ values or you will get an execution error.]

**10** Use quadratic interpolation to find the minimum of $f(x_1, x_2) = x_1^2 + 3x_2^2 + 2x_1x_2$ along the line $\boldsymbol{\alpha} + \lambda\mathbf{d}$ where $\boldsymbol{\alpha} = \begin{pmatrix} 1 \\ 1 \end{pmatrix}$ and $\mathbf{d} = \begin{pmatrix} 2 \\ 3 \end{pmatrix}$, correct to 2 decimal places.

**11** Verify the correctness of equations 2.11, 2.12 and 2.14.

**12** Verify the correctness of equation 2.20.

**13** Verify the equivalence of equations 2.24 and 2.25.

**14** For the curve $y = ax^2$ show that the tangent at $(x', y')$ meets the $x$-axis at $x'/2$. Hence or otherwise attempt to give the argument underlying equation 2.26.

**15** Solve the equation $e^x \sin x = 1$. Try to minimise the function $f(x) = (1 - e^x \sin x)^2$.

# 3
# Direct Search Methods—
# Functions of $n$ Variables

## 3.1 Preliminary Discussion

Much effort has been devoted to devising direct search methods to locate the minimum of a function of $n$ variables. A direct search method is one that uses function values only. A number of methods have been suggested. We shall only consider two in any detail. They are, however, two methods that experience has shown are very robust and capable of wide application.

Consider a function of two variables. Its contour lines are shown in Fig. 3.1. Its minimum is at $(x_1^*, x_2^*)$. The crudest search method is the alternating variable search method. We start at some point A and search in the direction of the $x_1$-axis for the minimum in this direction and thus find B at which the tangent to the contour is parallel to the $x_1$-axis. From B we then search in the direction of the $x_2$-axis and so proceed to C and then to D by searching parallel to the $x_1$-axis etc. In this way we proceed to the optimum point. Any of the univariate techniques of the previous chapter could be used for the searches. It is clearly possible to extend the idea to functions of $n$ variables.

In theory the method is reasonable if there is just one minimum. In practice it is generally too slow. Hence more sophisticated methods, which make more use of the information in the function values already obtained, have been devised.

A number of functions have been constructed which because of their nature provide severe tests for such methods. A few examples are given. Rosenbrock's function:

$$f(x_1, x_2) = 100(x_2 - x_1^2)^2 + (1 - x_1)^2; \ \mathbf{x}^* = (1, 1). \tag{3.1}$$

Powell's function:

$$f(\mathbf{x}) = (x_1 + 10x_2)^2 + 5(x_3 - x_4)^2 + (x_2 - 2x_3)^4 + 10(x_1 - x_4)^4 \ \text{with} \ \mathbf{x}^* = (0,0,0,0). \tag{3.2}$$

The two dimensional exponential function:

$$f(x_1, x_2) = \sum_a [(e^{-ax_1} - e^{-ax_2}) - (e^{-a} - e^{-10a})]^2 \quad \text{where} \ a = 0 \cdot 1(0 \cdot 1)1; \ \mathbf{x}^* = (1, 10). \tag{3.3}$$

Any optimisation procedure worthy of serious consideration should be able to handle these test problems (and others) efficiently.

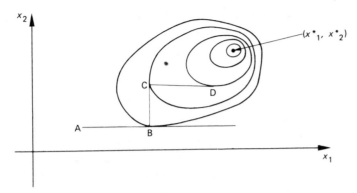

**Figure 3.1**

## 3.2  The Method of Hooke and Jeeves

This method dates back to 1961 but is none the less a very efficient and ingenious procedure. The search consists of a sequence of *exploration steps* about a *base point* which if successful are followed by *pattern moves.*

The procedure is as follows.

(A)   Choose an initial base point $b_1$ and a step length $h_j$ for each variable $x_j$; $j = 1, 2, ..., n$. The program given later uses a fixed step $h$ for each variable, but the modification indicated can be useful.

(B)   Carry out an exploration about $b_1$. The purpose of this is to acquire knowledge about the local behaviour of the function. This knowledge is used to find a likely direction for the *pattern move* by which it is hoped to obtain an even greater reduction in the value of the function. The exploration about $b_1$ proceeds as indicated.

 (i) Evaluate $f(b_1)$.

 (ii) Each variable is now changed in turn, by adding the step length. Thus we evaluate $f(b_1 + h_1e_1)$ where $e_1$ is a unit vector in the direction of the $x_1$-axis. If this reduces the function replace $b_1$ by $b_1 + h_1e_1$. If not find $f(b_1 - h_1e_1)$ and replace $b_1$ by $b_1 - h_1e_1$ if the function is reduced. If neither step gives a reduction leave $b_1$ unchanged and consider changes in $x_2$, i.e. find $f(b_1 + h_2e_2)$ etc. When we have considered all $n$ variables we will have a new base point $b_2$.

 (iii) If $b_2 = b_1$ i.e. no function reduction has been achieved, the exploration is repeated about the same base point $b_1$ but with a reduced step length. Reducing the step length(s) to one tenth of its former value appears to be satisfactory in practice.

 (iv) If $b_2 \neq b_1$ we make a *pattern move.*

(C)   Pattern moves utilise the information acquired by exploration, and accomplish the function minimisation by moving in the direction of the established 'pattern'. The procedure is as follows.

 (i) It seems sensible to move further from the base point $b_2$ in the direction

$b_2 - b_1$ since that move has already led to a reduction in the function value. So we evaluate the function at the next pattern point

$$P_1 = b_1 + 2(b_2 - b_1). \tag{3.4}$$

In general

$$P_i = b_i + 2(b_{i+1} - b_i). \tag{3.5}$$

(ii) Then continue with exploratory moves about $P_1(P_i)$.
(iii) If the lowest value at step C(ii) is less than the value at the base point $b_2$ ($b_{i+1}$ in general) then a new base point $b_3$ ($b_{i+2}$) has been reached. In this case repeat C(i). Otherwise abandon the pattern move from $b_2$ ($b_{i+1}$) and continue with an exploration about $b_2$ ($b_{i+1}$).

### Flow Chart for Hooke and Jeeves

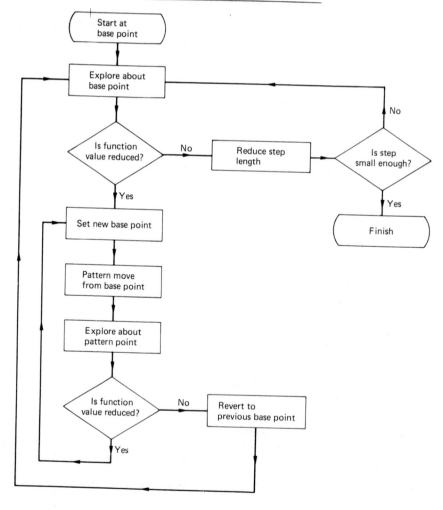

(D)   Terminate the process when the step length(s) has been reduced to a predetermined small value.

The various steps in the above procedure are explicitly indicated by comments in the following program.

We can give a flow chart representation of the method.

Flow Chart for an Exploration

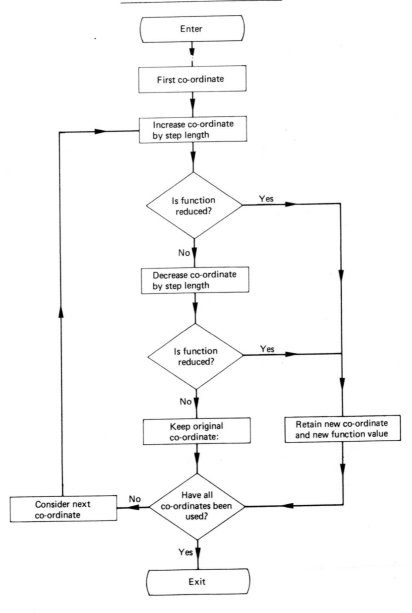

```
PROGRAM HookeandJeeves (input,output);
CONST
  n=3;                    { No. of variables in function f }      {**}
  hmin=1.0E-8;            { Minimum step length }                 {**}
  fwx=10; dpx=4;          { Output format constants for vector components }  {**}
  fwf=14;                 { Output format constant for function values }     {**}
  fws=14; dps=8;          { Output format constants for step length }        {**}
  reduction=0.1;          { Reduction factor in step length changes }        {**}
  smallvalue=1.0E-12;     { Used to avoid influence of round-off errors }    {**}
TYPE
  vector = ARRAY [1..n] OF real;
  point = RECORD
               x : vector;  f : real
          END;
  howobtained = PACKED ARRAY [1..12] OF char;

VAR
  b1, b2, b3, P : point;  { Base points and pattern point }
  fe : integer;           { Function evaluation counter }
  h : real;               { Step length for base change calculations }
  improvement : boolean;  { Indicator for better base point }
  i : integer;

FUNCTION f (x:vector): real;
{ The code here is dependent on the function being minimised }
BEGIN fe := fe+1;
  f := sqr(x[1]-2.0) + sqr(x[2]-5.0) + sqr(sqr(x[3]+2.0))          {**}
END; { f }

PROCEDURE inputdata;
VAR i : integer;
BEGIN writeln('     NUMBER OF VARIABLES =', n:3);
  writeln('    INITIAL POINT');
  FOR i:=1 TO n DO
  BEGIN
    write('    X[', i:2, ']'); read(b1.x[i]); writeln(b1.x[i]:fwx:dpx)
  END;
  write('    STEP LENGTH =');  read(h);  writeln(h:fws:dps);  writeln
END; { inputdata }

PROCEDURE outputline (step:real; s:howobtained; p:point);
VAR i : integer;
BEGIN write(step:fws:dps, '  ', p.f:fwf, '   ', s);
  FOR i:=1 TO n DO write(p.x[i]:fwx:dpx);  writeln
END; { outputline }

PROCEDURE initialise;
BEGIN fe:=0;  b1.f := f(b1.x)  { Step (B)(i) }  END; { initialise }

PROCEDURE exploration (oldbase:point; VAR newbase:point);
VAR i : integer; fval : real;
BEGIN  newbase := oldbase;
  FOR i:=1 TO n DO
```

```
  BEGIN  newbase.x[i] := oldbase.x[i] + h;  fval:=f(newbase.x);
    IF fval < newbase.f THEN newbase.f:=fval
    ELSE
    BEGIN  newbase.x[i] := oldbase.x[i] - h;  fval:=f(newbase.x);
        IF fval < newbase.f THEN newbase.f:=fval
        ELSE  newbase.x[i] := oldbase.x[i]
    END
  END;
    outputline(h, 'EXPLORATION ', newbase)
END; { exploration }

PROCEDURE patternmove (b1,b2:point; VAR P:point);
VAR  i : integer;
BEGIN
  FOR i:=1 TO n DO  P.x[i] := 2.0*b2.x[i] - b1.x[i];
  P.f := f(P.x);  outputline(h, 'PATTERN MOVE', P)
END; { patternmove }

BEGIN  { Main Program }
  writeln; writeln('    HOOKE & JEEVES'); writeln;
  inputdata;
  write(' ':fws-4, 'STEP ', ' ':fwf-4, 'F(X)    HOW OBTAINED');
  FOR i:=1 TO n DO write(' ':fwx-5, 'X[', i:2, ']'); writeln; writeln;
  initialise;  { Step (A) }   outputline(h, 'INITIAL BASE', b1);
  REPEAT  { Until step length is small enough }
    exploration(b1,b2);  { Step (B)(ii) }
    improvement :=  b2.f < b1.f - smallvalue;
    IF NOT improvement THEN h := h*reduction { Reduce step length }
    ELSE                                     { at Step (B)(iii)    }
      REPEAT  { From Step (B)(iv) or Step (C)(iii) }
        patternmove(b1,b2,P);  { Step (C)(i) }
        exploration(P,b3);  { Step (C)(ii) }
        improvement :=  b3.f < b2.f - smallvalue;
        { Now perform Step (C)(iii) }
        IF improvement THEN BEGIN b1:=b2; b2:=b3 END
        ELSE BEGIN b1:=b2; outputline(h, 'BASE CHANGE ', b1) END
      UNTIL NOT improvement
  UNTIL h<hmin;  { Step (D) }
  writeln; writeln('   FUNCTION MINIMUM =', b1.f);  writeln;
  writeln('   NO. OF FUNCTION EVALUATIONS =', fe:5)
END.  { HookeandJeeves }
```

The program given implements the procedure. One or two points are worth noting. The first point always needs to be borne in mind. The computer only works to *finite* accuracy and errors can accumulate during the course of a complicated calculation, particularly in this case if the step length is an awkward size. (Normally we would avoid this but the program should be robust.) Thus in the calculation of improvement in the outer REPEAT loop of the main program, where we are really asking if the base point has been changed, we avoid a reduction due to an accumulated error by subtracting *smallvalue* (set at $10^{-12}$ in the program constants but this could be changed to meet machine limitations).

The program as listed enables the function

$$f(x_1, x_2, x_3) = (x_1 - 2)^2 + (x_2 - 5)^2 + (x_3 + 2)^4$$

to be minimised. The minimum clearly is located at $(2, 5, -2)$. Some of the output with $(4, -2, 3)$ as the initial point and with initial step length as 1 is given. The progress of the explorations and pattern moves can be easily followed. A count of the number of function evaluations needed is kept. This is often used as a means of comparing the efficiency of different search methods. The better the method, the fewer evaluations needed in general.

HOOKE & JEEVES

NUMBER OF VARIABLES = 3
INITIAL POINT
X[ 1]     4.0000
X[ 2]    -2.0000
X[ 3]     3.0000
STEP LENGTH =     1.00000000

| STEP | F(X) | HOW OBTAINED | X[ 1] | X[ 2] | X[ 3] |
|---|---|---|---|---|---|
| 1.00000000 | 6.780000E+002 | INITIAL BASE | 4.0000 | -2.0000 | 3.0000 |
| 1.00000000 | 2.930000E+002 | EXPLORATION | 3.0000 | -1.0000 | 2.0000 |
| 1.00000000 | 1.060000E+002 | PATTERN MOVE | 2.0000 | 0.0000 | 1.0000 |
| 1.00000000 | 3.200000E+001 | EXPLORATION | 2.0000 | 1.0000 | 0.0000 |
| 1.00000000 | 5.000000E+000 | PATTERN MOVE | 1.0000 | 3.0000 | -2.0000 |
| 1.00000000 | 1.000000E+000 | EXPLORATION | 2.0000 | 4.0000 | -2.0000 |
| 1.00000000 | 2.000000E+001 | PATTERN MOVE | 2.0000 | 7.0000 | -4.0000 |
| 1.00000000 | 2.000000E+000 | EXPLORATION | 2.0000 | 6.0000 | -3.0000 |
| 1.00000000 | 1.000000E+000 | BASE CHANGE | 2.0000 | 4.0000 | -2.0000 |
| 1.00000000 | 0.000000E+000 | EXPLORATION | 2.0000 | 5.0000 | -2.0000 |
| 1.00000000 | 1.000000E+000 | PATTERN MOVE | 2.0000 | 6.0000 | -2.0000 |
| 1.00000000 | 0.000000E+000 | EXPLORATION | 2.0000 | 5.0000 | -2.0000 |
| 1.00000000 | 0.000000E+000 | BASE CHANGE | 2.0000 | 5.0000 | -2.0000 |
| 1.00000000 | 0.000000E+000 | EXPLORATION | 2.0000 | 5.0000 | -2.0000 |
| 0.10000000 | 0.000000E+000 | EXPLORATION | 2.0000 | 5.0000 | -2.0000 |
| 0.01000000 | 0.000000E+000 | EXPLORATION | 2.0000 | 5.0000 | -2.0000 |
| 0.00100000 | 0.000000E+000 | EXPLORATION | 2.0000 | 5.0000 | -2.0000 |
| 0.00010000 | 0.000000E+000 | EXPLORATION | 2.0000 | 5.0000 | -2.0000 |
| 0.00001000 | 0.000000E+000 | EXPLORATION | 2.0000 | 5.0000 | -2.0000 |
| 0.00000100 | 0.000000E+000 | EXPLORATION | 2.0000 | 5.0000 | -2.0000 |
| 0.00000010 | 0.000000E+000 | EXPLORATION | 2.0000 | 5.0000 | -2.0000 |
| 0.00000001 | 0.000000E+000 | EXPLORATION | 2.0000 | 5.0000 | -2.0000 |

FUNCTION MINIMUM = 0.0000000000000E+000

NO. OF FUNCTION EVALUATIONS =    89

## 3.3   Nelder and Mead's Method

Nelder and Mead's method is an extension of the simplex method of Spendley, Hext and Himsworth. A set of $(n + 1)$ mutually equidistant points in $n$-dimensional space is known as a regular simplex. This figure underlies the Spendley, Hext and Himsworth method. Thus in two dimensions the simplex is an equilateral triangle and in three dimensions it is a regular tetrahedron. The idea of the method is to compare the values of the function at the $(n + 1)$ vertices of the simplex and move the simplex towards the optimum point during the iterative process. The original simplex method maintained a regular simplex at each stage. Nelder and Mead proposed several modifications to the method which allow the simplices to become non-regular. The result is a very robust direct search method which is extremely powerful provided that the number of variables does not exceed five or six.

The movement of the simplex in this method is achieved by the application of three basic operations *reflection*, *expansion* and *contraction*. The thinking underlying these operations will become clear as we consider the steps in the procedure.

(A)   We start with $(n + 1)$ points $x_1, x_2, ..., x_{n+1}$ and find

$$f_1 = f(x_1), \quad f_2 = f(x_2) ... f_{n+1} = f(x_{n+1}).$$

(B)   We find the highest function value $f_h$, the next highest function value $f_g$ and the lowest function value $f_l$ and the corresponding points $x_h$, $x_g$ and $x_l$.

(C)   Find the centroid of all the points except $x_h$. Let this be $x_0$ and evaluate $f(x_0) = f_0$.

$$x_0 = \frac{1}{n} \sum_{i \neq h} x_i \qquad (3.6)$$

(D)   It would seem reasonable to try to move away from $x_h$. We *reflect* $x_h$ in $x_0$ to find $x_r$ and find $f(x_r) = f_r$.

Reflection is illustrated in Fig. 3.2.

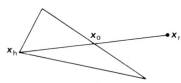

**Figure 3.2**

If $\alpha > 0$ is the *reflection* factor we find $x_r$ such that

$$x_r - x_0 = \alpha(x_0 - x_h)$$

i.e.   $x_r = (1 + \alpha)x_0 - \alpha x_h.$ $\qquad (3.7)$

N.B.   $\alpha = |x_r - x_0| / |x_0 - x_h|$ .

(E)   We now compare $f_r$ with $f_l$.

   (i) If $f_r < f_l$ we have obtained the lowest function value yet. The direction from $x_0$ to $x_r$ appears to be a good one to move along. We therefore make an *expansion* in this direction to find $x_e$ and evaluate $f_e = f(x_e)$. Figure 3.3

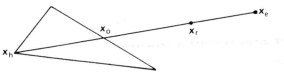

**Figure 3.3**

illustrates the operation of expanding the simplex. With an expansion factor $\gamma(>1)$ we shall have

$$\mathbf{x}_e - \mathbf{x}_0 = \gamma(\mathbf{x}_r - \mathbf{x}_0)$$

i.e.    $\mathbf{x}_e = \gamma\mathbf{x}_r + (1 - \gamma)\mathbf{x}_0.$                     (3.8)

N.B.    $\gamma = |\mathbf{x}_e - \mathbf{x}_0| / |\mathbf{x}_r - \mathbf{x}_0|.$

(a) if $f_e < f_l$ replace $\mathbf{x}_h$ by $\mathbf{x}_e$ and test the $(n + 1)$ points of the simplex for convergence to the minimum (see step (I)). If we have converged stop; if not return to step (B).

(b) If $f_e \not< f_l$ we abandon $\mathbf{x}_e$. We have evidently moved too far in the direction $\mathbf{x}_0$ to $\mathbf{x}_r$. Instead replace $\mathbf{x}_h$ by $\mathbf{x}_r$ which we know gave an improvement [step (E)(i)], test for convergence and if not return to step (B).

(ii) If $f_r > f_l$ but $f_r \not> f_g$, $\mathbf{x}_r$ is an improvement on the two worst points of the simplex and we replace $\mathbf{x}_h$ by $\mathbf{x}_r$, test for convergence and if not return to step (B); i.e. (i)(b) above.

(iii) If $f_r > f_l$ and $f_r > f_g$ proceed to step (F).

(F) We next compare $f_r$ and $f_h$.

(i) If $f_r > f_h$ proceed directly to the *contraction* step (F)(ii).

If $f_r < f_h$ replace $\mathbf{x}_h$ by $\mathbf{x}_r$ and $f_h$ by $f_r$. Remember $f_r > f_g$ from step (E)(iii) above.

Then proceed to step (F)(ii).

(ii) It this case $f_r > f_h$ so it would appear that we have moved too far in the direction $\mathbf{x}_h$ to $\mathbf{x}_0$. We try to rectify this by finding $\mathbf{x}_c$ (and then $f_c$) by a contraction step which is illustrated in Fig. 3.4.

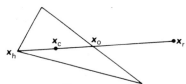

**Figure 3.4**

If $f_r > f_h$ we proceed directly to the contraction and find $\mathbf{x}_c$ from

$$\mathbf{x}_c - \mathbf{x}_0 = \beta(\mathbf{x}_h - \mathbf{x}_0)$$

where $\beta(0 < \beta < 1)$ is the contraction coefficient. Thus

$$\mathbf{x}_c = \beta\mathbf{x}_h + (1 - \beta)\mathbf{x}_0$$                     (3.9)

If however, $f_r < f_h$ we first replace $\mathbf{x}_h$ by $\mathbf{x}_r$ and then contract. Thus we find $\mathbf{x}_c$ from

$$\mathbf{x}_c - \mathbf{x}_0 = \beta(\mathbf{x}_r - \mathbf{x}_0)$$

i.e.    $\mathbf{x}_c = \beta\mathbf{x}_r + (1 - \beta)\mathbf{x}_0.$                     (3.10)

See Fig. 3.5.

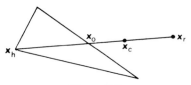

**Figure 3.5**

(G)  We now compare $f_c$ and $f_h$.
  (i)  If $f_c < f_h$ we replace $\mathbf{x}_h$ by $\mathbf{x}_c$, check for convergence and if not return to step (B).
  (ii)  If $f_c > f_h$ it would appear that all our efforts to find a value $< f_h$ have failed so we move to step (H).

(H)  At this step we reduce the size of the simplex by halving the distance of each point of the simplex from $\mathbf{x}_l$ the point generating the lowest function value.
  Thus $\mathbf{x}_i$ is replaced by $\mathbf{x}_l + \frac{1}{2}(\mathbf{x}_i - \mathbf{x}_l)$
i.e. replace $\mathbf{x}_i$ by

$$\tfrac{1}{2}(\mathbf{x}_i + \mathbf{x}_l). \tag{3.11}$$

We then calculate $f_i$ for $i = 1, 2, \ldots, (n+1)$, test for convergence and if not return to step (B).

(I)  The test of convergence is based on the standard deviation of the $(n+1)$ function values being less than some pre-determined small value $\varepsilon$. Thus we calculate

$$\sigma^2 = \sum_{i=1}^{n+1} (f_i - \bar{f})^2/(n+1) \tag{3.12}$$

where $\bar{f} = \sum f_i/(n+1)$.
  If $\sigma < \varepsilon$ all function values are very close together, and so hopefully are the points, near the minimum $\mathbf{x}_l$. This convergence criterion is thus reasonable although Box, Davies and Swann (reference 1) suggest what they regard as a 'safer' test.
  We give a flow chart for the steps in the procedure on the next page.
  There remain some important details to clarify. The first concerns the values of $\alpha$, $\beta$, $\gamma$ which occur as the reflection, contraction and expansion coefficients respectively. Nelder and Mead recommend $\alpha = 1$, $\beta = 0 \cdot 5$, $\gamma = 2$. This recommendation is based on trials with many different combinations. It appears to allow the method to work efficiently in many different situations.
  The choice of the initial simplex is at our discretion. The program given takes an initial point $\mathbf{x}_1$ and then forms

$$\begin{aligned} \mathbf{x}_2 &= \mathbf{x}_1 + k\mathbf{e}_1 \\ \mathbf{x}_3 &= \mathbf{x}_1 + k\mathbf{e}_2 \\ \mathbf{x}_{n+1} &= \mathbf{x}_1 + k\mathbf{e}_n \end{aligned} \tag{3.13}$$

where $k$ is an (arbitrary) step length of our choice and $\mathbf{e}_j$ is a unit vector in the direction of the $j$th co-ordinate.

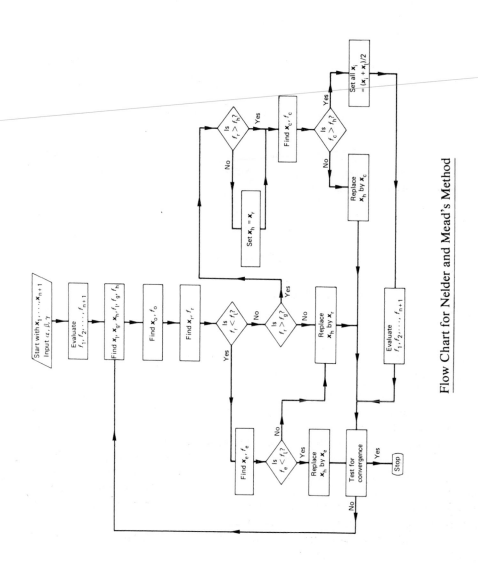

Flow Chart for Nelder and Mead's Method

In the program a point is denoted by its text subscript, e.g. $c$ refers to $\mathbf{x}_c$. The simplex $s$ is an array of points and the $j$th component of the $i$th point is referred to by $s[i] \cdot x[j]$.

$$s[i] \cdot x[j] = x_{ij} \qquad (3.14)$$

The program follows the steps (A)–(F) in the procedure previously outlined and the occurrence of each step is indicated by a comment. As listed the FUNCTION $f$ is appropriate for the minimisation of Rosenbrock's function (3.1).

Note that the test in the FUNCTION *convergence* uses the well known identity

$$\sum_{i=1}^{n+1} (f_i - \bar{f})^2 = \sum_{i=1}^{n+1} f_i^2 - (n+1)\bar{f}^2 \qquad (3.15)$$

to calculate the first quantity.

The program listing follows.

```
PROGRAM NelderandMead (input,output);
CONST
   n=2;  nl=3;     { n is no. of variables in function f, nl is n+1 }    {**}
   fwx=14; dpx=8;  { Output format constants for x-values }              {**}
   fwf=14; dpf=8;  { Output format constants for function values }       {**}

TYPE
   vector = ARRAY [1..n] OF real;
   point = RECORD
              x : vector;  f : real
           END;
   simplex = ARRAY [1..nl] OF point;
   howobtained = PACKED ARRAY [1..16] OF char;

VAR
   s : simplex;        { Simplex of points }
   e, g, h, l , r, c,  { Search points }
   centroid : point;   { Centroid of simplex minus point h }
   alpha, beta,        { Reflection, contraction }
   gamma : real;       { and expansion factors }
   epsilon : real;     { Required accurary in variance }
   k : real;           { Step length for simplex initialisation }
   fe, i, hindex : integer;

FUNCTION f (x:vector): real;
{ The code here is dependent on the function being minimised }
BEGIN  fe := fe+1;
   f := 100*sqr(x[2]-sqr(x[1])) + sqr(1.0-x[1])                          {**}
END; { f }

PROCEDURE inputdata;
VAR  i : integer;
BEGIN  writeln('    NUMBER OF VARIABLES =', n:3);
   writeln('    INITIAL ESTIMATE');
   WITH s[1] DO
     FOR i:=1 TO n DO
```

```
      BEGIN
        write('    X[', i:2, ']'); read(x[i]); writeln(x[i]:fwx:dpx)
      END;
    write('    STEP LENGTH ='); read(k); writeln(k:fwx:dpx); writeln;
    write('    ALPHA ='); read(alpha); writeln(alpha:6:2);
    write('    BETA ='); read(beta); writeln(beta:7:2);
    write('    GAMMA ='); read(gamma); writeln(gamma:6:2);
    write('    EPSILON = '); read(epsilon); writeln(epsilon)
END; { inputdata }


PROCEDURE outputline (p:point; s:howobtained);
VAR  i : integer;
BEGIN  write(p.f:fwf:dpf, '    ', s);
  FOR i:=1 TO n DO write(p.x[i]:fwx:dpx);   writeln
END; { outputline }


PROCEDURE initialise;
VAR  i : integer;
BEGIN  fe:=0;  s[1].f:=f(s[1].x);
  FOR i:=2 TO nl DO  { Initialise simplex }
    BEGIN s[i].x:=s[1].x; s[i].x[i-1]:=s[i].x[i-1]+k; s[i].f:=f(s[i].x) END
END; { initialise }


PROCEDURE findlgh;
{ Find the points l, g and h with the smallest, second largest    }
{ and largest function values respectively, i.e. perform Step (B) }
VAR  i : integer;
BEGIN  l:=s[1];  g:=s[1];  h:=s[1];  hindex:=1;
  FOR i:=2 TO nl DO
    WITH s[i] DO
    IF f<l.f THEN l:=s[i]
    ELSE IF f>g.f THEN
            IF f>h.f THEN
            BEGIN  g:=h; h:=s[i]; hindex:=i   END
            ELSE  g:=s[i]
END; { findlgh }


PROCEDURE findcentroid;
{ Find the centroid of all the points in simplex }
{ except h, i.e. perform Step (C).               }
VAR  i, j : integer;  sum : real;
BEGIN
  FOR j:=1 TO n DO
  BEGIN   sum:=0.0;
    FOR i:=1 TO hindex-1 DO sum := sum + s[i].x[j];
    FOR i:=hindex+1 TO nl DO sum := sum + s[i].x[j];
    centroid.x[j] := sum/n
  END;
  centroid.f := f(centroid.x)
END; { findcentroid }
```

```
PROCEDURE newpoint (VAR new:point; a:real; p1:point; b:real; p2:point);
{ Find the point whose vector is  a*p1.x + b*p2.x }
VAR  i : integer;
BEGIN
  FOR i:=1 TO n DO new.x[i] := a*p1.x[i] + b*p2.x[i];  new.f := f(new.x)
END; { newpoint }


FUNCTION convergence: boolean;
{ Test whether the process has converged, i.e. perform Step (I) }
VAR  sumf, sumfsq : real;  i : integer;
BEGIN   sumf:=0.0;  sumfsq:=0.0;
  FOR i:=1 TO n1 DO
    WITH s[i] DO BEGIN sumf := sumf + f; sumfsq := sumfsq + sqr(f) END;
  convergence := (sumfsq-sqr(sumf)/n1)/n1 < epsilon
END; { convergence }


BEGIN  { Main program }
  writeln;  writeln('    SIMPLEX METHOD OF NELDER & MEAD');  writeln;
  inputdata;  writeln;  write(' ':fwf-4, 'F(X)', '    HOW OBTAINED    ');
  FOR i:=1 TO n DO write(' ':fwx-5, 'X[', i:2, ']');  writeln;  writeln;
  initialise;  { Step (A) }
  REPEAT  { Until convergence achieved }
    findlgh;  { Step (B) }
    findcentroid;  { Step (C) }  outputline(centroid,'CENTROID        ');
    newpoint(r, 1.0+alpha, centroid, -alpha, h);  { Step (D) }
    outputline(r,'REFLECTION       ');
    IF r.f<l.f THEN  { Step (E)(i) }
    BEGIN  newpoint(e, gamma, r, 1.0-gamma, centroid);
      IF e.f<l.f THEN  { Step (E)(i)(a) }
      BEGIN s[hindex]:=e; outputline(e,'EXPANSION       ') END
      ELSE  { Step (E)(i)(b) }
      BEGIN s[hindex]:=r; outputline(r,'REFLECTION       ') END
    END
    ELSE
      IF r.f>g.f THEN  { Step (F) from Step (E)(iii) }
      BEGIN  { Step (F)(i) }
        IF r.f<h.f THEN h:=r;
        newpoint(c, beta, h, 1.0-beta, centroid);  { Step (F)(ii) }
        { Now perform Step (G) }
        IF c.f>h.f THEN  { Reduce simplex at Step (H) from Step (G)(ii) }
        BEGIN  FOR i:=1 TO n1 DO newpoint(s[i], 0.5, s[i], 0.5, 1);
          writeln('    REDUCTION OF SIMPLEX CARRIED OUT')
        END
        ELSE  { Step (G)(i) }
        BEGIN s[hindex]:=c; outputline(c,'CONTRACTION     ') END
      END
      ELSE  { Step (E)(ii) }
      BEGIN s[hindex]:=r; outputline(r,'REFLECTION       ') END
  UNTIL convergence;  { Step (I) }
  writeln; outputline(l,'MINIMUM OBTAINED');  writeln;
  writeln('    NO. OF FUNCTION EVALUATIONS =', fe:6)
END.
```

## Example 1

Use Nelder and Mead's method to minimise Rosenbrock's function

$$f(x_1, x_2) = 100(x_2 - x_1^2)^2 + (1 - x_1)^2.$$

Use the point $(1 \cdot 5, 2)$ as the initial estimate, take $k$ as $0 \cdot 5$, and use $\alpha = 1$, $\beta = 0 \cdot 5$ and $\gamma = 2$.

```
SIMPLEX METHOD OF NELDER & MEAD

NUMBER OF VARIABLES =   2
INITIAL ESTIMATE
X[ 1]    1.50000000
X[ 2]    2.00000000
STEP LENGTH =    0.50000000

ALPHA =   1.00
BETA  =   0.50
GAMMA =   2.00
EPSILON =   1.0000000000000E-010
```

| F(X) | HOW OBTAINED | X[ 1] | X[ 2] |
|---|---|---|---|
| 0.25000000 | CENTROID | 1.50000000 | 2.25000000 |
| 225.00000000 | REFLECTION | 1.00000000 | 2.50000000 |
| 66.07812500 | CONTRACTION | 1.25000000 | 2.37500000 |
| 0.25000000 | CENTROID | 1.50000000 | 2.25000000 |
| 88.45312500 | REFLECTION | 1.75000000 | 2.12500000 |
| 17.93847656 | CONTRACTION | 1.37500000 | 2.31250000 |
| 0.25000000 | CENTROID | 1.50000000 | 2.25000000 |
| 20.92285156 | REFLECTION | 1.62500000 | 2.18750000 |
| 4.80718994 | CONTRACTION | 1.43750000 | 2.28125000 |
| 5.66720963 | CENTROID | 1.46875000 | 2.39062500 |
| 51.29156494 | REFLECTION | 1.43750000 | 2.78125000 |
| 0.24111009 | CONTRACTION | 1.48437500 | 2.19531250 |
| 1.29287542 | CENTROID | 1.46093750 | 2.23828125 |
| 0.38197541 | REFLECTION | 1.42187500 | 1.97656250 |
| 0.38197541 | REFLECTION | 1.42187500 | 1.97656250 |
| 0.27103639 | CENTROID | 1.45312500 | 2.08593750 |
| 7.32736588 | REFLECTION | 1.46875000 | 1.89062500 |
| 1.09445943 | CONTRACTION | 1.44531250 | 2.18359375 |
| • • • • • • • • • • • • • • • • • • • • • • • • • • • • • • • • |
| 0.00006874 | REFLECTION | 1.00818480 | 1.01630452 |
| 0.00001944 | CENTROID | 1.00440899 | 1.00883076 |
| 0.00014342 | REFLECTION | 1.00811396 | 1.01717459 |
| 0.00002776 | CONTRACTION | 1.00255651 | 1.00465884 |
| 0.00000594 | CENTROID | 1.00159484 | 1.00300792 |
| 0.00003541 | REFLECTION | 0.99500488 | 0.98971131 |
| 0.00000880 | CONTRACTION | 0.99829986 | 0.99635961 |
| 0.00000085 | CENTROID | 0.99946652 | 0.99885830 |
| 0.00002163 | REFLECTION | 0.99637653 | 0.99305777 |
| 0.00000554 | CONTRACTION | 0.99792153 | 0.99595804 |
| 0.00000122 | MINIMUM OBTAINED | 1.00063318 | 1.00135699 |

```
NO. OF FUNCTION EVALUATIONS =   108
```

As given the progress of the procedure can be followed reasonably well. Of course it is possible to suppress the printout by removing all calls to the PROCEDURE *outputline* except the one outside the REPEAT loop and this will speed up the operations.

The true minimum has value 0 at (1, 1).

## 3.4   References

1   M. J. Box, D. Davies and W. H. Swann, *Non-linear Optimisation Techniques*, ICI Ltd., Monograph No. 5, Oliver and Boyd, 1969.
2   R. Hooke and T. A. Jeeves, 'Direct search solution of numerical and statistical problems', *J. Assn. Comp. Mach.*, **8**, 212–229, 1961.
3   J. A. Nelder and R. Mead, 'A simplex method for function minimisation', *The Comp. Journal*, 7, 308–313, 1965.
4   M. J. D. Powell, 'An iterative method for finding stationary values of a function of several variables', *The Comp. Journal*, 5, 147–151, 1962.
5   H. H. Rosenbrock, 'An automatic method for finding the greatest or least value of a function', *The Comp. Journal*, 3, 175–184, 1960.
6   W. Spendley, G. R. Hext and F. R. Himsworth, 'Sequential applications of simplex designs in optimisation and evolutionary operation', *Technometrics*, **4**, 441–461, 1962.

## Exercises 3

**1**   Try to write a Pascal program to implement the alternating variable search method. You can use any of the one-dimensional searches of Chapter 2 as a PROCEDURE for this method.

**2**   Use the program you have written in question 1 to find the minimum of (i) $(x_1 - 1)^2 + (x_2 - 2)^2 + (x_3 - 3)^2$   (ii)   Rosenbrock's   function   $100(x_2 - x_1^2)^2 + (1 - x_1)^2$.

**3**   Use the Hooke and Jeeves program to minimise the functions of question 2. Compare the number of function evaluations needed with the number needed for the alternating variable method.

**4**   Repeat questions 2 and 3 but with a variety of initial points.

**5**   Modify the Hooke and Jeeves method, changing the factor which reduces the step length. Instead of 10 use (a) 2 (b) 4 (c) 8 (d) 100. Repeat the examples given in questions 2 and 3 (and any others) and compare the number of function evaluations needed to obtain the final result.

**6**   Use the Nelder and Mead program to minimise (i) Rosenbrock's function (ii) Powell's function (iii) the two dimensional exponential function. [Equations 3.1, 3.2, 3.3.] Use different starting values and compare the number of function evaluations. Particularly awkward starting points are $(-1 \cdot 2, 1)$ for (i) $(3, -1, 0, 1)$ for (ii).

**7**   Consult the reference Box, Davies and Swann. Try to incorporate their convergence test in the Nelder and Mead program and test the result on the functions of question 6.

**8**  Modify the Nelder and Mead program by using different values for $\alpha$, $\beta$ and $\gamma$. Test the results. Consult the paper by Nelder and Mead and read their comments on this point.

**9**  Consult the reference by Spendley, Hext and Himsworth. Write a Pascal program to implement their method and test it. How does it compare with Nelder and Mead in terms of the number of function evaluations required?

**10**  Minimise the function

$$f(x_1, x_2) = x_1^4 + x_2^4 + 2x_1^2 x_2^2 - 4x_1 + 3.$$

**11**  Minimise the function

$$\phi(x_1, x_2) = (x_1^2 + x_2 - 11)^2 + (x_1 + x_2^2 - 7)^2.$$

**12**  Solve the equations

$$x_1^2 + x_2 = 11$$
$$x_1 + x_2^2 = 7.$$

Can you see how you can use question 11 to help you?

**13**  Solve the equations

$$x + y + z = 6$$
$$x^2 + y^2 + z^2 = 14$$
$$x^3 + y^3 + z^3 = 36.$$

**14**  The variables $F$ and $C$ should follow a relationship of the form $F = a + bC$ but there is error in the measured value of $F$.
   Estimate $a$ and $b$ given the data below

| F | 51 | 68 | 84 | 103 | 121 | 141 |
|---|----|----|----|-----|-----|-----|
| C | 10 | 20 | 30 | 40  | 50  | 60  |

Use the principle of least squares and choose $a$ and $b$ to minimise

$$S = \sum_{i=1}^{6} (F_i - a - bC_i)^2.$$

This is a simple linear regression problem. This topic is considered in many elementary statistics books and formulae for $a$ and $b$ exist which are easy to calculate. Check your answer using these results.

**15**  It is known that the variables $Q$ and $h$ are related (subject to measured error in $Q$) by $Q = ah^n$ where $a$ and $n$ are constants.
   Given the data below show that this appears to be reasonable and estimate $a$ and $n$.

| h | 4   | 6    | 8    | 10   | 12   |
|---|-----|------|------|------|------|
| Q | 650 | 1740 | 3640 | 6360 | 9790 |

N.B. If $Q = ah^n$, $\ln(Q) = \ln(a) + n \ln(h)$. Thus we can reduce the problem to one of linear regression with transformed variables $\ln(Q)$ and $\ln(h)$. Try it with and without the transformation from the point of view of the principle of least squares;

i.e. minimise (i) $\quad S_1 = \sum \left[ \ln(Q_i) - \ln(a) - n \ln(h_i) \right]^2$

(ii) $\quad S_2 = \sum (Q_i - ah_i^n)^2$

by choice of $a$ and $n$. Are the answers the same?

# 4
# Gradient Methods

## 4.1 The Method of Steepest Descent

In this chapter we consider search methods which use the gradient of the function as well as the function values. The alternating variable search which was briefly mentioned in Section 3.1 searched from a given point in a direction parallel to one of the axes for the minimum in that direction. It then searched in a direction parallel to one of the other axes etc. The directions are of course fixed. It seems reasonable to try to modify this method so that at each step the search for the minimum is carried out along the 'best' direction. What is best is not clear but the direction opposite to that of the gradient has a certain intuitive appeal. The direction of the gradient is the direction of steepest ascent. The opposite direction is thus the direction of steepest descent.

This property can be proved as follows. Suppose from a point $\mathbf{x}$ we move to a neighbouring point $\mathbf{x} + h\mathbf{d}$ where $\mathbf{d}$ is some direction and $h$ is some step length. Thus we move from $(x_1, x_2, ..., x_n)$ to $(x_1 + \delta x_1, x_2 + \delta x_2, ..., x_n + \delta x_n)$ where

$$\delta x_i = hd_i \tag{4.1}$$

and $d_i$ are the direction cosines of $\mathbf{d}$ so that

$$\sum_{i=1}^{n} d_i^2 = 1. \tag{4.2}$$

The change in the function value is given by

$$df = f(x_1 + \delta x_1, x_2 + \delta x_2, ..., x_n + \delta x_n) - f(x_1, x_2, ..., x_n)$$

$$= \frac{\partial f}{\partial x_1} \delta x_1 + \frac{\partial f}{\partial x_2} \delta x_2 + \cdots + \frac{\partial f}{\partial x_n} \delta x_n \tag{4.3}$$

to first order in the $\delta x_i$, where the partial derivatives are evaluated at $\mathbf{x}$ (refer to equation 1.4). How should we choose the $d_i$ subject to equation 4.2 so that we obtain the largest possible value for $df$?

We have here a constrained maximisation problem, and to solve it, we anticipate the results of the next chapter. Thus we use the method of Lagrange multipliers to define

$$\phi(d_1, d_2, ..., d_n) = df + \lambda(\sum d_i^2 - 1)$$

The maximum of $df$ subject to the constraint (equation 4.2) arises when

$\phi(d_1, d_2, ..., d_n)$ is maximised.

$$\phi(d_1, d_2, ..., d_n) = h\left(\frac{\partial f}{\partial x_1} d_1 + \frac{\partial f}{\partial x_2} d_2 + \cdots + \frac{\partial f}{\partial x_n} d_n\right) + \lambda(d_1^2 + d_2^2 + \cdots + d_n^2 - 1)$$

$$\frac{\partial \phi}{\partial d_j} = h\frac{\partial f}{\partial x_j} + 2\lambda d_j \ (j = 1, 2, ..., n). \tag{4.4}$$

When

$$\frac{\partial \phi}{\partial d_j} = 0, \quad d_j = -\frac{h}{2\lambda}\frac{\partial f}{\partial x_j}. \tag{4.5}$$

$$\therefore \quad \frac{d_1}{\dfrac{\partial f}{\partial x_1}} = \frac{d_2}{\dfrac{\partial f}{\partial x_2}} = \cdots = \frac{d_n}{\dfrac{\partial f}{\partial x_n}}. \tag{4.6}$$

Thus $d_i \propto \partial f/\partial x_i$ and the direction $\mathbf{d}$ is parallel to $\nabla f(\mathbf{x})$ at $\mathbf{x}$.

Thus the greatest *local* increase in the function for a given *small* step $h$ occurs when $\mathbf{d}$ is in the direction of $\nabla f(\mathbf{x})$ or $\mathbf{g}(\mathbf{x})$. So the direction of steepest descent is in the direction

$$-\nabla f(\mathbf{x}) \quad \text{or} \quad -\mathbf{g}(\mathbf{x}). \tag{4.7}$$

More simply we can write equation 4.3 as

$$df = |\nabla f(\mathbf{x})\| d\mathbf{x}| \ \cos\theta$$

where $\theta$ is the angle between $\nabla f(\mathbf{x})$ and $d\mathbf{x}$. For a given magnitude of $d\mathbf{x}$ we minimise $df$ by choosing $\theta$ to be $180°$ so that $d\mathbf{x}$ is in the direction $-\nabla f(\mathbf{x})$.

N.B. The gradient direction is orthogonal to the contours of the function at any point, for on a contour the function value does not change. Thus if $(d_1, d_2, ..., d_n)$ is a *small* step along the contour

$$f(x_1 + d_1, x_2 + d_2, ..., x_n + d_n) = f(x_1, x_2, ..., x_n)$$

$$\therefore \quad df = \sum_{j=1}^{n} \frac{\partial f}{\partial x_j} d_j = [\nabla f(\mathbf{x})]^{\mathsf{T}}\mathbf{d} = 0. \tag{4.8}$$

See Fig. 4.1.

The method of steepest descent seeks to exploit this property of the gradient direction. Thus if we are at the point $\mathbf{x}_i$ at any stage in the process we search for the function minimum along the direction $-\nabla f(\mathbf{x}_i)$. The method is an iterative process. At stage $i$ we have an approximation $\mathbf{x}_i$ for the minimum point. Our next approximation is

$$\mathbf{x}_{i+1} = \mathbf{x}_i - \lambda_i \nabla f(\mathbf{x}_i) \tag{4.9}$$

where $\lambda_i$ is the value of $\lambda$ that minimises

$$\phi(\lambda) = f[\mathbf{x}_i - \lambda\nabla f(\mathbf{x}_i)] \tag{4.10}$$

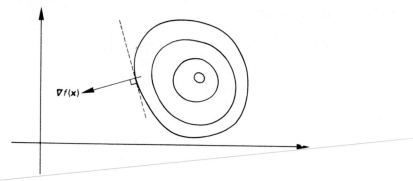

**Figure 4.1**

$\lambda_i$ can be found by using one of the univariate searches of Chapter 2. A flow chart for the method follows.

Flow Chart for Steepest Descent

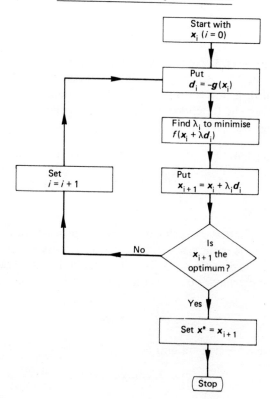

```
PROGRAM SteepestDescent (input,output);
CONST
  n=3;                  { Number of variables in function f }        {**}
  fwx=14; dpx=8;        { Output format constants for x-values }      {**}
  fwf=16; dpf=10;       { Output format constants for function values } {**}
TYPE
  vector = ARRAY [1..n] OF real;
  point1 = RECORD          { To represent a single point (x,f(x)) }
              x, f : real
           END;
  point = RECORD            { To represent values at a single point }
              x, g : vector;  { x-vector and gradient-vector }
              f, g0 : real    { function value and gradient value }
           END;
VAR
  P, Q : point;         { Search points }
  d : vector;           { Direction of search }
  epsilon,              { Required gradient accuracy in steepest descent }
  lambda,               { Step length in quadratic interpolation }
  E : real;             { Required accuracy in quadratic interpolation }
  p1, p2, p3 : point1;  { Search points in quadratic interpolation }
  it : integer;         { Iteration count for steepest descent }
  i : integer;

FUNCTION f (x:vector): real;
{ The code here is dependent on the function being minimised }
BEGIN
  f := sqr(x[1]-1.0) + sqr(x[2]-3.0) + 4.0*sqr(x[3]+5.0)             {**}
END; { f }

FUNCTION scalarmult (v1,v2:vector): real;
{ Perform scalar multiplication of vectors v1 and v2 }
VAR  i : integer;  sum : real;
BEGIN  sum:=0.0;
  FOR i:=1 TO n DO sum := sum +v1[i]*v2[i];
  scalarmult := sum
END; { scalarmult }

PROCEDURE gradients (VAR p:point);
{ Computes the gradients at p in each of the x-directions as }
{ well as the gradient of steepest ascent.                   }
{ The code here is dependent on the function being minimised }
VAR  i : integer;
BEGIN
  WITH p DO
  BEGIN  g[1] := 2.0*(x[1]-1.0);   g[2] := 2.0*(x[2]-3.0);          {**}
    g[3] := 8.0*(x[3]+5.0);                                         {**}
    g0:=0.0;  FOR i:=1 TO n DO g0 := g0 + sqr(g[i]);  g0 := sqrt(g0)
  END
END; { gradients }

PROCEDURE movepoint (VAR p1:point; p2:point; r:real);
{ p1 is made the point a distance r from p2 in the d-direction }
VAR  i : integer;
```

```
BEGIN   FOR i:=1 TO n DO pl.x[i] := p2.x[i] + r*d[i];
  pl.f:=f(pl.x);  gradients(pl)
END; { movepoint }


PROCEDURE inputdata;
VAR  i : integer;
BEGIN  writeln('    NUMBER OF VARIABLES =', n:3);
  writeln('    INITIAL POINT');
  FOR i:=1 TO n DO
  BEGIN write('    X[', i:2, ']'); read(P.x[i]); writeln(P.x[i]:fwx:dpx) END;
  write('    INITIAL STEP LENGTH ='); read(lambda); writeln(lambda:fwx:dpx);
  write('    REQUIRED ACCURACY IN GRADIENT =');
  read(epsilon); writeln(epsilon:fwf:dpf);
  write('    REQUIRED ACCURACY IN QUADRATIC INTERPOLATION =');
  read(E); writeln(E:fwx:dpx)
END; { inputdata }


PROCEDURE outputline (it:integer; p:point);
VAR  i : integer;
BEGIN  write(it:6, '    ', p.f:fwf);
  FOR i:=1 TO n DO write(p.x[i]:fwx:dpx); writeln
END; { outputline }


FUNCTION phi (lambda:real): real;
{ Computes the value of phi(lambda) which is the value of the  }
{ function f at the point a distance lambda in the d-direction }
{ from the current steepest descent point, Q.                  }
VAR  v : vector;  i : integer;
BEGIN FOR i:=1 TO n DO v[i] := Q.x[i] + lambda*d[i]; phi := f(v) END; { phi }


PROCEDURE quadint (VAR p1,p2,p3:point1; E:real);
{ This procedure uses the quadratic interpolation routine of Section 2.5 }
{ to find the point on the line through Q in the d-direction which mini- }
{ mises f(x). The code is identical to that of the appropriate parts of  }
{ the program QuadraticInterpolation, with function phi replacing f.      }
VAR  temp1, temp2, temp3, numerator, denominator : real;  p4 : point1;
  PROCEDURE order (VAR p,q:point1);
  { To put p,q in order based on their function values }
  VAR  r : point1;
  BEGIN
    IF p.f>q.f THEN BEGIN r:=p; p:=q; q:=r END
  END; { order }
BEGIN { quadint }
  REPEAT { Until required accuracy attained }
    temp1 := p2.x-p3.x;  temp2 := p3.x-p1.x;  temp3 := p1.x-p2.x;
    numerator := 0.5*(p1.f-p2.f)*temp1*temp2;
    denominator := temp1*p1.f + temp2*p2.f + temp3*p3.f;
    p4.x := 0.5*(p1.x+p2.x) + numerator/denominator;  p4.f:=phi(p4.x);
    { Perform a tournament sort to order p1, p2, p3, p4 }
    order(p1,p2); order(p3,p4); order(p1,p3); order(p2,p4); order(p2,p3);
    { Retain the best three points }
    IF ((p2.x>p1.x)=(p3.x>p1.x)) AND ((p2.x>p1.x)=NOT(p4.x>p1.x)) THEN p3:=p4
  UNTIL abs(p1.x-p2.x) < E
END; { quadint }
```

```
BEGIN  { Main Program }
  writeln; writeln('    STEEPEST DESCENT'); writeln;
  inputdata; writeln; write('ITERATION', ' ':fwf-4, 'F(X)');
  FOR i:=1 TO n DO write(' ':fwx-5, 'X[', i:2, ']'); writeln; writeln;
  it:=0;  { Initialise iteration count }
  P.f:=f(P.x); gradients(P); { Calculate function value and gradients at P }
  WHILE P.g0 >= epsilon DO  { Iterate until required accuracy }
  BEGIN                     { in gradient is attained.          }
    FOR i:=1 TO n DO d[i] := -P.g[i]/P.g0;  { Compute direction vector }
    p1.x:=0.0;  p1.f:=P.f;  lambda := lambda/2.0;  Q:=P;
    REPEAT  { Until minimum in d-direction is bracketed, see Fig. 4.2 }
      lambda := 2.0*lambda;  movepoint(P,Q,lambda)
    UNTIL  (P.f>=p1.f) OR (scalarmult(P.g,d)>=0.0);
    { Set values for p3, point at end of range and p2, midpoint of range }
    p3.x:=lambda;  p3.f:=P.f;  movepoint(P,Q,lambda/2.0);
    p2.x:=lambda/2.0;  p2.f:=P.f;
    quadint(p1,p2,p3,E);  { Find position of minimum in d-direction }
    movepoint(P,Q,p1.x);       { Set P to this new minimum point }
    it := it+1;  outputline(it,P);  lambda := lambda/2.0
  END;
  writeln; writeln('MINIMUM OF FUNCTION = ', P.f:fwf)
END. { SteepestDescent }
```

A program to carry out the procedure is given and it uses the notation of the flow chart. In the first statement of the WHILE loop in the main program the $\mathbf{d}_i$ is set equal to a unit vector in the direction of steepest descent.

We use quadratic interpolation to find the minimum of

$$\phi(\lambda) = f(\mathbf{x}_i + \lambda\mathbf{d}_i) \tag{4.11}$$

when we search from $\mathbf{x}_i$ in the direction $\mathbf{d}_i$.

At $\mathbf{x}_i$, $\lambda = 0$ and we choose our step length $\lambda$ so that we span the minimum of $\phi(\lambda)$. Note that

$$\frac{d\phi}{d\lambda} = \mathbf{g}(\mathbf{x}_i + \lambda\mathbf{d}_i)^{\mathsf{T}}\mathbf{d}_i. \tag{4.12}$$

See also equation 2.16. This is calculated in the FUNCTION *scalarmult* and we are sure to have spanned the minimum if either $\phi(\lambda) \geqslant \phi(0)$ or $d\phi(\lambda)/d\lambda$ (i.e. *scalarmult* $(P \cdot g, d)) \geqslant 0$.

N.B. $d\phi(0)/d\lambda = -\mathbf{g}(\mathbf{x}_i)^{\mathsf{T}}\mathbf{g}(\mathbf{x}_i) < 0$. See Fig. 4.2(i) and (ii.)

If we have not bracketed a minimum we double $\lambda$, repeatedly if necessary, until we do.

Having ascertained that $(0, \lambda)$ includes the minimum we choose our third point as $\lambda/2$ and proceed to find the minimum of $\phi(\lambda)$ using the routine implemented in the PROGRAM *QuadraticInterpolation* of Chapter 2.

We reset the point $\mathbf{x}_i \rightarrow \mathbf{x}_{i+1}$ ($=$ point $P$) using the PROCEDURE *movepoint* and if $|\mathbf{g}(\mathbf{x}_{i+1})|$ is small enough we terminate the WHILE loop. The step length *lambda* has been reduced in preparation for the next iteration. As the searches proceed we hope to converge on the optimum so it seems reasonable that the step length should get smaller for an efficient procedure. However the division by 2 is arbitrary.

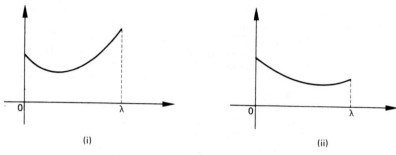

(i)                                                      (ii)

**Figure 4.2**

## Example 1

Use the program given to find the minimum of

$$f(x_1, x_2, x_3) = (x_1 - 1)^2 + (x_2 - 3)^2 + 4(x_3 + 5)^2.$$

The FUNCTIONs listed are appropriate for this problem. The minimum is clearly 0 when $x_1 = 1$, $x_2 = 3$ and $x_3 = -5$. With initial point $(4, -1, 2)$ and initial step length 4 the program found the minimum after 11 searches. The output is given.

```
STEEPEST DESCENT

NUMBER OF VARIABLES =   3
INITIAL POINT
X[ 1]      4.00000000
X[ 2]     -1.00000000
X[ 3]      2.00000000
INITIAL STEP LENGTH =     4.00000000
REQUIRED ACCURACY IN GRADIENT =      0.0000100000
REQUIRED ACCURACY IN QUADRATIC INTERPOLATION =      0.00005000
```

| ITERATION | F(X) | X[ 1] | X[ 2] | X[ 3] |
|---|---|---|---|---|
| 1 | 1.39512812E+001 | 3.23220500 | 0.02372667 | -5.16608668 |
| 2 | 8.80716055E-001 | 1.18938391 | 2.74748812 | -4.55810421 |
| 3 | 5.55978162E-002 | 1.14091457 | 2.81211391 | -5.01048471 |
| 4 | 3.50977724E-003 | 1.01195542 | 2.98405944 | -4.97210402 |
| 5 | 2.21565110E-004 | 1.00889565 | 2.98813913 | -5.00066188 |
| 6 | 1.39869555E-005 | 1.00075472 | 2.99899370 | -4.99823898 |
| 7 | 8.82968099E-007 | 1.00056156 | 2.99925125 | -5.00004178 |
| 8 | 5.57399831E-008 | 1.00004764 | 2.99993647 | -4.99988883 |
| 9 | 3.51875194E-009 | 1.00003545 | 2.99995273 | -5.00000264 |
| 10 | 2.22131659E-010 | 1.00000301 | 2.99999599 | -4.99999298 |
| 11 | 1.40227202E-011 | 1.00000224 | 2.99999702 | -5.00000017 |

```
MINIMUM OF FUNCTION =    1.40227202E-011
```

The criterion for terminating each search is that of the REPEAT loop in the PROCEDURE *quadint*. Experience has shown that it is not always economic to do the linear search thoroughly. All that is necessary is that we obtain a reduction in the function value from $f(\mathbf{x}_i)$. Thus it might be better to change the test to

$$p1 \cdot f < Q \cdot f$$

At first sight this may seem rather crude. The computation to find the minimum in this direction accurately might be considerable. Practical experience with these types of problem shows that it is just not worthwhile. What we lose on the 'accuracy swings' at this stage we make up for on the 'progress to the minimum via changes in direction roundabouts'. This amendment was made to deal with Example 2.

## Example 2

Find the minimum of $f(x_1, x_2, x_3) = (x_1 - 1)^4 + (x_2 - 3)^2 + 4(x_3 + 5)^4$.

Again the solution is clearly 0 at $(1, 3, -5)$. The output with initial point $(4, 2, -1)$ with step length 4 is given. Nine searches were needed to find the solution as given.

```
STEEPEST DESCENT

NUMBER OF VARIABLES =  3
INITIAL POINT
X[ 1]     4.00000000
X[ 2]     2.00000000
X[ 3]    -1.00000000
INITIAL STEP LENGTH =     4.00000000
REQUIRED ACCURACY IN GRADIENT =      0.0000100000
REQUIRED ACCURACY IN QUADRATIC INTERPOLATION =      0.00005000
```

| ITERATION | F(X) | X[ 1] | X[ 2] | X[ 3] |
|---|---|---|---|---|
| 1 | 4.45867849E+001 | 3.56967284 | 2.00796902 | -5.08013902 |
| 2 | 8.31635114E-001 | 0.73713983 | 2.09077024 | -5.07979536 |
| 3 | 2.76423755E-003 | 0.77350355 | 3.00097194 | -5.07572637 |
| 4 | 9.41437423E-005 | 1.01642718 | 2.99081193 | -5.03941129 |
| 5 | 9.25159531E-006 | 1.01641829 | 3.00002122 | -5.03892044 |
| 6 | 7.43944479E-006 | 1.01532148 | 2.99739171 | -4.98047631 |
| 7 | 6.29120724E-007 | 1.01531428 | 3.00000135 | -4.98053587 |
| 8 | 1.60305374E-007 | 1.01341701 | 2.99964364 | -4.99611719 |
| 9 | 3.32679008E-008 | 1.01341218 | 3.00000007 | -4.99611766 |

```
MINIMUM OF FUNCTION =    3.32679008E-008
```

Perhaps at this stage a caution should be given concerning the programs. On the face of it, it appears that all that is necessary is to change the FUNCTIONs for the function and gradient calculations. Would that things were that easy. There is to date no such thing as the 'universal optimiser' that can be guaranteed under all circumstances. The programs given are robust but care needs to be exercised in their application. They may fail on occasion and the device of changing the termination criterion slightly (from $<0\cdot000\ 01$ to $<0\cdot0001$ for example) may make all the difference. If more accuracy than the machine can give is demanded the program might loop infinitely. This is true of all the programs, so do be prepared to persevere with them in some cases.

Having said that, the method of steepest descent is NOT recommended as a serious optimisation procedure. It has an intuitive appeal but in practice it is far too slow. The point is that the steepest descent property is only a *local* property, and so, frequent changes of direction are necessary with it, and this leads to an inefficient computing procedure. It fails to take any account of the second derivatives.

The best way to do this is to develop methods which are based on quadratic functions. This is the simplest type of function and of course if we use the Taylor series expansion (equation 1.4) we notice that in the vicinity of its minimum any function can be approximated by a quadratic function (unless all its second derivatives are zero). Thus, methods based on procedures that work for quadratic functions should on the face of it stand a good chance of being successful with other functions.

In the next section we develop some of the important properties of the quadratic function of $n$ variables.

## 4.2   Quadratic Functions

The quadratic function

$$F(\mathbf{x}) = a + \mathbf{x}^T\mathbf{b} + \tfrac{1}{2}\mathbf{x}^T\mathbf{G}\mathbf{x} \tag{4.13}$$

where $a$ is a constant, $\mathbf{b}$ is a constant vector and $\mathbf{G}$ is a positive definite symmetric matrix has a minimum at the point $\mathbf{x}^*$ where $\mathbf{x}^*$ is given by,

$$\nabla F(\mathbf{x}^*) = \mathbf{b} + \mathbf{G}\mathbf{x}^* = \mathbf{0},$$
$$\text{i.e.} \quad \mathbf{x}^* = -\mathbf{G}^{-1}\mathbf{b}. \tag{4.14}$$

Now we have seen (equation 1.4) that subject to certain continuity conditions any function can be approximated in the region of a point $\mathbf{x}_0$ by

$$\phi(\mathbf{x}) = f(\mathbf{x}_0) + (\mathbf{x} - \mathbf{x}_0)^T\nabla f(\mathbf{x}_0) + \tfrac{1}{2}(\mathbf{x} - \mathbf{x}_0)^T\mathbf{G}(\mathbf{x}_0)(\mathbf{x} - \mathbf{x}_0) \tag{4.15}$$

where $\mathbf{G}(\mathbf{x}_0)$ is the Hessian matrix at $\mathbf{x}_0$.

A reasonable approximation to the minimum for $f(\mathbf{x})$ might be the minimum for $\phi(\mathbf{x})$. If the latter is at $\mathbf{x}_m$ we shall have

$$\nabla f(\mathbf{x}_0) + \mathbf{G}(\mathbf{x}_0)(\mathbf{x}_m - \mathbf{x}_0) = \mathbf{0},$$
$$\therefore \quad \mathbf{x}_m = \mathbf{x}_0 - \mathbf{G}^{-1}(\mathbf{x}_0)\nabla f(\mathbf{x}_0),$$

or

$$\mathbf{x}_m = \mathbf{x}_0 - \mathbf{G}^{-1}(\mathbf{x}_0)\mathbf{g}(\mathbf{x}_0), \tag{4.16}$$

Thus it appears that we should modify the iterative equation (4.9), and from a point $\mathbf{x}_i$ our next approximation to the minimum should be,

$$\mathbf{x}_{i+1} = \mathbf{x}_i - \mathbf{G}^{-1}(\mathbf{x}_i)\mathbf{g}(\mathbf{x}_i) \tag{4.17}$$

or more flexibly,

$$\mathbf{x}_{i+1} = \mathbf{x}_i - \lambda_i \mathbf{G}^{-1}(\mathbf{x}_i)\mathbf{g}(\mathbf{x}_i) \tag{4.18}$$

where $\lambda_i$ is determined by a search in the direction $\mathbf{G}^{-1}(\mathbf{x}_i)\mathbf{g}(\mathbf{x}_i)$.

The Newton–Raphson method is based on this last equation. We shall not consider it in detail but shall mention some features of it. As they stand equations 4.17 and 4.18 call for the evaluation and inversion of the Hessian matrix at each step and this can be a major computation. If $\mathbf{x}_i$ is close to $\mathbf{x}^*$ the convergence is fast since in general $\phi(\mathbf{x})$ will be a good approximation to $f(\mathbf{x})$ in this region. Both $|\mathbf{g}(\mathbf{x}_{i+1})|$ and $|\mathbf{x}_{i+1} - \mathbf{x}_i|$ should be checked as termination criteria. It is interesting to note that in contrast to the naive steepest descent, our search direction is not $-\mathbf{g}(\mathbf{x}_i)$, but $-\mathbf{G}^{-1}(\mathbf{x}_i)\mathbf{g}(\mathbf{x}_i)$ if second derivatives are taken into account. The Davidon–Fletcher–Powell method tries to get the best of all worlds by searching in the direction $-\mathbf{H}_i\mathbf{g}(\mathbf{x}_i)$ at the $i$th stage, where $\mathbf{H}_i$ is a positive define symmetric matrix which eventually equals $-\mathbf{G}^{-1}(\mathbf{x}^*)$. In this way it sidesteps both the evaluation and inversion of $\mathbf{G}(\mathbf{x}_i)$ at each step.

The direction of search at each stage is thus a crucial factor in the efficiency of iterative search methods. At any stage we want to make our next search in the 'best' direction. For a quadratic function of $n$ variables such as equation 4.13, the best direction in a certain sense is in a direction that is *conjugate* to the previous search directions. We first define this concept and then explain its usefulness.

Two directions $\mathbf{p}$ and $\mathbf{q}$ are said to be conjugate with respect to the symmetric positive definite matrix $\mathbf{G}$ if

$$\mathbf{p}^T\mathbf{G}\mathbf{q} = 0. \tag{4.19}$$

We can show from this definition that if $\mathbf{p}_0, \mathbf{p}_1, \mathbf{p}_2, \ldots, \mathbf{p}_{n-1}$ are $n$ mutually conjugate directions in $n$ dimensional space then they are linearly independent. For, if not, there will exist constants $\alpha_0, \alpha_1, \ldots, \alpha_{n-1}$, not all zero, such that,

$$\alpha_0\mathbf{p}_0 + \alpha_1\mathbf{p}_1 + \cdots + \alpha_{n-1}\mathbf{p}_{n-1} = \mathbf{0}.$$

Then for any $k(0 \leqslant k \leqslant n-1)$,

$$\mathbf{p}_k^T\mathbf{G} \sum_{j=0}^{n-1} \alpha_j\mathbf{p}_j = 0.$$

$$\therefore \quad \alpha_k\mathbf{p}_k^T\mathbf{G}\mathbf{p}_k = 0,$$

since all other terms vanish $(\mathbf{p}_k^T\mathbf{G}\mathbf{p}_j = 0, \; k \neq j)$ because of the mutual conjugacy.

Thus since $\mathbf{p}_k \neq \mathbf{0}$ and $\mathbf{G}$ is positive definite

$$\alpha_k = 0.$$

It follows that $\mathbf{p}_0, \mathbf{p}_1, \ldots, \mathbf{p}_{n-1}$ are linearly independent.

Before proceeding it is convenient to rewrite equation 4.13

$$F(\mathbf{x}) = a + \mathbf{x}^T\mathbf{b} + \tfrac{1}{2}\mathbf{x}^T\mathbf{G}\mathbf{x}$$

which has its optimum at

$$\mathbf{x}^* = -\mathbf{G}^{-1}\mathbf{b}$$

as

$$F(\mathbf{x}) = F(\mathbf{x}^*) + (\mathbf{x} - \mathbf{x}^*)^T \nabla F(\mathbf{x}^*) + \tfrac{1}{2}(\mathbf{x} - \mathbf{x}^*)^T \mathbf{G}(\mathbf{x} - \mathbf{x}^*)$$

$$= F(\mathbf{x}^*) + \tfrac{1}{2}(\mathbf{x} - \mathbf{x}^*)^T \mathbf{G}(\mathbf{x} - \mathbf{x}^*) \text{ (since } \nabla F(\mathbf{x}^*) = \mathbf{0})$$

$$= a + \mathbf{x}^{*T}\mathbf{b} + \tfrac{1}{2}\mathbf{x}^{*T}\mathbf{G}\mathbf{x}^* + \tfrac{1}{2}(\mathbf{x} - \mathbf{x}^*)^T \mathbf{G}(\mathbf{x} - \mathbf{x}^*)$$

$$= a - \tfrac{1}{2}\mathbf{b}^T\mathbf{G}^{-1}\mathbf{b} + \tfrac{1}{2}(\mathbf{x} - \mathbf{x}^*)^T \mathbf{G}(\mathbf{x} - \mathbf{x}^*)$$

$$\text{i.e. } F(\mathbf{x}) = c + \tfrac{1}{2}(\mathbf{x} - \mathbf{x}^*)^T \mathbf{G}(\mathbf{x} - \mathbf{x}^*) \tag{4.20}$$

where

$$c = a - \tfrac{1}{2}\mathbf{b}^T\mathbf{G}^{-1}\mathbf{b} \text{ is a constant.}$$

Suppose we use an iterative search technique to find the minimum of equation 4.20. It is clear that we should not decide on the search directions at the outset (alternating variable search for example) but rather should allow the knowledge gained by earlier searches to determine subsequent directions.

We start at $\mathbf{x}_0$ and search in the direction $\mathbf{p}_0$ to find the minimum at

$$\mathbf{x}_1 = \mathbf{x}_0 + \lambda_0\mathbf{p}_0 \tag{4.21}$$

where $\lambda_0$ is some scalar.

Note that at $\mathbf{x}_1, \mathbf{g}(\mathbf{x}_1) = \nabla F(\mathbf{x}_1)$ is orthogonal to $\mathbf{p}_0$,

$$\mathbf{g}(\mathbf{x}_1)^T\mathbf{p}_0 = 0. \tag{4.22}$$

See equations 2.16 and 4.12.

In general at step $i$ we search from a point $\mathbf{x}_i$ in the direction $\mathbf{p}_i$ to find the minimum in this direction at

$$\mathbf{x}_{i+1} = \mathbf{x}_i + \lambda_i\mathbf{p}_i \tag{4.23}$$

where

$$\mathbf{g}(\mathbf{x}_{i+1})^T\mathbf{p}_i = 0. \tag{4.24}$$

$$\mathbf{g}(\mathbf{x}_i) = \mathbf{G}(\mathbf{x}_i - \mathbf{x}^*) \tag{4.25}$$

for $F(\mathbf{x})$.

By repeated use of equation 4.23 we obtain after $n$ steps.

$$\mathbf{x}_n = \mathbf{x}_{n-1} + \lambda_{n-1}\mathbf{p}_{n-1}$$

$$= \mathbf{x}_{n-2} + \lambda_{n-2}\mathbf{p}_{n-2} + \lambda_{n-1}\mathbf{p}_{n-1}$$

$$= \mathbf{x}_{j+1} + \sum_{i=j+1}^{n-1} \lambda_i\mathbf{p}_i \tag{4.26}$$

for all $j$ in $0 \leqslant j < n - 1$.

Thus from equation 4.25

$$\mathbf{G}(\mathbf{x}_n - \mathbf{x}^*) = \mathbf{G}(\mathbf{x}_{j+1} - \mathbf{x}^*) + \sum_{i=j+1}^{n-1} \lambda_i\mathbf{G}\mathbf{p}_i. \tag{4.27}$$

Thus

$$\mathbf{g}(\mathbf{x}_n)^T\mathbf{p}_j = \mathbf{g}(\mathbf{x}_{j+1})^T\mathbf{p}_j + \sum_{i=j+1}^{n-1} \lambda_i\mathbf{p}_i^T\mathbf{G}\mathbf{p}_j \tag{4.28}$$

and so from equation 4.28

$$\mathbf{g}(\mathbf{x}_n)^T \mathbf{p}_j = \sum_{i=j+1}^{n-1} \lambda_i \mathbf{p}_i^T \mathbf{G} \mathbf{p}_j. \tag{4.29}$$

Now if all the vectors $\mathbf{p}_0, \mathbf{p}_1, \mathbf{p}_2, ..., \mathbf{p}_{n-1}$ are mutually conjugate so that

$$\mathbf{p}_i^T \mathbf{G} \mathbf{p}_j = 0 \quad \text{for } i \neq j. \tag{4.30}$$

then

$$\mathbf{g}(\mathbf{x}_n)^T \mathbf{p}_j = 0, \tag{4.31}$$

for all $j, j = 0, 1, ..., n - 1$. (It is true for $j = n - 1$ from equation 4.24).

But since in this case the $\mathbf{p}_0, \mathbf{p}_1, ..., \mathbf{p}_{n-1}$ are linearly independent and so form a basis it follows that

$$\mathbf{g}(\mathbf{x}_n) = \mathbf{0}, \tag{4.32}$$

whence

$$\mathbf{G}(\mathbf{x}_n - \mathbf{x}^*) = \mathbf{0} \tag{4.33}$$
$$\text{i.e.} \quad \mathbf{x}_n = \mathbf{x}^*.$$

It follows from this that if our searches are carried out in mutually conjugate directions we shall find the minimum of a quadratic function of $n$ variables in at most $n$ steps.

The Fletcher–Reeves method of Section 4.4 seeks to exploit this idea. We shall see however that it is pertinent to the Davidon–Fletcher–Powell method of the next section.

## 4.3  The Davidon–Fletcher–Powell Method

The Davidon–Fletcher–Powell (D.F.P.) method is based on equations 4.16 and 4.18, although it avoids calculating the inverse Hessian $\mathbf{G}^{-1}(\mathbf{x}_i)$ at each step by setting the search direction at stage $i$ as $-\mathbf{H}_i \mathbf{g}(\mathbf{x}_i)$, where $\mathbf{H}_i$ is a positive definite symmetric matrix which is *updated* at each stage in a manner that will be explained later. Ultimately $\mathbf{H}$ becomes equal to the inverse Hessian.

We start with an initial point $\mathbf{x}_0$ and an initial matrix $\mathbf{H}_0$, usually the unit matrix, although any symmetric positive definite matrix will do. The iterative procedure which will be justified shortly proceeds as follows. [N.B. It is convenient to write $\mathbf{g}(\mathbf{x}_i)$ as $\mathbf{g}_i$.]

1  At stage $i$ we have a point $\mathbf{x}_i$ and a positive definite symmetric matrix $\mathbf{H}_i$.
2  Set the direction of search

$$\mathbf{d}_i = -\mathbf{H}_i \mathbf{g}_i. \tag{4.34}$$

3  Carry out a linear search on the line $\mathbf{x}_i + \lambda \mathbf{d}_i$ to find the value $\lambda_i$ which minimises $f(\mathbf{x}_i + \lambda_i \mathbf{d}_i)$.
4  Put

$$\mathbf{v}_i = \lambda_i \mathbf{d}_i. \tag{4.35}$$

5    Put

$$x_{i+1} = x_i + v_i. \tag{4.36}$$

6    Find $f(x_{i+1})$ and $g_{i+1}$. Terminate the procedure if $|g_{i+1}|$ or $|v_i|$ are sufficiently small. Otherwise proceed.
N.B. From equation 4.24

$$g_{i+1}^T v_i = 0. \tag{4.37}$$

7    Put

$$u_i = g_{i+1} - g_i. \tag{4.38}$$

8    Update the **H** matrix by

$$H_{i+1} = H_i + A_i + B_i \tag{4.39}$$

where

$$A_i = v_i v_i^T / (v_i^T u_i) \tag{4.40}$$

$$B_i = -H_i u_i u_i^T H_i / (u_i^T H_i u_i). \tag{4.41}$$

9    Increase $i$ to $i+1$ and return to step 2.

We shall justify the procedure following the arguments of Fletcher and Powell.
(a) The process is stable, $v_i$ is downhill and $\lambda_i$ is positive. Since $g_i$ is the direction of steepest ascent, $v_i$ will be downhill if and only if

$$-v_i^T g_i = -g_i^T v_i$$
$$= \lambda_i g_i^T H_i g_i \tag{4.42}$$

is positive.

This will be so if $H_i$ is symmetric positive definite for all $i$. $H_0$ has these properties by assumption. The updating at equations 4.39, 4.40 and 4.41 maintains the symmetry. We prove that $H_i$ remains positive definite by induction.

Thus assume $H_i$ is symmetric positive definite. Then it has a square root $C_i$ such that

$$C_i^T C_i = C_i C_i^T = H_i. \tag{4.43}$$

Put

$$p = C_i \eta \quad \text{and} \quad q = C_i u_i \tag{4.44}$$

where $\eta$ is any vector.
Then

$$\eta^T H_{i+1} \eta = \eta^T H_i \eta + \frac{\eta^T v_i v_i^T \eta}{v_i^T u_i} - \frac{\eta^T H_i u_i u_i^T H_i \eta}{u_i^T H_i u_i}$$

$$= p^2 - \frac{(p^T q)^2}{q^2} + \frac{(\eta^T v_i)^2}{v_i^T u_i}$$

$$= \frac{p^2 q^2 - (\mathbf{p}^T \mathbf{q})^2}{q^2} + \frac{(\boldsymbol{\eta}^T \mathbf{v}_i)^2}{\mathbf{v}_i^T \mathbf{u}_i}$$

$$\geqslant \frac{(\boldsymbol{\eta}^T \mathbf{v}_i)^2}{\mathbf{v}_i^T \mathbf{u}_i} \tag{4.45}$$

because $\mathbf{p}^2 \mathbf{q}^2 \geqslant (\mathbf{p}^T \mathbf{q})^2$ by the Schwarz inequality.

Now the denominator of equation 4.45 is positive because

$$\mathbf{v}_i^T \mathbf{u}_i = \mathbf{v}_i^T [\mathbf{g}_{i+1} - \mathbf{g}_i]$$
$$= -\mathbf{v}_i^T \mathbf{g}_i \quad \text{since } \mathbf{v}_i^T \mathbf{g}_{i+1} = 0 \text{ from equation 4.37}$$
$$= \lambda_i \mathbf{g}_i^T \mathbf{H}_i \mathbf{g}_i$$
$$> 0 \quad \text{because } \lambda_i > 0 \text{ and } \mathbf{H}_i \text{ is positive definite.} \tag{4.46}$$

Thus $\boldsymbol{\eta}^T \mathbf{H}_{i+1} \boldsymbol{\eta} > 0$ which proves $\mathbf{H}_{i+1}$ to be positive definite. Thus the induction proof is complete.

(b) We next show that if the D.F.P. method is applied to the quadratic function (equation 4.13) with $\mathbf{G}$ symmetric positive definite, then $\mathbf{H}_n = \mathbf{G}^{-1}$ and the process will terminate after $n$ stages. We do this by showing that $\mathbf{v}_0, \mathbf{v}_1, \dots, \mathbf{v}_k$ are linearly independent eigenvectors of $\mathbf{H}_{k+1} \mathbf{G}$ with eigenvalue 1. Thus $\mathbf{H}_n \mathbf{G}$ must be the unit matrix.

We note from equation 4.38 that

$$\mathbf{u}_i = \mathbf{g}_{i+1} - \mathbf{g}_i$$
$$= \mathbf{G} \mathbf{x}_{i+1} - \mathbf{G} \mathbf{x}_i$$
$$= \mathbf{G} \mathbf{v}_i. \tag{4.47}$$

Also

$$\mathbf{H}_{i+1} \mathbf{G} \mathbf{v}_i = \mathbf{H}_{i+1} \mathbf{u}_i \quad \text{(from equation 4.47)}$$
$$= \mathbf{H}_i \mathbf{u}_i + \mathbf{A}_i \mathbf{u}_i + \mathbf{B}_i \mathbf{u}_i$$
$$= \mathbf{H}_i \mathbf{u}_i + \mathbf{v}_i - \mathbf{H}_i \mathbf{u}_i$$

using equations 4.39, 4.40 and 4.41 and noting that $\mathbf{v}_i^T \mathbf{u}_i$ and $\mathbf{u}_i^T \mathbf{H}_i \mathbf{u}_i$ are scalars which can be cancelled.

Thus

$$\mathbf{H}_{i+1} \mathbf{G} \mathbf{v}_i = \mathbf{v}_i. \tag{4.48}$$

We next show that for $k = 2, 3, \dots, n$

$$\mathbf{v}_i^T \mathbf{G} \mathbf{v}_j = 0, \quad 0 \leqslant i < j < k \tag{4.49}$$

$$\mathbf{H}_k \mathbf{G} \mathbf{v}_i = \mathbf{v}_i, \quad 0 \leqslant i < k \tag{4.50}$$

We do this by induction on $k$. If we put $i = 0$ in equation 4.48 we obtain $\mathbf{H}_1 \mathbf{G} \mathbf{v}_0 = \mathbf{v}_0$ which is equation 4.50 when $k = 1$. Equations 4.50 with $k = 2$ are

$$\mathbf{H}_2 \mathbf{G} \mathbf{v}_0 = \mathbf{v}_0 \quad \text{and} \quad \mathbf{H}_2 \mathbf{G} \mathbf{v}_1 = \mathbf{v}_1.$$

The second of these comes from equation 4.48 with $i = 1$.

For the first

$$H_2Gv_0 = H_1Gv_0 + v_1 \frac{v_1^T Gv_0}{v_1^T u_1} - \frac{H_1u_1u_1^T H_1 Gv_0}{u_1^T H_1 u_1}$$

The last two terms on the right are both zero since

$$v_1^T Gv_0 = v_0^T Gv_1 = v_0^T G(-\lambda_1 H_1 g_1)$$
$$= -\lambda_1 g_1^T H_1 Gv_0$$
$$= -\lambda_1 g_1^T v_0 \quad \text{(from equation 4.48 with } i = 0)$$
$$= 0 \quad \text{(from equation 4.37 with } i = 0).$$

Also $u_1 = Gv_1$, so that $u_1^T H_1 Gv_0 = v_1^T Gv_0$. Thus equations 4.50 are shown to be true for $k = 2$ and the result just established, when transposed gives

$$v_0^T Gv_1 = 0$$

which is equation 4.49 when $k = 2$.

We now proceed with the induction and try to show that if equations 4.49 and 4.50 are true for values up to $k$ they are also true for values up to $k + 1$.

We have

$$g_k = b + Gx_k$$
$$= b + G(x_{k-1} + v_{k-1})$$
$$= b + G(x_{k-2} + v_{k-2} + v_{k-1}) \text{ etc.}$$
$$= g_{i+1} + G(v_{i+1} + v_{i+2} + \cdots + v_{k-1}). \tag{4.51}$$

Thus from equation 4.49, when $i < k - 1$

$$v_i^T g_k = v_i^T g_{i+1} = 0 \quad \text{by equation 4.37}$$

and from equation 4.37 directly

$$v_{k-1}^T g_k = 0.$$

Thus

$$v_i^T g_k = 0, \quad 0 \leqslant i < k, \tag{4.52}$$

so that from equations 4.50

$$v_i^T GH_k g_k = 0 \quad 0 \leqslant i < k$$

so that

$$-v_i^T Gd_k = 0$$

so that

$$-v_i^T Gv_k = 0 \quad \text{since } v_k = \lambda_k d_k.$$

Thus we have established that

$$v_i^T Gv_k = 0 \quad \text{for } 0 \leqslant i < k \tag{4.53}$$

i.e. $\quad v_i^T Gv_j = 0 \quad \text{for } 0 \leqslant i < j < k + 1. \tag{4.54}$

We also have from equations 4.47 and 4.50

$$(\mathbf{u}_k)^{\mathsf{T}}\mathbf{H}_k\mathbf{G}\mathbf{v}_i = \mathbf{u}_k^{\mathsf{T}}\mathbf{v}_i$$
$$= \mathbf{v}_k^{\mathsf{T}}\mathbf{G}\mathbf{v}_i = 0 \quad \text{for } 0 \leqslant i < k(<k+1). \tag{4.55}$$

Hence from equations 4.39, 4.40, 4.41, 4.50

$$\mathbf{H}_{k+1}\mathbf{G}\mathbf{v}_i = \mathbf{H}_k\mathbf{G}\mathbf{v}_i + \frac{\mathbf{v}_k\mathbf{v}_k^{\mathsf{T}}\mathbf{G}\mathbf{v}_i}{\mathbf{v}_k^{\mathsf{T}}\mathbf{u}_k} - \frac{\mathbf{H}_k\mathbf{u}_k\mathbf{u}_k^{\mathsf{T}}\mathbf{H}_k\mathbf{G}\mathbf{v}_i}{\mathbf{u}_k^{\mathsf{T}}\mathbf{H}_k\mathbf{u}_k}$$

$$= \mathbf{H}_k\mathbf{G}\mathbf{v}_i,$$

since

$$\mathbf{v}_k^{\mathsf{T}}\mathbf{G}\mathbf{v}_i = 0$$

and

$$\mathbf{u}_k^{\mathsf{T}}\mathbf{H}_k\mathbf{G}\mathbf{v}_i = \mathbf{u}_k^{\mathsf{T}}\mathbf{v}_i$$
$$= \mathbf{v}_k^{\mathsf{T}}\mathbf{G}\mathbf{v}_i = 0 \quad \text{for } 0 \leqslant i < k.$$

Thus we have shown that

$$\mathbf{H}_{k+1}\mathbf{G}\mathbf{v}_i = \mathbf{H}_k\mathbf{G}\mathbf{v}_i = \mathbf{v}_i \quad \text{for } 0 \leqslant i < k. \tag{4.56}$$

Also for $i = k$

$$\mathbf{H}_{k+1}\mathbf{G}\mathbf{v}_k = \mathbf{H}_k\mathbf{G}\mathbf{v}_k + \frac{\mathbf{v}_k\mathbf{v}_k^{\mathsf{T}}\mathbf{G}\mathbf{v}_k}{\mathbf{v}_k^{\mathsf{T}}\mathbf{u}_k} - \frac{\mathbf{H}_k\mathbf{u}_k\mathbf{u}_k^{\mathsf{T}}\mathbf{H}_k\mathbf{G}\mathbf{v}_k}{\mathbf{u}_k^{\mathsf{T}}\mathbf{H}_k\mathbf{u}_k}$$

$$= \mathbf{H}_k\mathbf{u}_k + \mathbf{v}_k - \mathbf{H}_k\mathbf{u}_k$$

since

$$\mathbf{v}_k^{\mathsf{T}}\mathbf{G}\mathbf{v}_k = \mathbf{v}_k^{\mathsf{T}}\mathbf{u}_k \quad \text{and} \quad \mathbf{u}_k^{\mathsf{T}}\mathbf{H}_k\mathbf{G}\mathbf{v}_k = \mathbf{u}_k^{\mathsf{T}}\mathbf{H}_k\mathbf{u}_k$$

Thus $\mathbf{H}_{k+1}\mathbf{G}\mathbf{v}_k = \mathbf{v}_k$ and this combined with equation 4.56 gives

$$\mathbf{H}_{k+1}\mathbf{G}\mathbf{v}_i = \mathbf{v}_i \quad 0 \leqslant i < k+1. \tag{4.57}$$

Equations 4.54 and 4.57 extend equations 4.49 and 4.50 to the next value of $k$ and so complete the induction proof of the latter.

Equation 4.49 shows that $\mathbf{v}_0, \mathbf{v}_1, ..., \mathbf{v}_{n-1}$ are linearly independent. They are mutually conjugate with respect to $\mathbf{G}$. From equations 4.50 $\mathbf{v}_0, \mathbf{v}_1, ..., \mathbf{v}_{n-1}$ are eigenvectors of $\mathbf{H}_n\mathbf{G}$ with eigenvalue 1. Thus $\mathbf{H}_n\mathbf{G}$ must be a unit matrix.

$$\therefore \quad \mathbf{H}_n = \mathbf{G}^{-1}. \tag{4.58}$$

That the minimum is found by $n$ iterations follows from equation 4.52. $\mathbf{g}_n$ must be orthogonal to each of the $n$ independent vectors $\mathbf{v}_0, \mathbf{v}_1, ..., \mathbf{v}_{n-1}$. Thus

$$\mathbf{g}_n = \mathbf{0}. \tag{4.59}$$

(c) The updating of the $\mathbf{H}$ matrix follows equation 4.39.

$$\mathbf{H}_n = \mathbf{H}_0 + \sum_{i=0}^{n-1} \mathbf{A}_i + \sum_{i=0}^{n-1} \mathbf{B}_i.$$

We show that $\mathbf{G}^{-1} = \sum_{i=0}^{n-1} \mathbf{A}_i$. The orthogonality conditions (equation 4.49) imply that

$$\mathbf{V}^T\mathbf{G}\mathbf{V} = \Delta$$

where $\mathbf{V}$ is the matrix of vectors $\mathbf{v}_i$ and $\Delta$ is the diagonal matrix with elements $\mathbf{v}_i^T\mathbf{G}\mathbf{v}_i$. Thus

$$\mathbf{G} = (\mathbf{V}^T)^{-1} \Delta \mathbf{V}^{-1}$$
$$\therefore \quad \mathbf{G}^{-1} = \mathbf{V} \Delta^{-1} \mathbf{V}^T$$

and since $\Delta$ is a diagonal matrix we can do the inversion and matrix multiplication to obtain

$$\mathbf{G}^{-1} = \sum_{i=0}^{n-1} \frac{\mathbf{v}_i\mathbf{v}_i^T}{\mathbf{v}_i^T\mathbf{G}\mathbf{v}_i} = \sum_{i=0}^{n-1} \frac{\mathbf{v}_i\mathbf{v}_i^T}{\mathbf{v}_i^T\mathbf{u}_i} \quad \text{by equation 4.47.}$$

Thus

$$\mathbf{G}^{-1} = \sum_{i=0}^{n-1} \mathbf{A}_i. \tag{4.60}$$

Since equation 4.48 must be valid

$$\mathbf{H}_{i+1}\mathbf{G}\mathbf{v}_i = \mathbf{v}_i \quad \text{implies} \quad \mathbf{v}_i = \mathbf{H}_i\mathbf{G}\mathbf{v}_i + \mathbf{A}_i\mathbf{G}\mathbf{v}_i + \mathbf{B}_i\mathbf{G}\mathbf{v}_i.$$

Thus since

$$\mathbf{A}_i\mathbf{G}\mathbf{v}_i = \mathbf{A}_i\mathbf{u}_i = \frac{\mathbf{v}_i\mathbf{v}_i^T\mathbf{u}_i}{\mathbf{v}_i^T\mathbf{u}_i} = \mathbf{v}_i$$

$$\mathbf{B}_i\mathbf{G}\mathbf{v}_i = -\mathbf{H}_i\mathbf{G}\mathbf{v}_i = -\mathbf{H}_i\mathbf{u}_i. \tag{4.61}$$

Thus a simple form (though not necessarily the only form) for $\mathbf{B}_i$ is

$$\mathbf{B}_i = \frac{-\mathbf{H}_i\mathbf{u}_i\mathbf{z}^T}{\mathbf{z}^T\mathbf{G}\mathbf{v}_i} = \frac{-\mathbf{H}_i\mathbf{u}_i\mathbf{z}^T}{\mathbf{z}^T\mathbf{u}_i} \quad \text{where } \mathbf{z} \text{ is any vector.}$$

Since we want $\mathbf{B}_i$ to be symmetric we take $\mathbf{z} = \mathbf{H}_i\mathbf{u}_i$ so that

$$\mathbf{B}_i = \frac{-\mathbf{H}_i\mathbf{u}_i\mathbf{u}_i^T\mathbf{H}_i}{\mathbf{u}_i^T\mathbf{H}_i\mathbf{u}_i}. \tag{4.62}$$

This completes the theory of the D.F.P. method. The method uses both the ideas of the Newton–Raphson method and conjugate directions. When applied to a quadratic function of $n$ variables it converges in at most $n$ iterations. It is a very powerful optimisation procedure and works very efficiently for most functions whether they are quadratic or not.

We give a flow chart of the procedure and a program to implement the method. The linear searches required are carried out by cubic interpolation and the procedure given is very robust. These searches are not carried out to ultimate convergence but instead an improvement in the function is sought. In theory of course this means that the method loses the convergence properties for quadratic functions. In practice it is still very efficient and rapid. It is doubtful that the extra work involved in carrying out the linear searches completely would be worthwhile.

The program given follows the flow chart, uses the notation given there and has explanatory comments. The linear searches in the PROCEDURE *cubintmod* use the cubic interpolation routine of Section 2.6 except that they do not follow through to convergence. Thus a search, which is controlled by the boolean variable *minfound*, is terminated if the interpolated function value is less than both of the values used in the routine. Each search interval is decided at the bottom of the REPEAT loop in *cubintmod*.

**Example 1**

Use $(3, -1, 0, 1)$ as a starting point in order to minimise Powell's function

$$f(x_1, x_2, x_3, x_4) = (x_1 + 10x_2)^2 + 5(x_3 - x_4)^2 + (x_2 - 2x_3)^4 + 10(x_1 - x_4)^4.$$

The FUNCTIONs written are correct for this function. The starting point suggested is a particularly awkward one for this function. The minimum is 0 at $(0, 0, 0, 0)$. The way the method proceeds to this value can be seen in the output which are given.

Flow Chart for the Davidon–Fletcher–Powell Method

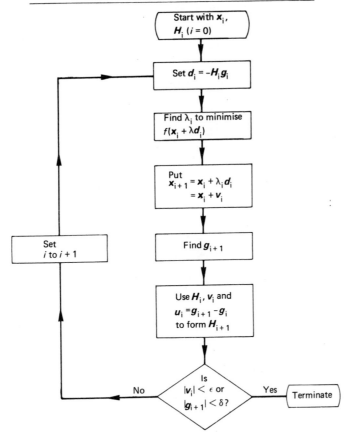

```
PROGRAM DavidonFletcherPowell (input,output);
CONST
  n=4;                  { Number of variables in funcion f }           {**}
  fwx=14; dpx=8;        { Output format constants for x-values }        {**}
  fwf=16; dpf=10;       { Output format constants for function values } {**}
TYPE
  vector = ARRAY [1..n] OF real;
  matrix = ARRAY [1..n] OF vector;
  point = RECORD              { To represent values at a single point }
            x, g : vector;    { x-vector and gradient-vector }
            f, g0 : real      { function value and gradient value }
          END;
VAR
  P, Q : point;      { Search points }
  H : matrix;        { Positive definite symmetric matrix }
  d,                 { Direction of search vector }
  v, u,              { Difference vectors for x-vectors and gradient vectors }
  m     : vector;    { For storing H*u }
  epsilon,           { Required accuracy in x-values }
  delta : real;      { Required accuracy in gradient }
  it : integer;      { Iteration count for Davidon-Fletcher-Powell }
  i, j, k : integer;   mu, vu : real;


FUNCTION f (x:vector): real;
{ The code here is dependent on the function being minimised }
BEGIN
  f := sqr(x[1]+10.0*x[2]) + 5.0*sqr(x[3]-x[4])                         {**}
       + sqr(sqr(x[2]-2.0*x[3])) + 10.0*sqr(sqr(x[1]-x[4]))             {**}
END; { f }


PROCEDURE gradients (VAR p:point);
{ Computes the gradients at p in each of the x-directions as }
{ well as the gradient of steepest ascent.                   }
{ The code here is dependent on the function being minimised }
VAR  i : integer;  t12, t23, t34, t14 : real;                          {**}
BEGIN
  WITH p DO
    BEGIN t12 := x[1]+10.0*x[2];  t34 := x[3]-x[4];  t23 := x[2]-2.0*x[3]; {**}
          t23 := t23*sqr(t23);  t14 := x[1]-x[4];  t14 := t14*sqr(t14);    {**}
      g[1] := 2.0*t12 + 40.0*t14;  g[2] := 20.0*t12 + 4.0*t23;            {**}
      g[3] := 10.0*t34 - 8.0*t23;  g[4] := -10.0*t34 - 40.0*t14;          {**}
      g0:=0.0;  FOR i:=1 TO n DO g0 := g0 + sqr(g[i]);  g0 := sqrt(g0)
    END
END; { gradients }


FUNCTION scalarmult (v1,v2:vector): real;
{ Perform scalar multiplication of vectors v1 and v2 }
VAR  i : integer;  sum : real;
BEGIN  sum:=0.0;
  FOR i:=1 TO n DO sum := sum + v1[i]*v2[i];
  scalarmult := sum
END; { scalarmult }
```

```
PROCEDURE movepoint (VAR p1:point; p2:point; r:real);
{ p1 is made the point a distance r from p2 in the d-direction }
VAR  i : integer;
BEGIN    FOR i:=1 TO n DO p1.x[i] := p2.x[i] + r*d[i];
  p1.f:=f(p1.x);  gradients(p1)
END; { movepoint }


PROCEDURE cubintmod (VAR p:point; d:vector);
{ A modification of the cubic interpolation routine of Section 2.6. }
{ The differences are :                                             }
{ (a)  iteration terminates when a point, r, is found with a        }
{      function value lower than both those of p and q, the ends    }
{      of the bracketing range.                                     }
{ (b)  phim is zero.                                                }
CONST  phim=0.0;
VAR  q, r : point;       { Search points, together with p }
  Gp, Gq, Gr : real;     { Gradient values in d-direction at p, q, r }
  qx, rx : real;         { Distances between points in iterative process }
  qx0, z, w : real;   minfound : boolean;
BEGIN
  REPEAT   { A search in the d-direction until gradient is negative }
    Gp := scalarmult(p.g,d);   qx := abs(2.0*(p.f-phim)/Gp);
    IF qx>1.0 THEN qx:=1.0;
    IF Gp>0.0 THEN movepoint(p,p,-qx)
  UNTIL Gp<=0.0;
  { Find next point, q }   qx0:=qx;
  REPEAT   { Until minimum has been bracketed }
    movepoint(q,p,qx0);  Gq := scalarmult(q.g,d);   qx:=qx0;  qx0:=2.0*qx0;
  UNTIL  (Gq>0.0) OR (q.f>p.f);
  REPEAT { Until r is found with function value lower than those at p and q }
    z := 3.0*(p.f-q.f)/qx + Gp + Gq;   w := sqr(z) - Gp*Gq;
    IF w<0.0 THEN w:=0.0;   w:=sqrt(w);   rx := qx*(z+w-Gp)/(Gq-Gp+2.0*w);
    movepoint(r,p,rx);   Gr := scalarmult(r.g,d);
    minfound := (r.f<p.f) AND (r.f<q.f);
    IF NOT minfound THEN
       IF Gr>0.0 THEN BEGIN  qx:=rx;  q:=r;  Gq:=Gr  END
       ELSE BEGIN  qx := qx-rx;  p:=r;  Gp:=Gr  END
  UNTIL minfound;
  p:=r;  { Return point in p }
END; { cubintmod }


PROCEDURE inputdata;
VAR  i :integer;
BEGIN  writeln('    NUMBER OF VARIABLES =', n:3);
  writeln('    INITIAL POINT');
  FOR i:=1 TO n DO
  BEGIN write('    X[', i:2, ']'); read(P.x[i]); writeln(P.x[i]:fwx:dpx) END;
  write('    REQUIRED ACCURACY, EPSILON, IN X-VALUES =');
  read(epsilon);  writeln(epsilon:fwx:dpx);
  write('    REQUIRED ACCURACY, DELTA, IN GRADIENT VALUE =');
  read(delta);  writeln(delta:fwf:dpf)
END; { inputdata }
```

```
PROCEDURE outputline (it:integer; p:point);
VAR  i : integer;
BEGIN  write(it:6, ´     ´, p.f:fwf);
  FOR i:=1 TO n DO write(p.x[i]:fwx:dpx);   writeln
END; { outputline }


PROCEDURE initialise;
VAR  zero : vector;  i : integer;
BEGIN  it:=0;   FOR i:=1 TO n DO zero[i]:=0.0;
  FOR i:=1 TO n DO BEGIN  H[i] := zero;  H[i,i]:=1.0  END
END; { initialise }


BEGIN   { Main Program }
  writeln;  writeln(´     DAVIDON-FLETCHER-POWELL´);   writeln;
  inputdata;  writeln;  initialise;
  write(´ITERATION´, ´  ´:fwf-4, ´F(X)´);
  FOR i:=1 TO n DO write(´  ´:fwx-5, ´X[´, i:2, ´]´); writeln; writeln;
  P.f := f(P.x);  gradients(P);
  REPEAT  { Until required accuracy in x-values or gradient attained }
    outputline(it,P);  Q:=P;
    FOR j:=1 TO n DO d[j] := -scalarmult(H[j],P.g);
    cubintmod(P,d);  it:=it+1;
    FOR j:=1 TO n DO BEGIN u[j] := P.g[j]-Q.g[j];  v[j] := P.x[j]-Q.x[j] END;
    FOR j:=1 TO n DO m[j] := scalarmult(H[j],u);
    mu := scalarmult(m,u);  vu := scalarmult(v,u);
    IF (mu<>0.0) AND (vu<>0.0) THEN
      FOR k:=1 TO n DO
        FOR j:=1 TO n DO  H[k,j] := H[k,j] - m[k]*m[j]/mu + v[k]*v[j]/vu;
  UNTIL  (sqrt(scalarmult(v,v)) < epsilon) OR (P.g0 < delta);
  writeln; writeln(´MINIMISATION COMPLETE - FINAL DETAILS ARE :´);
  writeln; outputline(it,P)
END. { DavidonFletcherPowell }
```

```
   DAVIDON-FLETCHER-POWELL

   NUMBER OF VARIABLES =  4
   INITIAL POINT
   X[ 1]     3.00000000
   X[ 2]    -1.00000000
   X[ 3]     0.00000000
   X[ 4]     1.00000000
   REQUIRED ACCURACY, EPSILON, IN X-VALUES =    0.00005000
   REQUIRED ACCURACY, DELTA, IN GRADIENT VALUE =    0.0000100000
```

| ITERATION | F(X) | X[ 1] | X[ 2] | X[ 3] | X[ 4] |
|---|---|---|---|---|---|
| 0 | 2.15000000E+002 | 3.00000000 | −1.00000000 | 0.00000000 | 1.00000000 |
| 1 | 3.08924630E+001 | 1.94987428 | −0.50582319 | 0.00686357 | 2.06385286 |
| 2 | 1.77325487E+001 | 1.95209393 | −0.14604276 | 0.11391275 | 1.98320490 |
| 3 | 9.91939375E+000 | 1.67208858 | −0.13261443 | 0.61733862 | 1.74023851 |
| 4 | 5.25920226E−002 | 0.12127709 | −0.00913126 | 0.23143438 | 0.21547037 |
| 5 | 2.54637279E−002 | 0.11244156 | −0.01592421 | 0.17549056 | 0.20519227 |

| | | | | |
|---|---|---|---|---|
| 6  | 4.77526369E−003 | 0.01728322  | −0.00013372 | 0.11865750  | 0.10683405 |
| 7  | 1.54571215E−003 | 0.00033036  | −0.00063799 | 0.08205684  | 0.08805791 |
| 8  | 7.35072134E−004 | −0.03342934 | 0.00362678  | 0.05560626  | 0.05257912 |
| 9  | 5.47393396E−004 | −0.04615749 | 0.00454798  | 0.03664320  | 0.03835074 |
| 10 | 4.76317501E−004 | −0.06776335 | 0.00685758  | 0.01622717  | 0.01484356 |
| 11 | 4.03787901E−004 | −0.09535005 | 0.00953730  | −0.01774760 | −0.01633796 |
| 12 | 3.95568823E−004 | −0.10379357 | 0.01037788  | −0.02704598 | −0.02578406 |
| 13 | 3.83488195E−004 | −0.10375865 | 0.01039584  | −0.02555629 | −0.02583233 |
| 14 | 2.38846639E−004 | −0.10256321 | 0.01075605  | −0.04140741 | −0.04177617 |
| 15 | 3.69797959E−005 | −0.01358959 | 0.00194769  | 0.00673806  | 0.00705002 |
| 16 | 9.69537459E−007 | −0.00981117 | 0.00097567  | 0.00762816  | 0.00762830 |
| 17 | 2.59135427E−007 | 0.00107519  | −0.00010262 | 0.01029894  | 0.01028331 |
| 18 | 2.00252552E−007 | 0.00113880  | −0.00012644 | 0.00939017  | 0.00943344 |
| 19 | 2.15389441E−008 | 0.00069496  | −0.00006245 | 0.00499591  | 0.00497136 |
| 20 | 5.52515759E−009 | 0.00061516  | −0.00006347 | 0.00388321  | 0.00389007 |
| 21 | 8.16231155E−010 | 0.00040898  | −0.00003953 | 0.00221975  | 0.00221486 |
| 22 | 2.09187169E−010 | 0.00035852  | −0.00003622 | 0.00173350  | 0.00173484 |
| 23 | 3.07191438E−011 | 0.00026419  | −0.00002615 | 0.00098481  | 0.00098383 |
| 24 | 8.06641768E−012 | 0.00024086  | −0.00002415 | 0.00078404  | 0.00078429 |
| 25 | 1.12150877E−012 | 0.00019691  | −0.00001964 | 0.00043602  | 0.00043583 |

```
MINIMISATION COMPLETE - FINAL DETAILS ARE :
```

| | | | | |
|---|---|---|---|---|
| 26 | 3.04015378E−013 | 0.00018661 | −0.00001867 | 0.00035136 | 0.00035140 |

## 4.4   The Fletcher–Reeves Method

The Fletcher–Reeves method tries to exploit the fact that for a quadratic function of $n$ variables, $n$ linear searches along *mutually conjugate* directions will locate the minimum.

Consider the function given by equation 4.13, i.e.

$$f(\mathbf{x}) = a + \mathbf{b}^T\mathbf{x} + \tfrac{1}{2}\mathbf{x}^T\mathbf{G}\mathbf{x}.$$

We seek to make our searches along directions which are mutually conjugate with respect to $\mathbf{G}$.

Our first search direction from our first point $\mathbf{x}_1$ is made in the direction of steepest descent (which seems reasonable);

$$\mathbf{d}_1 = -\mathbf{g}_1 \tag{4.63}$$

to find the value $\lambda_1$ which minimises

$$f(\mathbf{x}_1 + \lambda\mathbf{d}_1).$$

Put

$$\mathbf{x}_2 = \mathbf{x}_1 + \lambda_1\mathbf{d}_1 \tag{4.64}$$

and search in a direction $\mathbf{d}_2$, conjugate to $\mathbf{d}_1$ (we choose $\mathbf{d}_2$ to be a linear combination of $\mathbf{d}_1$ and $-\mathbf{g}_2$) to find

$$\mathbf{x}_3 = \mathbf{x}_2 + \lambda_2\mathbf{d}_2 \tag{4.65}$$

to minimise $f(\mathbf{x}_2 + \lambda \mathbf{d}_2)$. The search direction $\mathbf{d}_3$ from $\mathbf{x}_3$ is chosen conjugate to both $\mathbf{d}_1$ and $\mathbf{d}_2$. At the $(k+1)$th stage we choose $\mathbf{d}_{k+1}$ to be a linear combination of $-\mathbf{g}_{k+1}$, $\mathbf{d}_1, \mathbf{d}_2, ..., \mathbf{d}_k$ that is conjugate to all of $\mathbf{d}_1, \mathbf{d}_2, ..., \mathbf{d}_k$.

Thus $\mathbf{d}_{k+1} = -\mathbf{g}_{k+1} + \sum_{r=1}^{k} \alpha_r \mathbf{d}_r$, $k = 1, 2, ....$ It transpires that all the $\alpha_r$ are zero except for $\alpha_k$ and that

$$\mathbf{d}_{k+1} = -\mathbf{g}_{k+1} + \alpha_k \mathbf{d}_k \tag{4.66}$$

and

$$\alpha_k = \mathbf{g}_{k+1}^2 / \mathbf{g}_k^2. \tag{4.67}$$

We first establish equations 4.66 and 4.67 for $k = 1$, before proceeding by induction.

Since $f(\mathbf{x}_2) = f(\mathbf{x}_1 + \lambda_1 \mathbf{d}_1)$ is the minimum of $f(\mathbf{x}_1 + \lambda \mathbf{d}_1)$ along the line,

$$\mathbf{g}_2^T \mathbf{d}_1 = -\mathbf{g}_2^T \mathbf{g}_1 = 0. \tag{4.68}$$

We have had this result many times before (equations 4.37, 4.22, 4.24), and of course for a quadratic

$$\mathbf{g}_2 = \mathbf{b} + \mathbf{G}\mathbf{x}_2, \quad \mathbf{g}_1 = \mathbf{b} + \mathbf{G}\mathbf{x}_1$$

Thus if $\mathbf{d}_1$ and $\mathbf{d}_2 = -\mathbf{g}_2 + \alpha_1 \mathbf{d}_1$ are conjugate

$$\mathbf{d}_2^T \mathbf{G} \mathbf{d}_1 = 0,$$

$$\text{i.e.} \quad -\mathbf{g}_2^T \mathbf{G} \mathbf{d}_1 + \alpha_1 \mathbf{d}_1^T \mathbf{G} \mathbf{d}_1 = 0$$

$$\therefore \quad \frac{(-\mathbf{g}_2^T - \alpha_1 \mathbf{g}_1^T)\mathbf{G}(\mathbf{x}_2 - \mathbf{x}_1)}{\lambda_1} = 0.$$

$$\therefore \quad (-\mathbf{g}_2^T - \alpha \mathbf{g}_1^T)(\mathbf{g}_2 - \mathbf{g}_1) = 0$$

$$\therefore \quad -\mathbf{g}_2^2 + \alpha_1 \mathbf{g}_1^2 = 0,$$

the other terms vanishing from equation 4.68.

$$\therefore \quad \alpha_1 = \mathbf{g}_2^2 / \mathbf{g}_1^2$$

as required. This is just equation 4.67 when $k = 1$.

We now prove equations 4.66 and 4.67 by induction, so that we assume that $\mathbf{d}_1, \mathbf{d}_2, ..., \mathbf{d}_k$ are derived from these results and are mutually conjugate.

The point

$$\mathbf{x}_{k+1} = \mathbf{x}_k + \lambda_k \mathbf{d}_k$$

minimises $f(\mathbf{x}_k + \lambda \mathbf{d}_k)$ along the line $\mathbf{x}_k + \lambda \mathbf{d}_k$.

Thus

$$\mathbf{g}_{k+1}^T \mathbf{d}_k = 0. \tag{4.69}$$

We have

$$\mathbf{x}_{k+1} = \mathbf{x}_k + \lambda_k \mathbf{d}_k$$

$$= \mathbf{x}_{k-1} + \lambda_{k-1}\mathbf{d}_{k-1} + \lambda_k\mathbf{d}_k \text{ etc.}$$

$$\therefore \quad \mathbf{x}_{k+1} = \mathbf{x}_{j+1} + \sum_{i=j+1}^{k} \lambda_i \mathbf{d}_i; \quad 1 \leqslant j \leqslant k-1. \tag{4.70}$$

$$\therefore \quad \mathbf{Gx}_{k+1} = \mathbf{Gx}_{j+1} + \sum_{i=j+1}^{k} \lambda_i \mathbf{Gd}_i$$

$$\therefore \quad \mathbf{g}_{k+1}^T = \mathbf{g}_{j+1}^T + \sum_{i=j+1}^{k} \lambda_i \mathbf{d}_i^T \mathbf{G}, \quad 1 \leqslant j \leqslant k-1.$$

$$\therefore \quad \mathbf{g}_{k+1}^T \mathbf{d}_j = \mathbf{g}_{j+1}^T \mathbf{d}_j + \sum_{i=j+1}^{k} \lambda_i \mathbf{d}_i^T \mathbf{Gd}_j$$

Now $\mathbf{g}_{j+1}^T \mathbf{d}_j = 0$ (in the manner of equations 4.68 and 4.69) and because of the mutual conjugacy $\mathbf{d}_i^T \mathbf{Gd}_j = 0$ for $j < i$. Thus each term on the right is zero.

$$\therefore \quad \mathbf{g}_{k+1}^T \mathbf{d}_j = 0, \quad j = 1, 2, ..., k-1, \tag{4.71}$$

and from equation 4.69 we finally have,

$$\mathbf{g}_{k+1}^T \mathbf{d}_j = 0, \quad j = 1, 2, ..., k. \tag{4.72}$$

Thus we have shown that $\mathbf{g}_{k+1}$ is orthogonal to each of the directions $\mathbf{d}_1, \mathbf{d}_2, ..., \mathbf{d}_k$.

We can also show that $\mathbf{g}_{k+1}$ is orthogonal to each of $\mathbf{g}_1, \mathbf{g}_2, ..., \mathbf{g}_k$.

From equation 4.72

$$\mathbf{g}_{k+1}^T \mathbf{d}_j = 0, \quad j = 1, 2, ..., k$$

and since by the induction hypothesis

$$\mathbf{d}_j = -\mathbf{g}_j + \alpha_{j-1}\mathbf{d}_{j-1},$$

this becomes

$$-\mathbf{g}_{k+1}^T \mathbf{g}_j + \alpha_{j-1}\mathbf{g}_{k+1}^T \mathbf{d}_{j-1} = 0.$$

$$\therefore \quad -\mathbf{g}_{k+1}^T \mathbf{g}_j = 0$$

because $\mathbf{g}_{k+1}^T \mathbf{d}_{j-1} = 0$ from equation 4.72.

Thus

$$\mathbf{g}_{k+1}^T \mathbf{g}_j = 0 \quad \text{for } j = 1, 2, ..., k. \tag{4.73}$$

The induction proof is completed by showing that $\mathbf{d}_{k+1}$ defined by equation 4.66 is conjugate to $\mathbf{d}_1, \mathbf{d}_2, ..., \mathbf{d}_k$.

For $j = 1, 2, ..., k-1$

$$\mathbf{d}_{k+1}^T \mathbf{Gd}_j = -\mathbf{g}_{k+1}^T \mathbf{Gd}_j + \alpha_k \mathbf{d}_k^T \mathbf{Gd}_j$$

$$= -\mathbf{g}_{k+1}^T \mathbf{Gd}_j$$

because of the mutual conjugacy.

Now

$$-\mathbf{g}_{k+1}^T \mathbf{G} \mathbf{d}_j = -\mathbf{g}_{k+1}^T \mathbf{G} \frac{(\mathbf{x}_{j+1} - \mathbf{x}_j)}{\lambda_j}$$

$$= -\mathbf{g}_{k+1}^T \frac{(\mathbf{g}_{j+1} - \mathbf{g}_j)}{\lambda_j}$$

$$= 0$$

on account of equation 4.73.

Thus $\mathbf{d}_{k+1}^T \mathbf{G} \mathbf{d}_j = 0$ for $j = 1, 2, ..., k-1$ and this will be true whatever the value of $\alpha_k$. To complete the proof we must determine $\alpha_k$ so that

$$\mathbf{d}_{k+1}^T \mathbf{G} \mathbf{d}_k = 0.$$

$$\mathbf{d}_{k+1}^T \mathbf{G} \mathbf{d}_k = -\mathbf{g}_{k+1}^T \mathbf{G} \mathbf{d}_k + \alpha_k \mathbf{d}_k^T \mathbf{G} \mathbf{d}_k$$

$$= -\mathbf{g}_{k+1}^T \frac{(\mathbf{g}_{k+1} - \mathbf{g}_k)}{\lambda_k} + \alpha_k(-\mathbf{g}_k^T + \alpha_{k-1}\mathbf{d}_{k-1}^T) \frac{(\mathbf{g}_{k+1} - \mathbf{g}_k)}{\lambda_k}.$$

Thus

$$\mathbf{d}_{k+1}^T \mathbf{G} \mathbf{d}_k = \frac{-\mathbf{g}_{k+1}^2 + \alpha_k \mathbf{g}_k^2}{\lambda_k};$$

all other terms on the right vanish on account of equations 4.72 and 4.73.

Thus $\mathbf{d}_{k+1}$ will be conjugate to $\mathbf{d}_k$ if

$$\alpha_k = \mathbf{g}_{k+1}^2 / \mathbf{g}_k^2 \quad \text{as required.}$$

Thus the successive search directions in the Fletcher–Reeves method are conjugate and the method will find the minimum of a quadratic function of $n$ variables after at most $n$ searches. This assumes that the linear searches are carried out exactly and neglects any rounding errors that may arise.

The method will of course be applied to non-quadratic functions. As it homes in on the minimum it will hope to achieve the quadratic convergence property when the quadratic approximation becomes valid. Fletcher and Reeves suggest that in this situation every $n$th search direction should be along the direction of steepest descent and that the construction of conjugate directions should then *restart*.

The flow chart and the program given include this idea. In general the method does not appear to be so efficient or robust as the Davidon–Fletcher–Powell procedure. Nonetheless it is a useful method.

## Flow Chart for Fletcher–Reeves Method

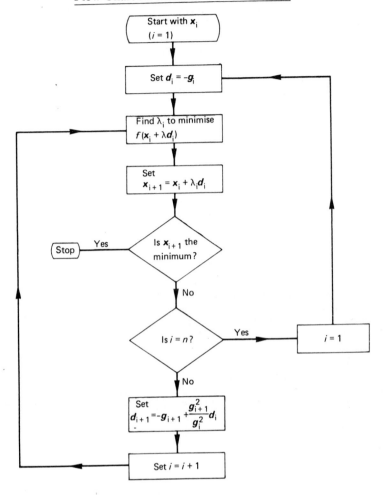

```
PROGRAM FletcherReeves (input,output);
CONST
  n=2;                { Number of variables in funcion f }              {**}
  fwx=14; dpx=8;      { Output format constants for x-values }           {**}
  fwf=16; dpf=10;     { Output format constants for function values }    {**}
TYPE
  vector = ARRAY [1..n] OF real;
  point = RECORD              { To represent values at a single point }
            x, g : vector;    { x-vector and gradient-vector }
            f, g0 : real      { function value and gradient value }
          END;
  howobtained = PACKED ARRAY [1..16] OF char;
```

```
VAR
    P, Q : point;            { Search points }
    d : vector;              { Direction of search vector }
    delta : real;            { Required accuracy in gradient }
    ak : real;               { Multiplier required to obtain conjugate direction }
    itnewdir,                { Iteration count for new direction }
    itrestart : integer;     { Iteration count for restart }
    fe : integer;            { Function evaluation counter }
    i, k : integer;
```

```
FUNCTION f (x:vector): real;
{ The code here is dependent on the function being minimised }
BEGIN
    f := 100.0*sqr(x[2]-sqr(x[1])) + sqr(1.0-x[1]);   fe := fe+1          {**}
END; { f }
```

```
PROCEDURE gradients (VAR p:point);
{ Computes the gradients at p in each of the x-directions as }
{ well as the gradient of steepest ascent.                   }
{ The code here is dependent on the function being minimised }
VAR  i : integer;  t : real;
BEGIN
    WITH p DO
    BEGIN  t := x[2]-sqr(x[1]);                                           {**}
        g[1] := -400.0*x[1]*t - 2.0*(1-x[1]);  g[2] := 200.0*t;          {**}
        g0:=0.0;  FOR i:=1 TO n DO g0 := g0 + sqr(g[i]);  g0 := sqrt(g0)
    END
END; { gradients }
```

```
FUNCTION scalarmult (v1,v2:vector): real;
{ Perform scalar multiplication of vectors v1 and v2 }
VAR  i : integer;  sum : real;
BEGIN  sum:=0.0;
    FOR i:=1 TO n DO sum := sum + v1[i]*v2[i];
    scalarmult := sum
END; { scalarmult }
```

```
PROCEDURE movepoint (VAR p1:point; p2:point; r:real);
{ p1 is made the point a distance r from p2 in the d-direction }
VAR  i : integer;
BEGIN    FOR i:=1 TO n DO p1.x[i] := p2.x[i] + r*d[i];
    p1.f:=f(p1.x);  gradients(p1)
END; { movepoint }
```

```
PROCEDURE cubintmod (VAR p:point; d:vector);
{ A modification of the cubic interpolation routine of Section 2.6. }
{ The differences are :                                            }
{ (a)   iteration terminates when a point, r, is found with a      }
{       function value lower than both those of p and q, the ends  }
{       of the bracketing range.                                   }
{ (b)   phim is zero.                                              }
CONST   phim=0.0;
VAR   q, r : point;       { Search points, together with p }
   Gp, Gq, Gr : real;    { Gradient values in d-direction at p, q, r }
   qx, rx : real;        { Distances between points in iterative process }

BEGIN
   REPEAT   { A search in the d-direction until gradient is negative }
     Gp := scalarmult(p.g,d);   qx := abs(2.0*(p.f-phim)/Gp);
     IF qx>1.0 THEN qx:=1.0;
     IF Gp>0.0 THEN movepoint(p,p,-qx)
   UNTIL Gp<=0.0;
   { Find next point, q }   qx0:=qx;
   REPEAT   { Until minimum has been bracketed }
     movepoint(q,p,qx0);   Gq := scalarmult(q.g,d);   qx:=qx0;   qx0:=2.0*qx0;
   UNTIL  (Gq>0.0) OR (q.f>p.f);
   REPEAT   { Until r found with function value less than those at p and q }
     z := 3.0*(p.f-q.f)/qx + Gp + Gq;   w := sqr(z) - Gp*Gq;
     IF w<0.0 THEN w:=0.0;  w:=sqrt(w);   rx := qx*(z+w-Gp)/(Gq-Gp+2.0*w);
     movepoint(r,p,rx);   Gr := scalarmult(r.g,d);
     minfound := (r.f<p.f) AND (r.f<q.f);
     IF NOT minfound THEN
        IF Gr>0.0 THEN BEGIN   qx:=rx;   q:=r;   Gq:=Gr   END
        ELSE BEGIN   qx := qx-rx;   p:=r;   Gp:=Gr   END
   UNTIL minfound;
   p:=r;   { Return point in p }
END; { cubintmod }


PROCEDURE inputdata;
VAR  i :integer;
BEGIN  writeln('     NUMBER OF VARIABLES =', n:3);
   writeln('    INITIAL POINT');
   FOR i:=1 TO n DO
   BEGIN write('    X[', i:2, ']'); read(P.x[i]); writeln(P.x[i]:fwx:dpx) END;
   write('    REQUIRED ACCURACY, DELTA, IN GRADIENT VALUE =');
   read(delta);   writeln(delta:fwf:dpf)
END; { inputdata }


PROCEDURE outputline (s:howobtained; itl,it2:integer; p:point);
VAR  i : integer;
BEGIN   write(s, itl:5, it2:8, ' ':4, p.f:fwf);
   FOR i:=1 TO n DO write(p.x[i]:fwx:dpx);   writeln
END; { outputline }


PROCEDURE initialise;
BEGIN   itrestart:=1;   itnewdir:=0;   fe:=0  END; { initialise }
```

```
BEGIN   { Main Program }
  writeln; writeln('     FLETCHER-REEVES');   writeln;
  inputdata; writeln;  initialise;
  writeln(' ':16, 'ITERATIONS');
  write('HOW OBTAINED    RESTART  NEW DIR ', ' ':fwf-4, 'F(X)');
  FOR i:=1 TO n DO write(' ':fwx-5, 'X[', i:2, ']'); writeln; writeln;
  P.f := f(P.x);  gradients(P);
  FOR i:=1 TO n DO d[i] := -P.g[i];  k:=1;  Q:=P;
  outputline('INITIAL POINT   ', itrestart, itnewdir, P);
  REPEAT   { Until required accuracy in gradient attained }
    cubintmod(P,d);
    IF P.g0>delta THEN
    BEGIN   { Required accuracy not yet attained }
      IF k<>N THEN   { Search in new conjugate direction }
      BEGIN   k:=k+1;   ak := sqr(P.g0/Q.g0);
        FOR i:=1 TO n DO d[i] := -P.g[i] + ak*d[i];  itnewdir := itnewdir+1;
        outputline('NEW DIRECTION   ', itrestart, itnewdir, P)
      END
      ELSE   { Restart along direction of steepest descent }
      BEGIN   FOR i:=1 TO n DO d[i] := -P.g[i];
        itrestart := itrestart+1;  itnewdir := itnewdir+1;  k:=1;
        outputline('RESTART        ', itrestart, itnewdir, P)
      END;
      Q:=P
    END
  UNTIL P.g0 < delta;
  writeln; writeln('MINIMISATION COMPLETE - FINAL DETAILS ARE :');
  writeln; outputline('FINAL VALUES    ', itrestart, itnewdir, P);
  writeln('NUMBER OF FUNCTION EVALUATIONS =', fe:6)
END. { FletcherReeves }
```

**Example 1**

Use the Fletcher–Reeves method with starting point $(-1 \cdot 2, 1)$ to minimise
Rosenbrock's function

$$f(x_1, x_2) = 100(x_2 - x_1^2)^2 + (1 - x_1)^2.$$

This is a particularly awkward starting point for this function. The function itself
is also a very tricky one to minimise. The minimum is zero at $(1, 1)$. The start and
finish of the output is shown.

```
  writeln('NUMBER OF FUNCTION EVALUATIONS =', te:6)
END. { FletcherReeves }
```

```
FLETCHER-REEVES

NUMBER OF VARIABLES = 2
INITIAL POINT
X[ 1]   -1.20000000
X[ 2]    1.00000000
REQUIRED ACCURACY, DELTA, IN GRADIENT VALUE =    0.0000010000
```

| HOW OBTAINED | ITERATIONS RESTART | NEW DIR | F(X) | X[ 1] | X[ 2] |
|---|---|---|---|---|---|
| INITIAL POINT | 0 | 0 | 2.42000000E+001 | −1.20000000 | 1.00000000 |
| NEW DIRECTION | 0 | 1 | 4.12810253E+000 | −1.03019958 | 1.06930629 |
| RESTART | 1 | 2 | 3.58377979E+000 | −0.73433301 | 0.46335895 |
| NEW DIRECTION | 1 | 3 | 2.87171480E+000 | −0.69222010 | 0.48817196 |
| RESTART | 2 | 4 | 2.65206475E+000 | −0.59684785 | 0.32426774 |
| NEW DIRECTION | 2 | 5 | 2.48450156E+000 | −0.57269815 | 0.33852930 |
| RESTART | 3 | 6 | 2.37428538E+000 | −0.52576089 | 0.25489799 |
| NEW DIRECTION | 3 | 7 | 2.27886429E+000 | −0.50469558 | 0.26686485 |
| RESTART | 4 | 8 | 2.18364054E+000 | −0.46700792 | 0.20034018 |
| NEW DIRECTION | 4 | 9 | 2.10883486E+000 | −0.44592933 | 0.21231522 |
| RESTART | 5 | 10 | 1.99723694E+000 | −0.40090080 | 0.14208979 |
| NEW DIRECTION | 5 | 11 | 1.91772803E+000 | −0.37858325 | 0.15645397 |
| RESTART | 6 | 12 | 1.76746793E+000 | −0.30930273 | 0.07260429 |
| NEW DIRECTION | 6 | 13 | 1.66491916E+000 | −0.28557574 | 0.09260528 |
| RESTART | 7 | 14 | 1.45302140E+000 | −0.17094482 | 0.00060227 |
| NEW DIRECTION | 7 | 15 | 1.32601224E+000 | −0.14898296 | 0.02984471 |
| RESTART | 8 | 16 | 1.07453835E+000 | 0.00384821 | −0.02865921 |
| NEW DIRECTION | 8 | 17 | 9.71748394E−001 | 0.01481926 | 0.00363621 |
| RESTART | 9 | 18 | 7.49601342E−001 | 0.17200939 | 0.00428251 |
| NEW DIRECTION | 9 | 19 | 6.86267105E−001 | 0.17158876 | 0.02930424 |
| RESTART | 10 | 20 | 5.10852144E−001 | 0.32017307 | 0.08044555 |
| NEW DIRECTION | 10 | 21 | 4.70079046E−001 | 0.31463406 | 0.09711689 |
| RESTART | 11 | 22 | 3.35953922E−001 | 0.45236934 | 0.18564997 |
| NEW DIRECTION | 11 | 23 | 3.07722569E−001 | 0.44570590 | 0.19646145 |
| RESTART | 12 | 24 | 2.76114258E−001 | 0.64255462 | 0.37436060 |
| NEW DIRECTION | 12 | 25 | 1.40856065E−001 | 0.62512130 | 0.38898213 |
| RESTART | 13 | 26 | 7.78217434E−002 | 0.75577542 | 0.55771461 |
| NEW DIRECTION | 13 | 27 | 6.24754858E−002 | 0.75029464 | 0.56183426 |
| RESTART | 14 | 28 | 3.19785747E−002 | 0.84168994 | 0.70012540 |
| NEW DIRECTION | 14 | 29 | 2.61477960E−002 | 0.83844372 | 0.70229965 |
| RESTART | 15 | 30 | 1.06374572E−002 | 0.91417224 | 0.82999158 |
| NEW DIRECTION | 15 | 31 | 7.76409482E−003 | 0.91196104 | 0.83130912 |
| RESTART | 16 | 32 | 1.94991513E−003 | 0.96666449 | 0.93154428 |
| NEW DIRECTION | 16 | 33 | 1.18847269E−003 | 0.96555373 | 0.93215518 |
| RESTART | 17 | 34 | 9.18379468E−005 | 0.99539031 | 0.98996170 |
| NEW DIRECTION | 17 | 35 | 2.44123861E−005 | 0.99506304 | 0.99013075 |
| RESTART | 18 | 36 | 4.42370147E−008 | 0.99998629 | 0.99995159 |
| NEW DIRECTION | 18 | 37 | 4.87664217E−010 | 0.99997793 | 0.99995578 |

MINIMISATION COMPLETE − FINAL DETAILS ARE :

| FINAL VALUES | 18 | 37 | 1.60266829E−018 | 1.00000000 | 1.00000000 |

NUMBER OF FUNCTION EVALUATIONS =   94

## Example 2

Find the minimum of

$$f(x_1, x_2, x_3) = 3(x_1 - 1)^2 + 2(x_2 - 2)^2 + (x_3 - 3)^2.$$

In contrast to Example 1 this is a trivial problem. The starting point used was

(9, −7, 11). The output given illustrates that, in accordance with theory, the Fletcher–Reeves method locates the minimum after three searches. Note that the output format constants have been altered in the program.

```
FLETCHER-REEVES

NUMBER OF VARIABLES =   3
INITIAL POINT
X[ 1]    9.0000
X[ 2]   -7.0000
X[ 3]   11.0000
REQUIRED ACCURACY, DELTA, IN GRADIENT VALUE =    0.000001
```

|  | ITERATIONS | | | | | |
| HOW OBTAINED | RESTART | NEW DIR | F(X) | X[ 1] | X[ 2] | X[ 3] |
|---|---|---|---|---|---|---|
| INITIAL POINT | 1 | 0 | 4.1800E+002 | 9.0000 | -7.0000 | 11.0000 |
| NEW DIRECTION | 1 | 1 | 3.7141E+001 | -0.4820 | 0.1115 | 7.8393 |
| NEW DIRECTION | 1 | 2 | 4.9655E+000 | 1.2069 | 2.8276 | 4.8621 |

MINIMISATION COMPLETE - FINAL DETAILS ARE :

| FINAL VALUES | 1 | 2 | 0.0000E+000 | 1.0000 | 2.0000 | 3.0000 |
| NUMBER OF FUNCTION EVALUATIONS = | | 8 | | | | |

## 4.5  References

The last twenty-five years have witnessed a great deal of research activity in the area discussed in this chapter. Many papers have been published and many advances have been made. The methods discussed in this chapter are but three among many that have been suggested. The ideas of conjugate directions and the property of quadratic functions as suggested by equation 4.17 are fundamental. It was mentioned in Section 4.3 that the updating of the **H** matrix in the D.F.P. method was not the only one possible. Indeed Huang has shown that there is a whole family of methods based on these ideas, of which the Davidon–Fletcher–Powell and the Fletcher–Reeves are but two special cases. The references below are just a selection from many which could have been quoted.

1   C. G. Broyden, 'Quasi-Newton methods and their application to function minimisation', *Maths. of Comp.*, **21**, 368–381, 1967.
2   C. G. Broyden, 'The convergence of single-rank quasi-Newton methods', *Maths. of Comp.*, **24**, 376–382, 1970.
3   R. Fletcher, 'A new approach to variable metric algorithms', *The Comp. Journal*, **13**, 317–322, 1970.
4   R. Fletcher and M. J. D. Powell, 'A rapidly convergent descent method for minimisation', *The Comp. Journal*, **6**, 163–168, 1963.
5   R. Fletcher and C. M. Reeves, 'Function minimisation by conjugate gradients', *The Comp. Journal*, **7**, 149–154, 1964.
6   H. Y. Huang, 'Unified approach to quadratically convergent algorithms for function minimisation', *J. Opt. Theory App.*, **5**, 405–423, 1970.

7  H. Y. Huang, and A. V. Levy, 'Numerical experiments on quadratically convergent algorithms for function minimisation', *J. Opt. Theory App.*, **6**, 269–282, 1970.

8  M. J. D. Powell, 'On the convergence of the variable metric algorithm', *J. Inst. Maths. Appl.*, **7**, 21–36, 1971.

9  M. J. D. Powell, 'Quadratic termination properties of minimisation algorithms. I. Statement and discussion of results', *J. Inst. Maths. App.*, **10**, 333–342, 1972.

10  M. J. D. Powell, 'Quadratic termination properties of minimisation algorithms. II. Proofs of theorems', *J. Inst. Maths. App.*, **10**, 343–357, 1972.

## Exercises 4

**1**  Modify the steepest descent program given in Section 4.1 to carry out the linear searches (i) by Fibonacci search (ii) by Golden search (iii) by cubic interpolation. Try to use your program to solve the problems of the worked examples. Note any difficulties that arise.

**2**  Attempt to solve Examples 1 and 2 of Section 4.1 with different starting points. Do any difficulties arise?

**3**  If $P_0, P_1$, and $P_2$ are successive points obtained from using the method of steepest descent it has been suggested that the method can be accelerated by making the next search in the direction $P_0P_2$. Draw a sketch of the contours of a function near its minimum to illustrate the thinking behind this suggestion. Try to incorporate this idea into the program given in Section 4.1.

**4**  If $f(\mathbf{x})$ is a positive definite quadratic function of two variables, whose minimum is at the origin, and $\mathbf{x}_0$, $\mathbf{x}_1$, and $\mathbf{x}_2$ are three successive points in a sequence using the method of steepest descent, show that the line through $\mathbf{x}_0$ and $\mathbf{x}_2$ passes through the minimum point of the function. See the acceleration technique of the previous question.

**5**  Consider the quadratic function $f(x, y) = x^2/a^2 + y^2/b^2$ where $a$ and $b$ are constants. The contours of this function are the ellipses

$$\frac{x^2}{a^2} + \frac{y^2}{b^2} = c^2,$$

where $c^2$ is the function value. The function minimum is of course zero at the origin. Show that the line

$$y = mx \pm c\sqrt{(a^2m^2 + b^2)}$$

is tangential to this ellipse and touches it at the point P,

$$\left[ \pm \frac{ma^2c}{\sqrt{(a^2m^2 + b^2)}}, \pm \frac{cb^2}{\sqrt{(a^2m^2 + b^2)}} \right].$$

Thus a search from a point on this line along the line will find the function minimum at P. The gradient of the line joining P to the origin (the minimum point) is $m'$. Show that

$$mm' = -b^2/a^2.$$

Show that this is equivalent to

$$\mathbf{p}^T \begin{pmatrix} 1/a^2 & 0 \\ 0 & 1/b^2 \end{pmatrix} \mathbf{q} = 0$$

where $\mathbf{p}^T = (\cos \alpha, \sin \alpha)$, $\mathbf{q}^T = (\cos \beta, \sin \beta)$ and $m = \tan \alpha$, $m' = \tan \beta$. Thus $\mathbf{p}$ and $\mathbf{q}$ are conjugate, and a search along $\mathbf{p}$, followed by a search in the direction $\mathbf{q}$ will find the minimum after two searches.

**6**   Minimise

$$f(\mathbf{x}) = 3(x_1 - 4)^2 + 5(x_2 + 3)^2 + 7(2x_3 + 1)^2$$

using (a) the D.F.P. method (b) the Fletcher–Reeves method. Show that as expected (a) needs 3 iterations and (b) needs 3 searches whatever starting point is used.

**7**   Minimise

$$f(x_1, x_2) = 1 - 2x_1 - 2x_2 - 4x_1 x_2 + 10x_1^2 + 2x_2^2.$$

**8**   Minimise

$$x_1^4 + x_2^4 + 2x_1^2 x_2^2 - 4x_1 + 3.$$

**9**   Minimise

$$(x_1^2 + x_2 - 11)^2 + (x_1 + x_2^2 - 7)^2.$$

**10**   Minimise

$$f(x_1, x_2) = x_1^3 + x_2^3 - 3x_1 - 2x_2 + 2.$$

# Part II
# Constrained Optimisation

# 5
# General Theory

## 5.1 Equality Constraints

Consider the two variable problem to minimise

$$z = f(x, y)$$

where the two variables $x$ and $y$ are constrained by the relationship

$$g(x, y) = 0. \tag{5.1}$$

In principle we can use the constraint $g(x, y) = 0$ to solve for $y$ as a function of $x$, viz. $y = h(x)$. In practice of course, it might be difficult or even impossible to find an explicit form for $h(x)$. However, subject to certain differentiability conditions (which must be satisfied for our results to hold) we shall have for the derivative of $h(x)$

$$\frac{dy}{dx} = \frac{d}{dx} h(x) = -\frac{\partial g}{\partial x} \bigg/ \frac{\partial g}{\partial y}. \tag{5.2}$$

We can then regard

$$z = f(x, y) = f[x, h(x)] \tag{5.3}$$

as a function of the one independent variable $x$. For a minimum of $z$ the necessary condition is

$$\frac{dz}{dx} = \frac{\partial f}{\partial x} + \frac{\partial f}{\partial y} \frac{dy}{dx} = 0$$

$$\text{i.e. } \frac{\partial f}{\partial x} + \left( \frac{-\dfrac{\partial f}{\partial y}}{\dfrac{\partial g}{\partial y}} \right) \cdot \frac{\partial g}{\partial x} = 0. \tag{5.4}$$

5.1 and 5.4 are equations which in principle can be solved to yield values $x^*, y^*$ at the minimum.

We can put this result in a slightly different form. If we define

$$\lambda = \frac{-\partial f}{\partial y} (x, y) \bigg/ \frac{\partial g}{\partial y} (x, y) \tag{5.5}$$

when $x = x^*, y = y^*$, then at the minimum we shall have

$$g(x, y) = 0,$$

$$\frac{\partial f}{\partial x}(x, y) + \lambda \frac{\partial g}{\partial x}(x, y) = 0,$$

and

$$\frac{\partial f}{\partial y}(x, y) + \lambda \frac{\partial g}{\partial y}(x, y) = 0,$$

the last result following directly from equation 5.5.

A neat way of generating these three necessary conditions is to consider the *Lagrange function*

$$F(x, y, \lambda) = f(x, y) + \lambda g(x, y) \qquad (5.6)$$

which is the sum of the objective function and the product of $\lambda$ (the Lagrange multiplier) with the constraint. The necessary conditions for a constrained minimum of $f(x, y)$ can then be written as:

$$\left.\begin{array}{l} \dfrac{\partial F}{\partial x}(x, y, \lambda) = \dfrac{\partial f}{\partial x}(x, y) + \lambda \dfrac{\partial g}{\partial x}(x, y) = 0 \\[3mm] \dfrac{\partial F}{\partial y}(x, y, \lambda) = \dfrac{\partial f}{\partial y}(x, y) + \lambda \dfrac{\partial g}{\partial y}(x, y) = 0 \\[3mm] \dfrac{\partial F}{\partial \lambda}(x, y, \lambda) = g(x, y) = 0 \end{array}\right\} \qquad (5.7)$$

These provide three equations for $x^*, y^*$ and $\lambda^*$, the values of $x, y,$ and $\lambda$ at the minimum.

## Example 1

Find the minimum of $x^2 + y^2$ subject to $x + y = 4$. Here $f(x, y) = x^2 + y^2$ and $g(x, y) = 4 - x - y = 0$.

The Lagrange function is

$$F(x, y, \lambda) = x^2 + y^2 + \lambda(4 - x - y),$$

$$\frac{\partial F}{\partial x} = 2x - \lambda = 0$$

$$\frac{\partial F}{\partial y} = 2y - \lambda = 0$$

$$\frac{\partial F}{\partial \lambda} = 4 - x - y = 0.$$

The solution to these equations is easily seen to be $x = y = 2, \lambda = 4$.

The function minimum is $2^2 + 2^2 = 8$. It is left as an exercise for the reader to verify this result by considering the function of one variable $x$ obtained by eliminating $y$,

$$z = x^2 + (4 - x)^2.$$

The result (equation 5.7) can be generalised to functions of $n$ variables which are subject to $m$ equation constraints although we argue the case somewhat differently. Thus we consider the problem of minimising

$$z = f(\mathbf{x}) = f(x_1, x_2, ..., x_n)$$

where the variables $\mathbf{x}$ are constrained by

$$g_1(\mathbf{x}) = 0, \ g_2(\mathbf{x}) = 0, \ ..., \ g_m(\mathbf{x}) = 0. \tag{5.8}$$

In principle we can use the constraints to express $m$ of the variables (which we can without loss of generality take to be $x_1, x_2, ..., x_m$) in terms of the other $n - m$. We can think of these as being the $n - m$ independent variables. Provided this can be done in principle we can say that at the constrained minimum

$$f(\mathbf{x} + \mathbf{h}) - f(\mathbf{x}) \geqslant 0 \quad \text{for all } \mathbf{h} \text{ which satisfy } g_i(\mathbf{x} + \mathbf{h}) = g_i(\mathbf{x}) = 0; \quad i = 1, ..., m$$

Thus to first order in $h_j$ we shall have

$$\sum_{j=1}^{n} h_j \frac{\partial f}{\partial x_j} = 0 \quad \text{where the } h_j \text{ must satisfy}$$

$$\sum_{j=1}^{n} h_j \frac{\partial g_i}{\partial x_j} = 0, \quad \text{for } i = 1, 2, ..., m.$$

This we can write as

$$\sum_{j=1}^{n} h_j \left( \frac{\partial f}{\partial x_j} + \sum_{i=1}^{m} \lambda_i \frac{\partial g_i}{\partial x_j} \right) = 0, \tag{5.9}$$

where $\lambda_1, \lambda_2, ..., \lambda_m$ are the $m$ Lagrange multipliers.

Since $h_{m+1}, h_{m+2}, ..., h_n$ are independent increments their coefficients must be zero;

$$\text{i.e. } \frac{\partial f}{\partial x_j} + \sum_{i=1}^{m} \lambda_i \frac{\partial g_i}{\partial x_j} = 0, \quad j = m + 1, ..., n.$$

The increments $h_1, h_2, ..., h_m$ are not independent but we can make their coefficients in equation 5.9 zero by choice of $\lambda_1, \lambda_2, ..., \lambda_m$.

Thus we choose $\lambda_1, \lambda_2, ..., \lambda_m$ to make

$$\frac{\partial f}{\partial x_j} + \sum_{i=1}^{m} \lambda_i \frac{\partial g_i}{\partial x_j} = 0 \quad \text{for } j = 1, 2, ..., m.$$

Thus we have finally

$$\frac{\partial f}{\partial x_j} + \sum_{i=1}^{m} \lambda_i \frac{\partial g_i}{\partial x_j} = 0, \quad j = 1, 2, ..., n. \tag{5.10}$$

Thus if we define the Lagrange function

$$F(\mathbf{x}, \boldsymbol{\lambda}) = f(\mathbf{x}) + \sum_{i=1}^{m} \lambda_i g_i(\mathbf{x}) \tag{5.11}$$

then the necessary conditions for the constrained minimum of $f(\mathbf{x})$ can be expressed as

$$\frac{\partial F}{\partial x_j} = \frac{\partial f}{\partial x_j} + \sum_{i=1}^{m} \lambda_i \frac{\partial g_i}{\partial x_j} = 0, \quad j = 1, 2, \dots, n \qquad (5.12)$$

$$\frac{\partial F}{\partial \lambda_i} = g_i(\mathbf{x}) = 0; \quad i = 1, \dots, m. \qquad (5.13)$$

We note that for feasible values of $\mathbf{x}$ (i.e. those which satisfy the constraints)

$$F(\mathbf{x}, \boldsymbol{\lambda}) = f(\mathbf{x}) + \sum_{i=1}^{m} \lambda_i g_i(\mathbf{x}) = f(\mathbf{x}).$$

At the constrained minimum $\mathbf{x}^*$

$$f(\mathbf{x}^* + \mathbf{h}) - f(\mathbf{x}^*) \geqslant 0 \quad \text{where } \mathbf{h} \text{ satisfies } g_i(\mathbf{x}^* + \mathbf{h}) = 0 \text{ for all } i.$$

We shall thus have

$$F(\mathbf{x}^* + \mathbf{h}) - F(\mathbf{x}^*) = \sum_{j=1}^{n} \frac{\partial F}{\partial x_j} h_j + \frac{1}{2} \sum_{i=1}^{n} \sum_{j=1}^{n} h_i \frac{\partial^2 F}{\partial x_i \partial x_j} h_j + \dots \geqslant 0,$$

where the derivatives are evaluated at $\mathbf{x}^*, \boldsymbol{\lambda}^*$.

On account of equation 5.12 this gives

$$\frac{1}{2} \sum_{i=1}^{n} \sum_{j=1}^{n} h_i \frac{\partial^2 F}{\partial x_i \partial x_j} h_j \geqslant 0, \quad \text{for all } \mathbf{h} \text{ which satisfy the constraints.}$$

Sufficient conditions for a constrained minimum are thus equation 5.12, and equation 5.13 and the quadratic form

$$\frac{1}{2} \sum_{i=1}^{n} \sum_{j=1}^{n} h_i \frac{\partial^2 F}{\partial x_i \partial x_j} h_j \qquad (5.14)$$

is positive definite for values for $\mathbf{h}$ satisfying the constraints.

N.B. It is not always easy to put this last condition in a useful form.

**Example 2**

Verify that (2,2) is the constrained minimum of $x_1^2 + x_2^2$ subject to $x_1 + x_2 = 4$. With $F(\mathbf{x}, \lambda) = x_1^2 + x_2^2 + \lambda(4 - x_1 - x_2)$ we have seen that

$$\frac{\partial F}{\partial x_1} = 0, \quad \frac{\partial F}{\partial x_2} = 0, \quad \frac{\partial F}{\partial \lambda} = 0 \quad \text{when } x_1 = x_2 = 2 \text{ and } \lambda = 4.$$

The Hessian matrix for $F$ is $\begin{pmatrix} 2 & 0 \\ 0 & 2 \end{pmatrix}$ and this is simply positive definite, which establishes the result.

## 5.2  Inequality Constraints

In this section we extend the ideas of Lagrange multipliers to the case of inequality constraints. Thus we consider the general mathematical programming problem:

minimise $\qquad\qquad\qquad\qquad f(\mathbf{x})$

subject to the $m$ constraints $g_i(\mathbf{x}) \leqslant b_i$   $(i = 1, 2, ..., m)$.

There is of course no loss of generality in assuming that all constraints are of the less than or equal to variety. (The constraint $\phi(\mathbf{x}) \geqslant c$ can be written as $-\phi(\mathbf{x}) \leqslant -c$.)

Perhaps at the outset we should say that there is no solution to the problem posed in all cases. To date no method has been devised which is guaranteed to solve every problem of the type just given. Perhaps the reader will remedy this situation.

The inequality constraints can be transformed into equation constraints by the addition of a non-negative *slack variable* $u_i^2$ to each one (note $u_i^2$ is always positive) to obtain

$$g_i(\mathbf{x}) + u_i^2 = b_i$$

i.e. $g_i(\mathbf{x}) + u_i^2 - b_i = 0.$ \hfill (5.15)

Thus the problem is to minimise $f(\mathbf{x})$ subject to the $m$ equation constraints $g_i(\mathbf{x}) + u_i^2 - b_i = 0$. In line with the previous section we form the Lagrange function

$$F(\mathbf{x}, \boldsymbol{\lambda}, \mathbf{u}) = f(\mathbf{x}) + \sum_{i=1}^{m} \lambda_i [\, g_i(\mathbf{x}) + u_i^2 - b_i \,]. \qquad (5.16)$$

The necessary conditions to be satisfied at a stationary point are:

$$\frac{\partial F}{\partial x_j} = 0 = \frac{\partial f}{\partial x_j} + \sum_{i=1}^{m} \lambda_i \frac{\partial g_i}{\partial x_j}; \quad j = 1, 2, ..., n \qquad (5.17)$$

$$\frac{\partial F}{\partial \lambda_i} = 0 = g_i(\mathbf{x}) + u_i^2 - b_i; \quad i = 1, 2, ..., m \qquad (5.18)$$

$$\frac{\partial F}{\partial u_i} = 0 = 2\lambda_i u_i. \quad i = 1, 2, ..., m. \qquad (5.19)$$

The last condition when multiplied by $u_i/2$ gives

$$\lambda_i u_i^2 = 0$$

i.e. $\lambda_i [\, b_i - g_i(\mathbf{x}) \,] = 0, \quad i = 1, 2, ..., m.$ \hfill (5.20)

Equations 5.17, 5.18 and 5.20 are necessary conditions for a constrained minimum $\mathbf{x}^*$. Equations 5.18 are just a restatement of the constraints $g_i(\mathbf{x}) \leqslant 0$. Condition 5.20 states that one of $\lambda_i$ or $b_i - g_i(\mathbf{x}^*)$ is zero. If $\lambda_i$ is not zero then $g_i(\mathbf{x}^*) = b_i$, and the constraint is *active* and satisfied as an equation. On the other hand if the constraint is satisfied as a strict inequality so the $g_i(\mathbf{x}^*) < b$ then the corresponding Lagrange multiplier $\lambda_i$ is zero. This makes sense intuitively. As far as the constrained minimum is concerned if $g_i(\mathbf{x}^*) < b_i$, this constraint is inactive and could be ignored, and the corresponding $\lambda_i$ is zero. Of course at the outset we do not know which constraints can be ignored.

There is also an extra condition which must be satisfied at a constrained minimum, viz. $\lambda_i \geqslant 0$.

Suppose that equations 5.17, 5.18 and 5.20 are satisfied at the point $(\mathbf{x}^*, \boldsymbol{\lambda}^*, \mathbf{u}^*)$. If the actual constrained function minimum is $z = f(\mathbf{x}^*)$ then we can regard $z$ as a function of the $b_i$, in that changing the $b_i$ will modify the constraints and so will change $z$. We shall show that

$$\frac{\partial z}{\partial b_i} = -\lambda_i^*.$$

$$\frac{\partial z}{\partial b_i} = \sum_{j=1}^{n} \frac{\partial f}{\partial x_j} \cdot \frac{\partial x_j}{\partial b_i}$$

where the partial derivatives are evaluated at $\mathbf{x}^*$.

Since $g_k(\mathbf{x}) + u_k^2 = b_k$

$$\frac{\partial g_k}{\partial b_i} = \sum_{j=1}^{n} \frac{\partial g_k}{\partial x_j} \cdot \frac{\partial x_j}{\partial b_i} = \begin{array}{ll} 0 & \text{if } i \neq k \\ 1 & \text{if } i = k. \end{array}$$

Thus

$$\frac{\partial z}{\partial b_i} + \sum_{k=1}^{m} \lambda_k^* \frac{\partial g_k}{\partial b_i} = \frac{\partial z}{\partial b_i} + \lambda_i^* = \sum_{j=1}^{n} \left( \frac{\partial f}{\partial x_j} + \sum_{k=1}^{m} \lambda_k^* \frac{\partial g_k}{\partial x_j} \right) \frac{\partial x_j}{\partial b_j}.$$

But this is zero because of equations 5.17.

Thus

$$\frac{\partial z}{\partial b_i} = -\lambda_i^*. \tag{5.21}$$

Now as $b_i$ is increased the constraint region is enlarged which cannot possibly result in a higher value for $z$, the minimum of $f(\mathbf{x})$ within this region, although it could reduce $z$. So we shall have

$$\frac{\partial z}{\partial b_i} \leqslant 0$$

i.e. $\lambda_i^* \geqslant 0.$ \tag{5.22}

The necessary conditions to be satisfied at the minimum of $f(\mathbf{x})$ where $\mathbf{x}$ must satisfy $g_i(\mathbf{x}) \leqslant b_i (i = 1, 2, ..., m)$ are that we can find $\mathbf{x}$ and $\boldsymbol{\lambda}$ which satisfy

$$\left. \begin{array}{ll} \dfrac{\partial f}{\partial x_j} + \displaystyle\sum_{i=1}^{m} \lambda_i \dfrac{\partial g_i}{\partial x_j} = 0, & j = 1, ..., n. \\[2ex] g_i(\mathbf{x}) \leqslant b_i & i = 1, 2, ..., m. \\[1ex] \lambda_i [\, g_i(\mathbf{x}) - b_i ] = 0 & i = 1, 2, ..., m. \\[1ex] \lambda_i \geqslant 0. & i = 1, ..., m. \end{array} \right\} \tag{5.23}$$

[The sign of the $\lambda_i$ is reversed if we are dealing with a maximum.] These conditions are known as the Kuhn–Tucker conditions.

## Example 1

Write down the Kuhn–Tucker conditions for the minimum of $3x_1^2 + 4x_1x_2 + 5x_2^2$ subject to $x_1 \geqslant 0$, $x_2 \geqslant 0$ and $x_1 + x_2 \geqslant 4$.

The problem can be written, minimise

$$3x_1^2 + 4x_1x_2 + 5x_2^2$$

subject to

$$-x_1 \leqslant 0$$
$$-x_2 \leqslant 0$$
$$-x_1 - x_2 \leqslant -4.$$

The Lagrange function $F(\mathbf{x}, \mathbf{u}, \boldsymbol{\lambda})$ is

$$F = 3x_1^2 + 4x_1x_2 + 5x_2^2 + \lambda_1(u_1^2 - x_1) + \lambda_2(u_2^2 - x_2) + \lambda_3(u_3^2 - x_1 - x_2 + 4).$$

The necessary conditions are thus

$$6x_1 + 4x_2 - \lambda_1 - \lambda_3 = 0$$
$$4x_1 + 10x_2 - \lambda_2 - \lambda_3 = 0$$
$$-x_1 \leqslant 0, \quad -x_2 \leqslant 0, \quad -x_1 - x_2 \leqslant -4,$$
$$\lambda_1 x_1 = 0, \quad \lambda_2 x_2 = 0, \quad \lambda_3(4 - x_1 - x_2) = 0$$
$$\lambda_1, \lambda_2, \lambda_3 \geqslant 0.$$

It is easy to verify that these conditions are satisfied by $x_1 = 3$, $x_2 = 1$, $\lambda_1 = 0$, $\lambda_2 = 0$, $\lambda_3 = 22$, the function minimum being 44 at A(3, 1).

The contours of $f(\mathbf{x})$ are the ellipses

$$3x_1^2 + 4x_1x_2 + 5x_2^2 = c.$$

The unconstrained minimum of $f(\mathbf{x})$ is zero at the origin. The constrained region is shown shaded in Fig. 5.1 which illustrates the problem.

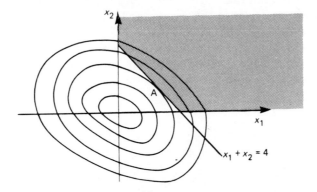

**Figure 5.1**

## 5.3 Convexity and Concavity

The general mathematical programming problem posed at the beginning of the previous section is a very hard problem. Indeed it is one to which there is no complete solution as yet. Some of the difficulties can be illustrated graphically for some

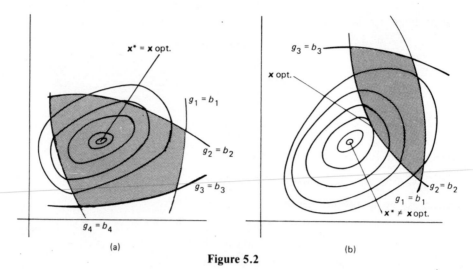

(a)                                    (b)

**Figure 5.2**

two variable problems. Figures 5.2(a) and (b) show the contours of a function. The values increase as we move from $\mathbf{x}^*$, the unconstrained minimum. Also shown are the constraint boundaries $g_i(\mathbf{x}) = b_i$, the constrained region being shaded.

In (a) the constrained minimum is the same as the unconstrained minimum. All the constraints are satisfied as strict inequalities and if we *had only known* we could have ignored the constraints and treated this problem by the methods of Part I of this book. In (b) the constrained minimum lies on $g_2(\mathbf{x}) = b_2$ and the other two constraints are inactive. If we *had only known* we could have ignored $g_1$ and $g_3$ and treated this an an equation constraint problem just involving $g_2(\mathbf{x}) = b_2$. Incidentally, we notice from this that at the constrained minimum $\mathbf{x}$ opt., $\nabla f(\mathbf{x}) = \lambda \nabla g_2(\mathbf{x})$ since $\nabla f(\mathbf{x})$ is perpendicular to the contour and the boundary at this point. (Compare this with equation 5.17.)

It is also possible for the constraints to introduce local minima into the problem. This can occur even if the function itself only has one minimum point in the unconstrained situation. Figure 5.3 illustrates this.

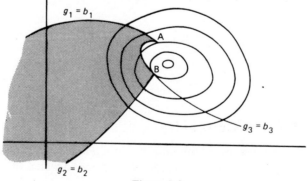

**Figure 5.3**

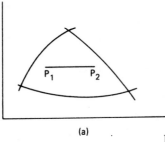

(a)                                                                (b)

**Figure 5.4**

The function has only one unconstrained minimum point. However, for the constrained problem both A and B are local minima since no feasible point in the immediate neighbourhood of A or B gives smaller function values.

Some of the problems just discussed are eliminated if we restrict our problems to constraint regions that are convex and the function to be minimised (maximised) is convex (concave).

We first define these terms. A region is *convex* if the line segment joining any two points in the region lies entirely within the region. Thus if $x_1$ and $x_2$ are in the region so is every point $\theta x_2 + (1 - \theta)x_1$ where $0 < \theta < 1$. Figure 5.4(a) illustrates a convex region, Fig. 5.4(b) a non convex region.

A function $f(\mathbf{x})$ is said to be *convex* over the convex domain $X$ if for any two points $\mathbf{x}_1, \mathbf{x}_2 \in X$,

$$f[\theta\mathbf{x}_2 + (1 - \theta)\mathbf{x}_1] \leqslant \theta f(\mathbf{x}_2) + (1 - \theta)f(\mathbf{x}_1) \qquad (5.24)$$

for $0 < \theta < 1$.

For a function of one variable this means that it lies below the chord joining any two points on its graph (Fig. 5.5).

For a *concave* function defined on a convex domain we reverse the inequality to obtain,

$$f[\theta\mathbf{x}_2 + (1 - \theta)\mathbf{x}_1] \geqslant \theta f(\mathbf{x}_2) + (1 - \theta)f(\mathbf{x}_1). \qquad (5.25)$$

Such a function lies above the chord joining two points on its graph.

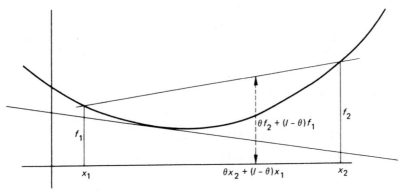

**Figure 5.5**

If the inequalities in equations 5.24 and 5.25 are replaced by strict inequalities $f(\mathbf{x})$ is said to be strictly convex or strictly concave.

There are two further important properties of convex (concave) functions which can be deduced from equations 5.24 and 5.25.

If $f(\mathbf{x})$ is convex over the convex domain $X$ and $\mathbf{x}_1, \mathbf{x}_2 \in X$, then

$$f(\mathbf{x}_2) \geqslant f(\mathbf{x}_1) + (\mathbf{x}_2 - \mathbf{x}_1)^T \nabla f(\mathbf{x}_1). \tag{5.26}$$

The inequality is reversed for a concave function.

This is established by the following argument. Since $f(\mathbf{x})$ is convex, for $0 < \theta < 1$

$$f[\theta \mathbf{x}_2 + (1 - \theta)\mathbf{x}_1] \leqslant \theta f(\mathbf{x}_2) + (1 - \theta)f(\mathbf{x}_1)$$

$$\therefore \quad f[\mathbf{x}_1 + \theta(\mathbf{x}_2 - \mathbf{x}_1)] - f(\mathbf{x}_1) \leqslant \theta[f(\mathbf{x}_2) - f(\mathbf{x}_1)]$$

$$\therefore \quad f(\mathbf{x}_2) \geqslant f(\mathbf{x}_1) + \frac{f[\mathbf{x}_1 + \theta(\mathbf{x}_2 - \mathbf{x}_1)] - f(\mathbf{x}_1)}{\theta}.$$

But by the first mean value theorem

$$f[\mathbf{x}_1 + \theta(\mathbf{x}_2 - \mathbf{x}_1)] = f(\mathbf{x}_1) + \theta(\mathbf{x}_2 - \mathbf{x}_1)^T \nabla f[\mathbf{x}_1 + \lambda\theta(\mathbf{x}_2 - \mathbf{x}_1)]$$

where $\lambda$ is some value in $0 < \lambda < 1$; i.e. the derviative is evaluated at some point between $\mathbf{x}_1$ and $\mathbf{x}_1 + \theta(\mathbf{x}_2 - \mathbf{x}_1)$.

$$\therefore \quad f(\mathbf{x}_2) \geqslant f(\mathbf{x}_1) + (\mathbf{x}_2 - \mathbf{x}_1)^T \nabla f[\mathbf{x}_1 + \theta\lambda(\mathbf{x}_2 - \mathbf{x}_1)].$$

As $\theta \to 0$ we obtain the result (equation 5.26).

For convex functions of one (two) variable(s) equation 5.26 says that such a function lies above any tangent line (plane) to the function (see Fig. 5.5).

A function is convex if the Hessian matrix

$$\mathbf{H} = \left(\frac{\partial^2 f}{\partial x_i \partial x_j}\right)$$

is positive definite. By Taylor's theorem we can write

$$f(\mathbf{x}) = f(\mathbf{x}_1) + (\mathbf{x} - \mathbf{x}_1)^T \nabla f(\mathbf{x}_1) + \tfrac{1}{2}(\mathbf{x} - \mathbf{x}_1)^T \mathbf{H}(\mathbf{x} - \mathbf{x}_1)$$

where $\mathbf{H}$ is evaluated at the point $\mathbf{x}_1 + \lambda(\mathbf{x} - \mathbf{x}_1)$ and $0 < \lambda < 1$.

Thus we really have to show that a positive definite quadratic function $\tfrac{1}{2}\mathbf{x}^T\mathbf{H}\mathbf{x}$ is convex. This is not difficult. Let $\mathbf{x}_2$ and $\mathbf{x}_1$ be any values for $\mathbf{x}$ and let $\bar{\mathbf{x}} = \theta\mathbf{x}_2 + (1 - \theta)\mathbf{x}_1, 0 < \theta < 1$.

Then

$$\bar{\mathbf{x}}^T\mathbf{H}\bar{\mathbf{x}} - \theta\mathbf{x}_2^T\mathbf{H}\mathbf{x}_2 - (1 - \theta)\mathbf{x}_1^T\mathbf{H}\mathbf{x}_1$$

$$= \theta^2\mathbf{x}_2^T\mathbf{H}\mathbf{x}_2 + 2\theta(1 - \theta)\mathbf{x}_2^T\mathbf{H}\mathbf{x}_1 + (1 - \theta)^2\mathbf{x}_1^T\mathbf{H}\mathbf{x}_1 - \theta\mathbf{x}_2^T\mathbf{H}\mathbf{x}_2 - (1 - \theta)\mathbf{x}_1^T\mathbf{H}\mathbf{x}_1$$

$$= -\theta(1 - \theta)(\mathbf{x}_2 - \mathbf{x}_1)^T\mathbf{H}(\mathbf{x}_2 - \mathbf{x}_1).$$

Since $0 < \theta < 1$, $(1 - \theta) > 0$ and so if $\mathbf{H}$ is positive definite the final expression is less than or equal to zero. Thus

$$[\theta\mathbf{x}_2 + (1 - \theta)\mathbf{x}_1]^T\mathbf{H}[\theta\mathbf{x}_2 + (1 - \theta)\mathbf{x}_1] \leqslant \theta\mathbf{x}_2^T\mathbf{H}\mathbf{x}_2 + (1 - \theta)\mathbf{x}_1^T\mathbf{H}\mathbf{x}_1. \tag{5.27}$$

For convex functions of one variable this says that the second derivative is non-negative so that the first derivative is an increasing function which can only be zero at one point. Thus such a function will have one minimum point.

## Example 1

If $g_i(\mathbf{x}), (i = 1, 2, ..., m)$, are convex functions over the convex domain $X$, show that $\sum \lambda_i g_i(\mathbf{x})$ where the $\lambda_i \geq 0$ is also convex.

Let

$$h(\mathbf{x}) = \sum_{i=1}^{m} \lambda_i g_i(\mathbf{x}).$$

Then if $\mathbf{x}_1, \mathbf{x}_2 \in X$

$$h[\theta \mathbf{x}_2 + (1 - \theta)\mathbf{x}_1] = \sum_{i=1}^{m} \lambda_i g_i[\theta \mathbf{x}_2 + (1 - \theta)\mathbf{x}_1]$$

$$\leq \sum_{i=1}^{m} \lambda_i [\theta g_i(\mathbf{x}_2) + (1 - \theta) g_i(\mathbf{x}_1)]$$

$$\leq \theta \sum_{i=1}^{m} \lambda_i g_i(\mathbf{x}_2) + (1 - \theta) \sum_{i=1}^{m} \lambda_i g_i(\mathbf{x}_1)$$

$$= \theta h(\mathbf{x}_2) + (1 - \theta) h(\mathbf{x}_1)$$

which proves $h(\mathbf{x})$ to be convex.

## Example 2

If the constraint region is defined by $g_i(\mathbf{x}) \leq b_i, (i = 1, ..., m)$ where the $g_i(\mathbf{x})$ are convex functions show that the constraint region is convex.

Suppose $\mathbf{x}_1$ and $\mathbf{x}_2$ are feasible points within the constraint region. Then

$$g_i(\mathbf{x}_1) \leq b_i \quad i = 1, ..., m$$

$$g_i(\mathbf{x}_2) \leq b_i \quad i = 1, ..., m.$$

Then, if $0 < \theta < 1$, for $i = 1, 2, ..., m$

$$g_i[\theta \mathbf{x}_2 + (1 - \theta)\mathbf{x}_1] \leq \theta g_i(\mathbf{x}_2) + (1 - \theta) g_i(\mathbf{x}_1)$$
$$\leq \theta b_i + (1 - \theta) b_i$$
$$= b_i.$$

Thus $\theta \mathbf{x}_2 + (1 - \theta)\mathbf{x}_1$ belongs to the set of feasible points which is thus a convex set.

We can use the results above to establish the theorem that if $f(\mathbf{x})$ is a convex function over the region constrained by $g_i(\mathbf{x}) \leq b_i$, where the $g_i(\mathbf{x})$ are convex, then a local minimum of $f(\mathbf{x})$ in this region is its global minimum in this region.

For suppose $\mathbf{x}^*$ is the global minimum and $\mathbf{x}_0$ is a local minimum with $f(\mathbf{x}^*) < f(\mathbf{x}_0)$. Both these points are feasible and since the feasible region is convex and $f(\mathbf{x})$ is convex

$$f[\theta\mathbf{x}^* + (1-\theta)\mathbf{x}_0] \leqslant \theta f(\mathbf{x}^*) + (1-\theta)f(\mathbf{x}_0)$$
$$\leqslant \theta f(\mathbf{x}_0) + (1-\theta)f(\mathbf{x}_0)$$
$$\leqslant f(\mathbf{x}_0)$$

for $0 < \theta < 1$.

But if $\theta$ is sufficiently small $\theta\mathbf{x}^* + (1-\theta)\mathbf{x}_0$ lies within $\delta$ of $\mathbf{x}_0$. Thus since $\mathbf{x}_0$ is a local minimum it is not possible for the function value at the first point to be less than $f(\mathbf{x}_0)$. Thus we have a contradiction and $\mathbf{x}^*$ and $\mathbf{x}_0$ must coincide.

## Example 3

Write down the Kuhn–Tucker conditions for the problem: minimise $-x^2 - y^2$ subject to $x, y \geqslant 0, x + 2y \leqslant 3$. The Lagrange function is

$$F(x, y, \boldsymbol{\lambda}, \mathbf{u}) = -x^2 - y^2 + \lambda_1(-x + u_1^2) + \lambda_2(-y + u_2^2) + \lambda_3(x + 2y + u_3^2 - 3).$$

The necessary conditions are:

$$-2x - \lambda_1 + \lambda_3 = 0$$
$$-2y - \lambda_2 + 2\lambda_3 = 0$$
$$\lambda_1 x = 0, \quad \lambda_2 y = 0, \quad \lambda_3(x + 2y - 3) = 0$$

$$x + 2y \leqslant 3$$

$$\lambda_1, \lambda_2, \lambda_3 \geqslant 0.$$

We try to find solutions for these conditions. If $x, y > 0$ then $\lambda_1 = \lambda_2 = 0$.

(a) If $\lambda_3 = 0$ then $x = y = 0$ and we have a maximum.

(b) If $\lambda_1 = \lambda_2 = 0, \lambda_3 > 0$, then $2x = \lambda_3 = y$ and $x + 2y - 3 = 0$. Thus $x = \frac{3}{5}$ and $y = \frac{6}{5}$ and $\lambda_3 = \frac{6}{5}$, all conditions are satisfied and

$$f = -\frac{45}{25}.$$

(c) If $\lambda_1 > 0, \lambda_2 = 0, \lambda_3 > 0$ then

$$x = 0, \quad y > 0, \quad x + 2y = 3 \quad \text{i.e. } y = \frac{3}{2}.$$
$$\therefore \quad \lambda_3 = \frac{3}{2}, \quad \lambda_1 = \frac{3}{2} \quad \text{and all conditions are satisfied.}$$
$$f = -\frac{9}{4}.$$

(d) If $\lambda_1 = 0, \lambda_2 > 0, \lambda_3 > 0$ then

$$x > 0, \quad y = 0, \quad x + 2y = 3, \quad \text{i.e. } x = 3, \quad \lambda_3 = 6, \quad \lambda_2 = 12$$

and all conditions are satisfied and $f = -9$.

Hence there are several points which satisfy the necessary conditions. The global minimum is $-9$ at $(3, 0)$. The problem is illustrated in Fig. 5.6.

The difficulty that arises in Example 3 is removed if $f(\mathbf{x})$ is convex and the constraint region is convex. For the problem, minimise $f(\mathbf{x})$ subject to $g_i(\mathbf{x}) \leqslant b_i$, where $f(\mathbf{x})$ is convex and the $g_i(\mathbf{x})$ are convex, the Kuhn–Tucker necessary conditions (equation 5.23) are also sufficient.

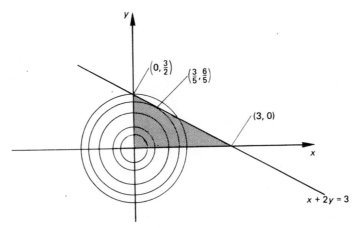

**Figure 5.6**

For in this case the Lagrange function (equation 5.16)

$$F(\mathbf{x}, \boldsymbol{\lambda}, \mathbf{u}) = f(\mathbf{x}) + \sum_{i=1}^{m} \lambda_i [\, g_i(\mathbf{x}) + u_i^2 - b_i ]$$

being the sum of convex functions is also convex. The $\lambda_i$ are of course non-negative. Hence $F$ has a global minimum at the point where its derivatives vanish and there is only one such point. Thus the necessary conditions are also sufficient.

Example 3 does not contradict this result. The $g_i(\mathbf{x})$ are certainly convex but $f(x, y) = -(x^2 + y^2)$ is *not* convex: it is concave.

## 5.4 References

1  B. Bernholtz, 'A new derivation of the Kuhn-Tucker conditions', *Operations Research,* **12**, No. 2, 295–299, 1964.
2  H. W. Kuhn and A. W. Tucker, 'Non Linear Programming', in *Proc. of 2nd Berkeley Symposium on Mathematical Statistics and Probability* (Editor J. Neyman), Berkeley, University of California Press, 481–492, 1951.
3  G. R. Walsh, *Methods of Optimisation,* John Wiley, 1975.
4  D. J. Wilde, 'Differential Calculus in Non Linear Programming', *Operations Research* **10**, No. 6, 764–773, 1962.
5  P. Wolfe, 'Methods of Non Linear Programming' in *Recent Advances in Mathematical Programming* (Editors R. L. Graves and P. Wolfe), McGraw-Hill, New York, 67–86, 1963.
6  P. Wolfe, 'Methods of Non Linear Programming' in *Non Linear Programming* (Editor J. Abadie), Nato Summer School, Menton, 1964, North Holland Publishing Co., Amsterdam, 1967.

## Exercises 5

**1**  Show that $f(x_1, x_2) = x_1^2 + x_2^2$ where $x_1 x_2 = 4$ has a minimum value of 8 when $(x_1, x_2) = (\pm 2, \pm 2)$.

**2**  Show that $f(x, y) = x^2 + y^2$ where $x$ and $y$ are constrained by $x - y = 5$ has a minimum when $x = 2 \cdot 5$, $y = -2 \cdot 5$.

**3**  If $a, b, c, k$ are positive constants, find positive $x, y, z$ such that $x + y + z = k$ and $w = ax^2 + by^2 + cz^2$ is a minimum.

**4**  If $a, b, c$ are all negative and

$$f(x_1, x_2, x_3) = ax_2x_3 + bx_3x_1 + cx_1x_2$$

where in addition $x_1 + x_2 + x_3 = 1$, show that $f(x_1, x_2, x_3)$ has a minimum value of $abc / [2(ab + bc + ca) - (a^2 + b^2 + c^2)]$, provided the denominator above is positive.

**5**  Find the stationary value(s) of $xy^2z^3$ if $x + y + z = 6$.

**6**  An open rectangular box made of thin sheet metal has height $z$, and a rectangular base of dimensions $x, y$. The base and the sides of length $x$ are of thickness $d$ (small) and the sides of length $y$ are of thickness $2d$. If the quantity of material is fixed, show that the volume of the box is a maximum when $x = 2y = 4z$.

**7**  Find the Kuhn–Tucker conditions for the problem:

$$\text{minimise} \quad x^2 + y^2$$

$$\text{subject to} \quad x \geqslant 0, \quad y \geqslant 0, \quad x + y \geqslant 5$$

and hence solve this problem.

**8**  Find the Kuhn–Tucker conditions for the problem.

$$\text{minimise} \quad f(x, y) = x^2 + 6xy - 4x - 2y$$

$$\text{subject to} \quad x^2 + 2y \leqslant 1$$

$$2x - 2y \leqslant 1.$$

Hence solve this problem.

**9**  If $f(\mathbf{x})$ is a convex function on the domain $X$ show that $g(\mathbf{x}) = -af(\mathbf{x})$ where $a$ is positive is a concave function on $X$.

**10**  The functions $g_i(\mathbf{x})$, $i = 1, 2, \ldots, m$ are all convex. Show that the set of points $\{\mathbf{x}: g_i(\mathbf{x}) \leqslant k\}$ where $k$ is a constant form a convex set.

**11**  $h(x)$ is a positive concave function of $x$ for $a \leqslant x \leqslant b$. By considering its second derivative or otherwise show that $g(x) = 1/h(x)$ is a convex function for $a \leqslant x \leqslant b$.

Generalise this result to the case where $h(\mathbf{x})$ is a positive concave function on the domain $X$. Show that the Hessian matrix of $g(\mathbf{x}) = 1/h(\mathbf{x})$ is positive definite.

**12**  Consider the problem of minimising the convex function $f(\mathbf{x})$ subject to the constraints $g_i(\mathbf{x}) \leqslant 0, i = 1, 2, \ldots, m$. Suppose that the unconstrained minimum of $f(\mathbf{x})$ is at $\mathbf{x}^*$ and that $g_1(\mathbf{x}^*)$, $g_2(\mathbf{x}^*)$, $g_3(\mathbf{x}^*) > 0$. If the constrained minimum is at $\mathbf{x}_0$, show that at least one of $g_1(\mathbf{x}_0)$, $g_2(\mathbf{x}_0)$, $g_3(\mathbf{x}_0)$ is zero. Explain the geometrical significance of this result.

**13** Find the maximum and minimum values of

$$x^2 + y^2$$

if $3x^2 + 4xy + 6y^2 = 140$. Interpret the result geometrically.

**14** The problem of minimising economic lot sizes can be expressed as one of minimising the function

$$f(x_1, x_2) = \frac{\alpha}{x_1} + \frac{\beta}{x_2} + \gamma(x_1 + x_2),$$

where $x_1, x_2 \geqslant 0$. $\alpha$ and $\beta$ are constants connected with the set-up costs for production runs of the two commodities and $\gamma$ is a constant connected to the cost of holding stock. (See Question 8, Exercise 1.)

Show that this function is minimised if $x_1 = \sqrt{\alpha/\gamma}$, $x_2 = \sqrt{\beta/\gamma}$.

In reality storage facilities mean that $x_1$ and $x_2$ must satisfy in addition $x_1 + x_2 \leqslant S$ where $S$ is some constant.

Write down the Kuhn–Tucker conditions for the resulting problem and hence obtain a solution.

**15** A parcel to be sent through the mail has a cuboid shape with dimensions $x_1, x_2, x_3$. The post office stipulates that $x_1 \leqslant 20$, $x_2 \leqslant 11$, $x_3 \leqslant 42$ and in addition $x_1 + 2x_2 + 2x_3 \leqslant 72$. Find the dimensions which maximise the volume. [This is Rosenbrock's *modified* Post Office Parcel Problem. See also the next chapter.]

**16** The standard Post Office Parcel Problem is similar to the above except that the constraints are

$$x_i \leqslant 42, \quad (i = 1, 2, 3), \quad x_1 + 2x_2 + 2x_3 \leqslant 72.$$

Write down the Kuhn–Tucker conditions for this problem and hence obtain the solution.

# 6
# Search Methods

## 6.1 Modified Hooke and Jeeves

We first discuss methods of solving the non-linear programming problem which only use function values. The direct search methods of Chapter 3, when applied to the unconstrained optimisation problem, were successful. One might suppose that they could be modified to take account of constraints. Indeed it has been suggested that merely giving the objective function a very large value (in a minimisation problem) whenever the constraints are violated will suffice. Certainly this idea has an obvious intuitive appeal and is easy to program.

For each trial point we check whether it lies within the constraint region. If so we evaluate the objective function in the normal way. If not we give the objective function a very large value. In this way the search method will be directed back into the feasible region and hence towards the minimum point within the feasible region.

To illustrate an attempt to implement this procedure we give a listing of a modified Hooke and Jeeves direct search program. The problem being considered is the following.

$$\text{Minimise} \quad f(x_1, x_2) = 3x_1^2 + 4x_1 x_2 + 5x_2^2$$
$$\text{subject to} \quad x_1 \geqslant 0, \quad x_2 \geqslant 0, \quad x_1 + x_2 \geqslant 4.$$

(See Example 1 of Section 5.2.).

The program is identical with the Hooke and Jeeves program in Section 3.2 except that the FUNCTION $f$ has been modified to take account of the constraints in the way just outlined. The minimum is 44 at (3, 1) on the constraint $x_1 + x_2 = 4$.

```
PROGRAM ModifiedHookeandJeeves (input,output);
CONST
  n=2;                  { No. of variables in function f }        {**}
  hmin=1.0E-8;          { Minimum step length }                   {**}
  fwx=10; dpx=4;        { Output format constants for vector components } {**}
  fwf=14;               { Output format constant for function values }    {**}
  fws=14; dps=8;        { Output format constants for step length }       {**}
  reduction=0.1;        { Reduction factor in step length changes }       {**}
  smallvalue=1.0E-12;   { Used to avoid influence of round-off errors }   {**}
  verylargevalue=       { Used as function value when }                   {**}
           1.0E30;      { constraints violated       }                    {**}
```

```
TYPE
  vector = ARRAY [1..n] OF real;
  point = RECORD
            x : vector;  f : real
          END;
  howobtained = PACKED ARRAY [1..12] OF char;


VAR
  b1, b2, b3, P : point;  { Base points and pattern point }
  fe : integer;           { Function evaluation counter }
  h : real;               { Step length for base change calculations }
  improvement : boolean;  { Indicator for better base point }
  i : integer;


FUNCTION f (x:vector): real;
{ The code here is dependent on the function being minimised }
{ and the constraints on the x-values.                       }
BEGIN  fe := fe+1;
  IF (x[1]<0.0) OR (x[2]<0.0) OR (x[1]+x[2]<4.0) THEN f:=verylargevalue  {**}
  ELSE  f := 3.0*sqr(x[1]) + 4.0*x[1]*x[2] + 5.0*sqr(x[2])               {**}
END; { f }


PROCEDURE inputdata;
VAR  i : integer;
BEGIN  writeln('     NUMBER OF VARIABLES =', n:3);
  writeln('    INITIAL POINT');
  FOR i:=1 TO n DO
  BEGIN
    write('    X[', i:2, ']'); read(b1.x[i]); writeln(b1.x[i]:fwx:dpx)
  END;
  write('    STEP LENGTH ='); read(h); writeln(h:fws:dps);  writeln
END; { inputdata }


PROCEDURE outputline (step:real; s:howobtained; p:point);
VAR  i : integer;
BEGIN  write(step:fws:dps, '   ', p.f:fwf, '    ', s);
  FOR i:=1 TO n DO write(p.x[i]:fwx:dpx);  writeln
END; { outputline }


PROCEDURE initialise;
BEGIN  fe:=0;  b1.f := f(b1.x)  { Step (B)(i) }  END; { initialise }


PROCEDURE exploration (oldbase:point; VAR newbase:point);
VAR  i : integer;  fval : real;
BEGIN  newbase := oldbase;
  FOR i:=1 TO n DO
  BEGIN  newbase.x[i] := oldbase.x[i] + h;  fval:=f(newbase.x);
    IF fval < newbase.f THEN newbase.f:=fval
    ELSE
```

```
    BEGIN  newbase.x[i] := oldbase.x[i] - h;  fval:=f(newbase.x);
      IF fval < newbase.f THEN newbase.f:=fval
      ELSE  newbase.x[i] := oldbase.x[i]
    END
  END;
    outputline(h, 'EXPLORATION ', newbase)
  END; { exploration }

PROCEDURE patternmove (b1,b2:point; VAR P:point);
VAR  i : integer;
BEGIN
    FOR i:=1 TO n DO  P.x[i] := 2.0*b2.x[i] - b1.x[i];
    P.f := f(P.x);  outputline(h, 'PATTERN MOVE', P)
END; { patternmove }


BEGIN  { Main Program }
    writeln;  writeln('    CONSTRAINED HOOKE & JEEVES');  writeln;
    inputdata;
    write(' ':fws-4, 'STEP ', ' ':fwf-4, 'F(X)    HOW OBTAINED');
    FOR i:=1 TO n DO write(' ':fwx-5, 'X[', i:2, ']'); writeln; writeln;
    initialise; { Step (A) }  outputline(h, 'INITIAL BASE', b1);
    REPEAT  { Until step length is small enough }
      exploration(b1,b2);  { Step (B)(ii) }
      improvement :=  b2.f < b1.f - smallvalue;
      IF NOT improvement THEN h := h*reduction  { Reduce step length }
      ELSE                                      { at Step (B)(iii)    }
        REPEAT  { From Step (B)(iv) or Step (C)(iii) }
          patternmove(b1,b2,P);  { Step (C)(i) }
          exploration(P,b3);  { Step (C)(ii) }
          improvement :=  b3.f < b2.f - smallvalue;
          { Now perform Step (C)(iii) }
          IF improvement THEN BEGIN b1:=b2; b2:=b3 END
          ELSE BEGIN b1:=b2; outputline(h, 'BASE CHANGE ', b1) END
        UNTIL NOT improvement
    UNTIL h<hmin; { Step (D) }
    writeln;  writeln('    FUNCTION MINIMUM =', b1.f);  writeln;
    writeln('   NO. OF FUNCTION EVALUATIONS =', fe:5)
END.  { ModifiedHookeandJeeves }
```

With initial point $(4, 3)$ and step length 1 the output given was obtained and the program was successful.

```
CONSTRAINED HOOKE & JEEVES

NUMBER OF VARIABLES =  2
INITIAL POINT
X[ 1]    4.0000
X[ 2]    3.0000
STEP LENGTH =    1.00000000
```

| STEP | F(X) | HOW OBTAINED | X[ 1] | X[ 2] |
|---|---|---|---|---|
| 1.00000000 | 1.410000E+002 | INITIAL BASE | 4.0000 | 3.0000 |
| 1.00000000 | 7.100000E+001 | EXPLORATION | 3.0000 | 2.0000 |
| 1.00000000 | 1.000000E+030 | PATTERN MOVE | 2.0000 | 1.0000 |

| | | | | |
|---|---|---|---|---|
| 1.00000000 | 4.400000E+001 | EXPLORATION | 3.0000 | 1.0000 |
| 1.00000000 | 1.000000E+030 | PATTERN MOVE | 3.0000 | 0.0000 |
| 1.00000000 | 4.800000E+001 | EXPLORATION | 4.0000 | 0.0000 |
| 1.00000000 | 4.400000E+001 | BASE CHANGE | 3.0000 | 1.0000 |
| 1.00000000 | 4.400000E+001 | EXPLORATION | 3.0000 | 1.0000 |
| 0.10000000 | 4.400000E+001 | EXPLORATION | 3.0000 | 1.0000 |
| 0.01000000 | 4.400000E+001 | EXPLORATION | 3.0000 | 1.0000 |
| 0.00100000 | 4.400000E+001 | EXPLORATION | 3.0000 | 1.0000 |
| 0.00010000 | 4.400000E+001 | EXPLORATION | 3.0000 | 1.0000 |
| 0.00001000 | 4.400000E+001 | EXPLORATION | 3.0000 | 1.0000 |
| 0.00000100 | 4.400000E+001 | EXPLORATION | 3.0000 | 1.0000 |
| 0.00000010 | 4.400000E+001 | EXPLORATION | 3.0000 | 1.0000 |
| 0.00000001 | 4.400000E+001 | EXPLORATION | 3.0000 | 1.0000 |

FUNCTION MINIMUM = 4.4000000000000E+001

NO. OF FUNCTION EVALUATIONS = 49

With initial point (3, 4) and step length 1 the program succeeded.

With initial point (5, 6) and step length 1 the program 'got stuck' at the point (1, 3) on the active constraint and got the wrong answer. The output is given

CONSTRAINED HOOKE & JEEVES

NUMBER OF VARIABLES = 2
INITIAL POINT
X[ 1]    5.0000
X[ 2]    6.0000
STEP LENGTH =    1.00000000

| STEP | F(X) | HOW OBTAINED | X[ 1] | X[ 2] |
|---|---|---|---|---|
| 1.00000000 | 3.750000E+002 | INITIAL BASE | 5.0000 | 6.0000 |
| 1.00000000 | 2.530000E+002 | EXPLORATION | 4.0000 | 5.0000 |
| 1.00000000 | 1.550000E+002 | PATTERN MOVE | 3.0000 | 4.0000 |
| 1.00000000 | 8.100000E+001 | EXPLORATION | 2.0000 | 3.0000 |
| 1.00000000 | 1.000000E+030 | PATTERN MOVE | 0.0000 | 1.0000 |
| 1.00000000 | 1.000000E+030 | EXPLORATION | 0.0000 | 1.0000 |
| 1.00000000 | 8.100000E+001 | BASE CHANGE | 2.0000 | 3.0000 |
| 1.00000000 | 6.000000E+001 | EXPLORATION | 1.0000 | 3.0000 |
| 1.00000000 | 1.000000E+030 | PATTERN MOVE | 0.0000 | 3.0000 |
| 1.00000000 | 6.000000E+001 | EXPLORATION | 1.0000 | 3.0000 |
| 1.00000000 | 6.000000E+001 | BASE CHANGE | 1.0000 | 3.0000 |
| 1.00000000 | 6.000000E+001 | EXPLORATION | 1.0000 | 3.0000 |
| 0.10000000 | 6.000000E+001 | EXPLORATION | 1.0000 | 3.0000 |
| 0.01000000 | 6.000000E+001 | EXPLORATION | 1.0000 | 3.0000 |
| 0.00100000 | 6.000000E+001 | EXPLORATION | 1.0000 | 3.0000 |
| 0.00010000 | 6.000000E+001 | EXPLORATION | 1.0000 | 3.0000 |
| 0.00001000 | 6.000000E+001 | EXPLORATION | 1.0000 | 3.0000 |
| 0.00000100 | 6.000000E+001 | EXPLORATION | 1.0000 | 3.0000 |
| 0.00000010 | 6.000000E+001 | EXPLORATION | 1.0000 | 3.0000 |
| 0.00000001 | 6.000000E+001 | EXPLORATION | 1.0000 | 3.0000 |

FUNCTION MINIMUM = 6.0000000000000E+001

NO. OF FUNCTION EVALUATIONS = 59

Similarly frustrating results were obtained with initial point (5, 6) and step length 0·5. A false solution was obtained at (1·5, 2·5). With initial point (4, 3) but a step length not of 1, which worked, but of 0·5, the false solution (2·5, 1·5) was obtained.

The problem is clear. The method is not able to move along the constraint and converges on the first point on the constraint that it locates as the solution. As was stressed in Chapter 5, the general constrained optimisation problem is a hard problem and more sophisticated procedures than this will be needed to obtain a practical solution method.

## 6.2   The Complex Method

Difficulties encountered in trying to implement the search methods then in existence, prompted Box in 1964 to devise his own method. Essentially it is a modification of the Simplex Method of Nelder and Mead so as to take account of constraints. Box called it the Complex Method.

The problem considered is that of minimising $f(\mathbf{x}) = f(x_1, x_2, ..., x_n)$ where the $\mathbf{x}$ are subject to the *explicit* constraints

$$l_j \leqslant x_j \leqslant u_j, \quad j = 1, 2, ..., n \tag{6.1}$$

and also the *implicit* constraints

$$g_i(\mathbf{x}) \leqslant b_i, \quad i = 1, 2, ..., m. \tag{6.2}$$

If the objective function $f(\mathbf{x})$ is convex and the implicit constraints $g_i(\mathbf{x})$ are convex the problem will have a unique solution. The $l_j$ and $u_j$ are lower and upper bounds for the variables. If in the actual problem certain variables are in theory unbounded, assuming 'safe' bounds which certainly include the optimum will enable the method to be implemented.

The method is an iterative procedure. It assumes that we know $n$ and $m$, the $l_j$ and the $u_j$ and have an initial point $\mathbf{x}_1$ that satisfies all the constraints (equations 6.1 and 6.2). We first have to generate a set of $k$ points which satisfy the constraints, and evaluate the objective function at those $k$ points. This set of points is called a complex. Box found that $k$ needed to be larger than $n + 1$, the number of points used in the Simplex Method of Nelder and Mead. He suggested the value $k = 2n$.

As we have mentioned it is assumed that $\mathbf{x}_1$, satisfying all the constraints is given. We can generate further points which satisfy equation 6.1 by

$$x_{ij} = l_j + r(u_j - l_j) \tag{6.3}$$

for $j = 1, 2, ..., n$ and $i = 2, 3, ..., k$ where $r$ is a pseudo-random rectangularly distributed variable on the range (0, 1). Such variables are obtained from a pseudo-random number generator provided in the program.

Points generated by equation 6.3 for a given value of $j$ will automatically satisfy equation 6.1. If they also satisfy equation 6.2 they are accepted as points of the initial complex. If the point generated by equation 6.3 does not satisfy equation 6.2 we move it halfway towards the centroid of already accepted points, i.e. we form

$$\mathbf{x}_i' = \frac{(\mathbf{x}_i + \mathbf{x}_c)}{2} \tag{6.4}$$

where

$$\mathbf{x}_c = \frac{1}{i-1} \sum_{e=1}^{i-1} \mathbf{x}_e. \tag{6.5}$$

If equation 6.4 is still not feasible we repeat this procedure again and again until it is. If the $g_i(\mathbf{x})$ are convex we will ultimately satisfy the constraints. Of course since $\mathbf{x}_1$ is in the constrained region we will always have a centroid of already accepted points.

In this way we obtain our initial complex of feasible points. It is convenient to order these points according to the magnitude of the corresponding function values. We can describe the procedure for the initialisation of the process by means of a flow chart. In the program listing this is implemented in the PROCEDURE *initiate complex*.

We now come to the iterative procedure of the Complex Method in which we seek to move towards the minimum point within the constrained region. The steps required are outlined below.

1   Find the point with the greatest function value $\mathbf{x}_h$ and form the centroid $\mathbf{x}_0$ of the other $(k - 1)$ points.

2   We try to move away from $\mathbf{x}_h$ and so form the point $\mathbf{x}_r$ by reflecting $\mathbf{x}_h$ in $\mathbf{x}_0$, using a reflection factor $\alpha(>1)$.

$$\text{i.e.} \quad \mathbf{x}_r = (1 + \alpha)\mathbf{x}_0 - \alpha\mathbf{x}_h \tag{6.6}$$

3   We next test if $\mathbf{x}_r$ is feasible.
  (i) If not and if $l_j$ is violated we set $x_{rj} = l_j + 10^{-6}$; if $u_j$ is violated set $x_{rj} = u_j - 10^{-6}$.
  (ii) If an implicit constraint is violated we move the point $\mathbf{x}_r$ halfway towards the centroid $\mathbf{x}_0$

$$\text{i.e.} \quad \mathbf{x}_r(\text{new}) = (\mathbf{x}_r + \mathbf{x}_0)/2 \tag{6.7}$$

We then retest for feasibility and repeat the procedures at step 3 until a feasible point is obtained.

4   If $\mathbf{x}_r$ is feasible we evaluate $f(\mathbf{x}_r)$ and compare it with $f(\mathbf{x}_k)$ the worst function value since the function values have been ordered.

If $f(\mathbf{x}_r) > f(\mathbf{x}_k)$ i.e. is worse than the worst value obtained so far we move $\mathbf{x}_r$ halfway towards $\mathbf{x}_0$

$$\text{i.e.} \quad \mathbf{x}_r(\text{new}) = (\mathbf{x}_r + \mathbf{x}_0)/2,$$

and then return to step 3.

5   If $f(\mathbf{x}_r) < f(\mathbf{x}_k)$ we replace $\mathbf{x}_k$ by $\mathbf{x}_r$ and reorder the points and function values of the complex.

6   We next calculate two quantities that are used to test whether the method has converged. These are the standard deviation of the $k$ function values, and the maximum distance $d_m$ between two points of the complex. The former is calculated as

$$\sigma = \left\{ \sum_{e=1}^{k} [f(\mathbf{x}_e) - \bar{f}]^2 / k \right\}^{1/2} \tag{6.8}$$

## Flow Chart to Initiate the Complex Method

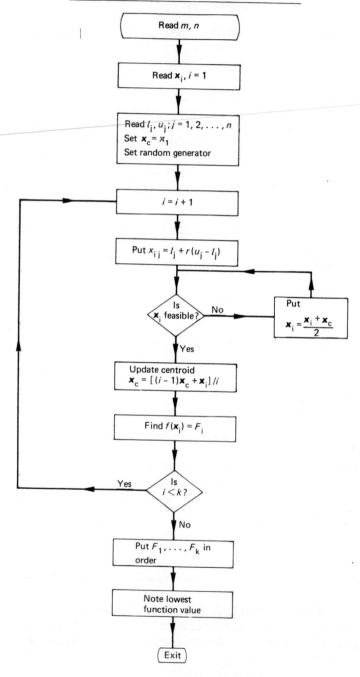

where

$$\bar{f} = \frac{1}{k} \sum_{e=1}^{k} f(\mathbf{x}_e) \tag{6.9}$$

but $\sigma^2$ is best calculated from the equivalent formula

$$\sigma^2 = \left\{ \sum_{e=1}^{k} f(\mathbf{x}_e)^2 - \frac{[\sum f(\mathbf{x})]^2}{k} \right\} \Big/ k \tag{6.10}$$

7   The test of convergence is made on $\sigma^2$ and $d_m$. If *both* are sufficiently small we terminate. Otherwise we return to step 1 and repeat the process.

In the program listed, intermediate information is output but only if the best (minimum) function value has been improved.

A flow chart indicating the steps 1 to 7 is given and in the program listing this is implemented in the PROCEDURE *iterativecomplex* where the occurrence of each step is indicated by a comment.

FUNCTION *f* evaluates the objective function. PROCEDURE *checkimplicit* and PROCEDURE *checkexplicit* test the implicit and explicit constraints respectively.

The function *f* and the PROCEDURE *implicitconstraints* in the program listing are appropriate to the modified Post Office Parcel Problem (see Exercises 5, question 15);

$$\text{minimise} \quad f(\mathbf{x}) = -x_1 x_2 x_3$$
$$\text{subject to} \quad 0 \leqslant x_1 \leqslant 20, \quad 0 \leqslant x_2 \leqslant 11, \quad 0 \leqslant x_3 \leqslant 42$$
$$\text{and} \quad x_1 + 2x_2 + 2x_3 \leqslant 72.$$

There is only one implicit constraint for this problem but it should be clear how the PROCEDURE would be modified for other constraints.

The procedure converges when the complex shrinks to lying within a small neighbourhood of the minimum point. Provided the variation in function values is also small the convergence test will terminate at this stage.

The choice of $k = 2n$ and $\alpha = 1\cdot3$ are empirical rules suggested by Box. The former is partly to prevent premature collapse of the complex. The overreflection factor $\alpha(>1)$ enables the complex to expand and move in the desired direction. The moves halfway to the centroid contract the complex. Thus the complex is able to move around the feasible region and is able to move along a constraint and turn a corner where two constraints intersect. The device of setting the variables just inside their bounds helps with this.

The way in which the initial complex is generated means that several runs can be made very easily. It is certainly suggested that more than one run should be made, just in case the method converges prematurely by some quirk of the particular points used. Indeed, it is probably a good idea to obtain some information on the likely magnitude of the minimum function value, and then subtract this in FUNCTION *f* so that, for the function actually minimised, the minimum is roughly zero. This will avoid any problems when calculating the variance at the test of convergence.

## The Iterative Routine of the Complex Method

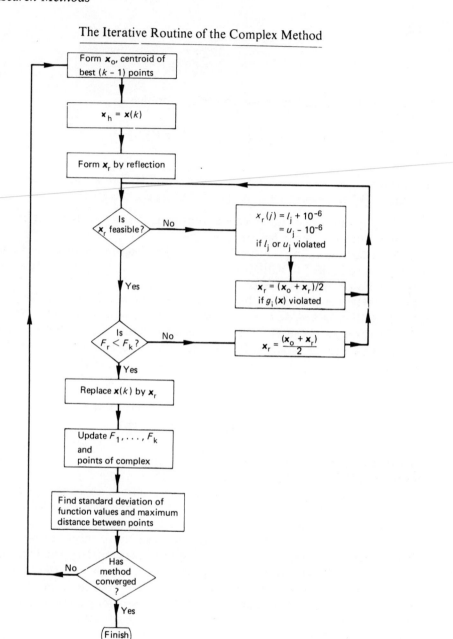

After all if the values were 9 digit values with the first 8 the same we could run into serious accuracy problems and might even obtain a negative variance!! (It would just be machine accuracy but would cause an execution error nonetheless.) This last point has been incorporated into the FUNCTION $f$. As stated the minimum value is in fact zero.

**Example 1**

Solve the modified Post Office Parcel Problem. The initial point used was (20, 10, 10). The random number generator was initialised with 7199 but this is irrelevant. The first and last parts of the computer output are given. The true minimum occurs at the point (20, 11, 15) so we have obtained good accuracy by our method. The number of function evaluations at 254, is fairly high (compared with many other runs that were made), but is in line with the results obtained by Box.

```
PROGRAM ComplexMethod (input,output);
CONST
  n=3;                       { No. of variables in function f}        {**}
  m=1;                       { No. of constraints }                   {**}
  k=6;                       { No. of points in complex }             {**}
  fwx=14; dpx=8;             { Output format constants for x-values } {**}
  fwf=16; dpf=10;            { Output format constant for function values }  {**}
  smallvalue=1.0E-6;

TYPE
  vector = ARRAY [1..n] OF real;
  point = RECORD
               x : vector;  f : real
          END;
  complex = ARRAY [1..k] OF point;
  garray = ARRAY [1..m] OF real;

VAR
  c : complex;            { Complex of points }
  l, u : vector;          { Lower and upper bounds for x-values }
  b : garray;             { Upper bounds on implicit function values }
  alpha : real;           { Reflection factor }
  epsilon,                { Required accuracy in variance and maximum }
  mdist : real;           { distance between points in final complex }
  fe, rseed : integer;    { Function evaluation counter and random number seed }
  i : integer;

FUNCTION f (x:vector): real;
{ The code here is dependent on the function being minimised }
BEGIN  fe := fe+1;
  f := -x[1]*x[2]*x[3] + 3300.0                                       {**}
END; { f }

PROCEDURE implicitconstraints (VAR g:garray; x:vector);
{ Compute the values of the implicit constraint function(s) at the point }
{ with vector x. The code here is dependent on the implicit constraints. }
BEGIN                                                                 {**}
  g[1] := x[1] + 2.0*x[2] + 2.0*x[3]
END; { implicitconstraints }

PROCEDURE inputdata;
VAR  i, j : integer;
```

```
BEGIN  writeln('     NUMBER OF CONSTRAINTS =', m:3);
  writeln('     NUMBER OF VARIABLES =', n:3);
  writeln('     INITIAL POINT');
  WITH c[1] DO
    FOR i:=1 TO n DO
    BEGIN write('     X[', i:2, ']'); read(x[i]); writeln(x[i]:fwx:dpx) END;
  writeln;   write('     EXPLICIT CONSTRAINTS    J');
  writeln(' ':fwx-4, 'L[J]', ' ':fwx-4, 'U[J]');
  FOR j:=1 TO n DO
  BEGIN  write(' ':24, j:4);   read(l[j], u[j]);
    writeln(l[j]:fwx:dpx, u[j]:fwx:dpx)
  END;  writeln;
  writeln('     IMPLICIT CONSTRAINT BOUNDS   I', ' ':fwf-4, 'B[I]');
  FOR i:=1 TO m DO
  BEGIN write(' ':30, i:4); read(b[i]); writeln(b[i]:fwf:dpf) END; writeln;
  write('     EPSILON ='); read(epsilon); writeln(epsilon:fwf);
  write('     MDIST ='); read(mdist); writeln(mdist:fwx);
  write('     ALPHA ='); read(alpha); writeln(alpha:6:2);
  write('     RANDOM NUMBER SEED ='); read(rseed); writeln(rseed:8)
END; { inputdata }


PROCEDURE outputline (p:point);
VAR  i : integer;
BEGIN  write(' ', p.f:fwf);
  FOR i:=1 TO n DO write(p.x[i]:fwx:dpx);   writeln
END; { outputline }


PROCEDURE newpoint (VAR new:point; a:real; p1:point; b:real; p2:point);
{ Find the point whose vector is a*p1.x + b*p2.x }
VAR  i : integer;
BEGIN
  FOR i:=1 TO n DO new.x[i] := a*p1.x[i] + b*p2.x[i]
END; { newpoint }


PROCEDURE bubblesort (VAR c:complex);
{ Sorts the points in the complex c into ascending order of function     }
{ value. The bubblesort method is particularly efficient when the complex }
{ is almost in order to start with, which is the case for each call from  }
{ the procedure iterativecomplex.                                         }
VAR  i, h, flag : integer;  temp : point;
BEGIN  flag:=k;
  WHILE flag>0 DO
  BEGIN  h := flag - 1;   flag:=0;
    FOR i:=1 TO h DO
      IF c[i].f > c[i+1].f THEN
        BEGIN temp:=c[i]; c[i]:=c[i+1]; c[i+1]:=temp; flag:=i END
  END
END; { bubblesort }


FUNCTION random : real;
{ This could be replaced by a library routine, if available }
CONST  m=524288; { This integer may be too large for some microcomputers }
BEGIN  rseed := (5*rseed) MOD m;   random := rseed/m  END; { random }
```

```
PROCEDURE checkimplicit (p:point; VAR violated:boolean);
VAR  g : garray;  i : integer;
BEGIN  violated := false;  implicitconstraints(g,p.x);
  FOR i:=1 TO m DO IF g[i]>b[i] THEN violated := true
END; { checkimplicit }


PROCEDURE initiatecomplex;
VAR i, j : integer;  violated : boolean;  centroid : point;
BEGIN  c[1].f := f(c[1].x);  centroid := c[1];
  FOR i:=2 TO k DO
  BEGIN
    FOR j:=1 TO n DO  c[i].x[j] := l[j] + random*(u[j]-l[j]);
    REPEAT
      checkimplicit(c[i], violated);
      IF violated THEN newpoint(c[i], 0.5, c[i], 0.5, centroid)
    UNTIL NOT violated;
    c[i].f := f(c[i].x);
    newpoint(centroid, (i-1)/i, centroid, 1/i, c[i]);
  END;
  bubblesort(c);  outputline(c[1])
END; { initialisecomplex }


PROCEDURE iterativecomplex;
VAR  centroid, r : point;  violated, improvement : boolean;
     sum : real;  i, j : integer;


FUNCTION varconvergence : boolean;
{ Test whether the variance of the function values in the }
{ complex is small enough, i.e. < epsilon                 }
VAR sumf, sumfsq : real;  i : integer;
BEGIN  sumf:=0.0;  sumfsq:=0.0;
  FOR i:=1 TO k DO
    WITH c[i] DO
    BEGIN  sumf := sumf + f;  sumfsq := sumfsq + sqr(f)  END;
  varconvergence := (sumfsq - sqr(sumf)/k)/k < epsilon
END; { varconvergence }


FUNCTION maxdistance : real;
{ Computes the maximum distance between pairs of points in the complex }
VAR  h, i, j : integer;  sum, max : real;
BEGIN  max:=0.0;
  FOR h:=1 TO k-1 Do
    FOR i:=h+1 TO k DO
    BEGIN  sum:=0.0;
      FOR j:=1 TO n DO  sum := sum + sqr(c[h].x[j]-c[i].x[j]);
      IF sum>max THEN max:=sum
    END;
  maxdistance := sqrt(max)
END; { maxdistance }


PROCEDURE checkexplicit (VAR p:point);
VAR  j : integer;
```

```
BEGIN
  FOR j:=1 TO n DO
    WITH p DO
      IF x[j]<l[j] THEN  x[j] := l[j] + smallvalue
      ELSE  IF x[j]>u[j] THEN  x[j] := u[j] - smallvalue
END; { checkexplicit }

BEGIN { iterativecomplex }
  REPEAT  { Until convergence achieved }
    REPEAT  { Until best point improved }
      FOR i:=1 TO n DO    { Step 1 - find centroid of    }
      BEGIN  sum:=0.0;   { first k-1 points of complex }
        FOR j:=1 TO k-1 DO  sum := sum + c[j].x[i];
        centroid.x[i] := sum/(k-1)
      END;
      newpoint(r, 1.0+alpha, centroid, -alpha, c[k]);  { Step 2 }
      REPEAT  { Until a better point than the current worst is found }
        REPEAT  { Until a feasible point is obtained, i.e. Step 3 }
          checkexplicit(r);
          checkimplicit(r, violated);
          IF violated THEN newpoint(r, 0.5, centroid, 0.5, r);
        UNTIL NOT violated;   r.f := f(r.x);
        { Step 4 }
        improvement := r.f < c[k].f;
        IF NOT improvement THEN newpoint(r, 0.5, centroid, 0.5, r)
      UNTIL improvement;
      c[k]:=r;  bubblesort(c)  { Step 5 }
    UNTIL  r.f=c[1].f;  outputline(c[1]);
    { Only perform convergence test when best point improved }
  UNTIL varconvergence AND (maxdistance < mdist)  { Steps 6 & 7 }
END; { iterativecomplex }

BEGIN  { Main Program }
  writeln; writeln('    COMPLEX METHOD'); writeln;
  inputdata; fe:=0;  writeln;  write(' ':fwf-13, 'NEW MINIMUM AT ');
  FOR i:=1 TO n DO write(' ':fwx-5, 'X[', i:2, ']'); writeln; writeln;
  initiatecomplex;
  iterativecomplex;
  writeln; writeln('    MINIMUM FOUND - FINAL DETAILS ARE:'); writeln;
  outputline(c[1]);  writeln;
  writeln('    NO. OF FUNCTION EVALUATIONS =', fe:5)
END. { ComplexMethod }
```

```
COMPLEX METHOD

NUMBER OF CONSTRAINTS =  1
NUMBER OF VARIABLES =  3
INITIAL POINT
X[ 1]    20.00000000
X[ 2]    10.00000000
X[ 3]    10.00000000
```

| EXPLICIT CONSTRAINTS | J | L[J] | U[J] |
|---|---|---|---|
| | 1 | 0.00000000 | 20.00000000 |
| | 2 | 0.00000000 | 11.00000000 |
| | 3 | 0.00000000 | 42.00000000 |

| IMPLICIT CONSTRAINT BOUNDS | I | B[I] |
|---|---|---|
| | 1 | 72.0000000000 |

EPSILON = 1.00000000E-006
MDIST = 1.000000E-004
ALPHA =   1.30
RANDOM NUMBER SEED =      7199

| NEW MINIMUM AT | X[ 1] | X[ 2] | X[ 3] |
|---|---|---|---|
| 1.27250543E+003 | 11.16204262 | 8.44561720 | 21.50723743 |
| 1.24901751E+003 | 18.92357035 | 10.99999900 | 9.85294885 |
| 4.48071197E+002 | 17.98067598 | 10.99999900 | 14.41916192 |
| 3.63678036E+002 | 18.51527047 | 10.05889192 | 15.76607076 |
| 3.31827363E+002 | 18.10698206 | 10.99999900 | 14.90220179 |
| 2.74305052E+002 | 18.43946763 | 10.73522361 | 15.28500788 |
| 2.38135999E+002 | 18.04903131 | 10.70231842 | 15.85090745 |
| 1.52279996E+002 | 19.33588243 | 10.30836000 | 15.79219581 |
| 1.50718999E+002 | 18.64475738 | 10.39417724 | 16.25041883 |
| 1.10021253E+002 | 19.16674233 | 10.79670457 | 15.41516818 |

. . . . . . . . . . . . . . . . . . . . . . . . . . . . . . . . . . . . . . . . . . .

| | | | |
|---|---|---|---|
| 1.28830952E-002 | 19.99992364 | 10.99999069 | 15.00001140 |
| 1.19121477E-002 | 19.99985200 | 10.99997234 | 15.00009457 |
| 1.09455148E-002 | 19.99986648 | 10.99996740 | 15.00009484 |
| 9.17332168E-003 | 19.99990685 | 10.99996779 | 15.00007210 |
| 9.06548780E-003 | 19.99990629 | 10.99996529 | 15.00007641 |
| 8.09277748E-003 | 19.99990810 | 10.99996342 | 15.00008202 |
| 7.46656129E-003 | 19.99993676 | 10.99995631 | 15.00007307 |
| 6.28769907E-003 | 19.99994815 | 10.99995986 | 15.00006504 |
| 5.24833186E-003 | 19.99998232 | 10.99995014 | 15.00005739 |
| 5.03477619E-003 | 19.99999020 | 10.99995389 | 15.00004734 |

MINIMUM FOUND - FINAL DETAILS ARE:

| | | | |
|---|---|---|---|
| 5.03477619E-003 | 19.99999020 | 10.99995389 | 15.00004734 |

NO. OF FUNCTION EVALUATIONS =  254

   The Complex Method is a useful procedure which can be applied to a wide range of constrained optimisation problems. It should not however, be regarded as the panacea in this field. If the objective function is convex and the constrained region is also convex, the method should succeed, although certain peculiarities of the problem may call for some modification of the termination criteria. If the objective function is concave or the constrained region not convex it is easy to see how the method *could* fail. Indeed, in the case of a non-convex constrained region it is not even clear that the centroid of feasible points will also be feasible. Thus the moves

$$x_r(\text{new}) = (x_r + x_0)/2$$

are not guaranteed to achieve their objective.

It is interesting to compare the situation with the conditions under which necessary Kuhn–Tucker conditions become sufficient (see Section 5.3).

Care also needs to be taken to check that the global minimum rather than a local minimum has been found. Box suggests that making more than one run from different initial points should resolve this difficulty, and this is easy to do with the method. The random manner in which the initial complex is generated should mean that initially we generate a good coverage of the constrained region, and so will tend to converge on the global minimum. Convergence of several runs to the same result should clarify the issue.

## 6.3   Reference

M. J. Box, 'A new method of constrained optimisation and a comparison with other methods', *The Comp. Journal*, **8**, 42–52, 1965.

## Exercises 6

**1**   Use the Complex Method to minimise

$$x^2 + y^2 \quad \text{if } x \geqslant 0, \quad y \geqslant 0, \quad x + y \geqslant 5.$$

**2**   Minimise $x^2 + 6xy - 4x - 2y$   if $x^2 + 2y \leqslant 1, 2x - 2y \leqslant 1$.

**3**   Minimise $3x_1^2 + 4x_1x_2 + 5x_2^2$   if $x_1, x_2 \geqslant 0$   and   $x_1 + x_2 > 4$.

**4**   Experiment with the program for the Complex Method by changing the values of (a) $k$, the number of points in the complex, a program constant, (b) $\alpha$, the over-reflection factor, an input value. Try it on the problems below and those in the text.

**5**   Consider the problem of minimising

$$f(x_1, x_2) = \frac{4}{x_1} + \frac{9}{x_2} + (x_1 + x_2)$$

where $x_1, x_2 \geqslant 0, x_1 + x_2 \leqslant S$. Consider the two cases (a) $S = 6$ (b) $S = 4$. [See also question 14 of Exercise 5.]

**6**   Minimise $f = -[9 - (x_1 - 3)^2] x_2^3/27\sqrt{3}$ where $x_1$ and $x_2$ satisfy

$$x_1 \geqslant 0, \quad 0 \leqslant x_2 \leqslant x_1/\sqrt{3}, \quad 0 \leqslant x_1 + \sqrt{3}x_2 \leqslant 6.$$

**7**   Minimise $x_1^4 + x_2^2$   if $x_1 \geqslant 0, \quad x_2 \geqslant 0, \quad x_1x_2 \geqslant 8$.

**8**   Minimise $x_1^2 + x_2^2 + x_3^2$   if $x_1 + x_2 + x_3 \geqslant 3, \quad x_1x_2x_3 \geqslant 3$. (Use $(1, 2, 3)$ as the initial point.)

**9** Minimise $(x_1 - 3)^2 + (x_2 - 4)^2$

$$\text{if} \quad 2x_1^2 + x_2^2 \leqslant 34$$
$$2x_1 + 3x_2 \leqslant 18$$
$$x_1, x_2 \geqslant 0.$$

**10** Minimise $-x_1 x_2 x_3$ for

$$x_1, x_2, x_3 \geqslant 0$$
$$2x_1^2 + x_2^2 + 3x_3^2 \leqslant 51.$$

# 7
# Sequential Unconstrained Optimisation

## 7.1  Penalty Functions

The idea underlying penalty function methods is to transform the problem of minimising

$$z = f(\mathbf{x})$$

subject to certain constraints on $\mathbf{x}$ into the problem of finding the *unconstrained* minimum of

$$Z = f(\mathbf{x}) + P(\mathbf{x}).$$

$P(\mathbf{x})$ is the penalty function. It is not unique but is required to have the property that if the constraints are violated then a high value will be given to $Z$ so that the minimum of $Z$ will not arise outside the constrained region.

It is convenient at this point to formulate the constrained problem in the form:

$$\text{minimise} \quad z = f(\mathbf{x}) \tag{7.1}$$

$$\text{subject to} \quad c_j(\mathbf{x}) \geqslant 0; \quad j = 1, 2, \ldots, m. \tag{7.2}$$

N.B. a 'less than or equal to' constraint $h(\mathbf{x}) \leqslant 0$ can always be written $-h(\mathbf{x}) \geqslant 0$ so there is no loss of generality.

A useful form for $P(\mathbf{x})$ is then

$$P(\mathbf{x}) = r \sum_{j=1}^{m} \frac{1}{c_j(\mathbf{x})}. \tag{7.3}$$

where $r$ is *positive*. The function $Z = \phi(\mathbf{x}, r)$ then takes the form

$$Z = \phi(\mathbf{x}, r) = f(\mathbf{x}) + r \sum_{j=1}^{m} \frac{1}{c_j(\mathbf{x})} \tag{7.4}$$

Now as $\mathbf{x}$ takes on feasible values, i.e. values for which $c_j(\mathbf{x}) \geqslant 0$, $Z$ takes on values which are greater than the corresponding values of $f(\mathbf{x})$ (the true objective function for our problem), although the difference may be reduced by allowing $r$ to become very small. However, if $\mathbf{x}$ takes on values, which though feasible, are close to the boundary of the constrained region, so that at least one of the $c_j(\mathbf{x})$ is near to zero, $P(\mathbf{x})$ and hence $Z$ will become very large. Thus the effect of $P(\mathbf{x})$ is to create a steep sided ridge along each of the constraint boundaries. Hence if we start with a feasible point and try to find the unconstrained minimum of $\phi(\mathbf{x}, r)$ it will certainly lie within the feasible region of our constrained problem. By giving $r$ a suitable small value, so that the effect of $P(\mathbf{x})$ is small at the minimum point, we may be able to make this *unconstrained* minimum point for $\phi(\mathbf{x}, r)$ coincide with the *constrained* minimum of $f(\mathbf{x})$.

Let us consider a very simple example, but one which allows us to appreciate 'what is going on'.

**Example 1**

Use the penalty function given by equation 7.4 to minimise

$$f(x) = x$$

where $x \geqslant 2$, i.e. $x - 2 \geqslant 0$. The minimum value is clearly 2, when $x = 2$. How does the penalty function method find the solution? Consider the function

$$\phi(x, r) = x + \frac{r}{x - 2}.$$

Figure 7.1 shows the graph of $\phi(x, r)$ and the position of its minimum point for various values of $r\ (= 1, 0 \cdot 25, 0 \cdot 01)$.

The constrained region is to the right of the vertical line $x = 2$. We can see that the sequence of points $Q_1$, $Q_2$, $Q_3$ is approaching the constrained minimum point Q. Indeed it is easy to find the minimum of $\phi(x, r)$ by the methods of Chapter 1.

$$\frac{\mathrm{d}\phi}{\mathrm{d}x} = 1 - \frac{r}{(x - 2)^2}$$

Thus when

$$\mathrm{d}\phi/\mathrm{d}x = 0, \quad (x - 2)^2 = r$$

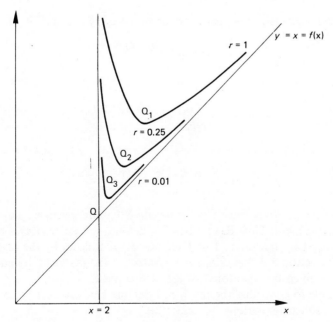

**Figure 7.1**

so that

$$x = 2 \pm \sqrt{r}.$$

$$\frac{d^2\phi}{dx^2} = \frac{2r}{(x-2)^3}$$

and the minimum arises when $x = 2 + \sqrt{r}$ (within the constrained region).

Thus $\phi(x, r)$ has a minimum of $2 + 2\sqrt{r}$ when $x = 2 + \sqrt{r}$. Thus $Q_1$ is the point $(3, 4)$, $Q_2$ $(2 \cdot 5, 3)$, $Q_3$ $(2 \cdot 1, 2 \cdot 2)$. Clearly as $r \to 0$ the unconstrained minimum of $\phi(x, r)$ approaches the value 2 and the location of the minimum point, the value $x = 2$.

In general it will not be possible to locate the position of the minimum of $\phi(x, r)$ analytically as a simple function of $r$, and it will be necessary to resort to numerical techniques for its calculation.

It should be noted that if the objective function $f(\mathbf{x})$ is convex, and the $c_j(\mathbf{x})$ are concave, then $\phi(\mathbf{x}, r)$ as given by equation 7.4 is also a convex function over the constrained region, which is itself a convex region. Thus $\phi(\mathbf{x}, r)$ has a unique minimum for a given value of $r$.

We can see that the feasible region is convex, for if $\mathbf{x}_1$ and $\mathbf{x}_2$ are points which belong to the feasible region, i.e. $c_j(\mathbf{x}_1) \geqslant 0$ and $c_j(\mathbf{x}_2) \geqslant 0$ for $j = 1, 2, ..., m$, then if $0 < \theta < 1$,

$$c_j(\theta\mathbf{x}_2 + (1 - \theta)\mathbf{x}_1) \geqslant \theta c_j(\mathbf{x}_2) + (1 - \theta)c_j(\mathbf{x}_1) \quad [\text{since } c_j(\mathbf{x}) \text{ is concave}]$$
$$\geqslant 0.$$

Thus $\theta\mathbf{x}_2 + (1 - \theta)\mathbf{x}_1$ for $0 < \theta < 1$ is also feasible. [Compare Example 2 of Section 5.3.]

In addition $1/c_j(\mathbf{x})$ is convex for all $\mathbf{x}$ for which $c_j(\mathbf{x}) \geqslant 0$. For if $h(\mathbf{x}) = 1/c_j(\mathbf{x})$,

$$\nabla h(\mathbf{x}) = \frac{-\nabla c_j(\mathbf{x})}{[c_j(\mathbf{x})]^2}.$$

Thus the Hessian matrix of $h(\mathbf{x})$ is given by

$$H(\mathbf{x}) = -\frac{C(\mathbf{x})}{[c_j(\mathbf{x})]^2} + \frac{2\nabla c_j(\mathbf{x}) \, \nabla c_j(\mathbf{x})^{\mathrm{T}}}{[c_j(\mathbf{x})]^3}$$

where $C(\mathbf{x})_{ik} = \partial^2 c_j(\mathbf{x})/\partial x_i \partial x_k$ is the Hessian matrix of $c_j(\mathbf{x})$. Thus if $\mathbf{p}$ is any vector

$$\mathbf{p}^{\mathrm{T}}H(\mathbf{x})\mathbf{p} = -\frac{\mathbf{p}^{\mathrm{T}}C(\mathbf{x})\mathbf{p}}{[c_j(\mathbf{x})]^2} + \frac{2[\mathbf{p}^{\mathrm{T}}\,\nabla c_j(\mathbf{x})]^2}{[c_j(\mathbf{x})]^3}$$

and this is always positive, since $C(\mathbf{x})$ is negative definite because $c_j(\mathbf{x})$ is concave, and of course $c_j(\mathbf{x}) \geqslant 0$. Thus $H(\mathbf{x})$ is positive definite so that $1/c_j(\mathbf{x})$ is convex over the region. (Compare question 11 of Exercises 5.) It follows by the result given in Example 1 of Section 5.3 that, since $r$ is positive, $P(\mathbf{x})$ (as given by equation 7.3) and $\phi(\mathbf{x}, r)$ (as given by equation 7.4) are also convex.

It is is possible to generalise the result of Example 1 of this section to the general constrained problem (equations 7.1 and 7.2).

Suppose $\mathbf{x}_1^*, \mathbf{x}_2^*, ..., \mathbf{x}_k^*$ are the minimum points of $\phi(\mathbf{x}, r_k)$ for the decreasing sequence of values $r_1, r_2, ..., r_k ...$ which tend to zero. Then the sequence of points $x_1^*, x_2^*, ..., x_k^* ...$ converges to the optimal solution of the constrained problem (equations 7.1 and 7.2) as $r_k \to 0$.

Thus

$$\underset{r_k \to 0}{\text{Lim}} \ x_k^* = x^* \tag{7.5}$$

and

$$\underset{r_k \to 0}{\text{Lim}} \ [\text{Min} \ \phi(x, r_k)] = f(x^*) \tag{7.6}$$

where $x^*$ is the constrained minimum point of $f(x)$.

We can prove this result as follows. Since $f(x)$ is continuous and $f(x^*) \leqslant f(x)$ for all feasible points, given any positive $\varepsilon$ however small we can find a feasible point $x'$ such that

$$f(x') < f(x^*) + \varepsilon/2. \tag{7.7}$$

Since $r_k$ is a decreasing sequence tending to zero we can find a value of $k$ so that for $k \geqslant K$

$$r_k \leqslant \left\{ \frac{\varepsilon}{2m} \ \underset{j}{\text{min}} \ \left[ \frac{1}{c_j(x')} \right] \right\}. \tag{7.8}$$

Since $P(x)$ is positive, from the definition of $\phi(x, r)$ we have

$$f(x^*) \leqslant \text{min} \ \phi(x, r_k) = \phi(x_k^*, r_k) \tag{7.9}$$

where $x_k^*$ is the unconstrained minimum point of $\phi(x, r_k)$.

In addition for $k > K$, $r_k < r_K$ and

$$\phi(x_k^*, r_k) \leqslant \phi(x_K^*, r_k) \tag{7.10}$$

This follows since $x_k^*$ minimises $\phi(x, r_k)$ and any other value for $x$, in particular the value $x_K^*$, will give a value at least as large as $\phi(x_k^*, r_k)$.

It is also true that

$$\phi(x_K^*, r_K) = f(x_K^*) + r_K \sum_{j=1}^{m} \frac{1}{c_j(x_K^*)}$$

$$> f(x_K^*) + r_k \sum_{j=1}^{m} \frac{1}{c_j(x_K^*)}$$

since $r_k < r_K$.

$$\therefore \quad \phi(x_K^*, r_K) > \phi(x_K^*, r_k).$$

Thus

$$f(x^*) \leqslant \phi(x_k^*, r_k) \leqslant \phi(x_K^*, r_k) < \phi(x_K^*, r_K). \tag{7.11}$$

But since $x_K^*$ minimises $\phi(x, r_K)$

$$\phi(x_K^*, r_K) \leqslant \phi(x', r_K) = f(x') + r_K \sum_{j=1}^{m} \frac{1}{c_j(x')}. \tag{7.12}$$

Thus from equations 7.11 and 7.12

$$f(\mathbf{x}^*) \leqslant \phi(\mathbf{x}_k^*, r_k) \leqslant f(\mathbf{x}') + r_K \sum_{j=1}^{m} \frac{1}{c_j(\mathbf{x}')} \tag{7.13}$$

$$\leqslant f(\mathbf{x}') + \frac{\varepsilon}{2} \quad \text{by equation 7.8} \tag{7.14}$$

Then from equation 7.7 we obtain

$$f(\mathbf{x}^*) \leqslant \phi(\mathbf{x}_k^*, r_k) < f(\mathbf{x}^*) + \frac{\varepsilon}{2} + \frac{\varepsilon}{2}$$

so that

$$\phi(\mathbf{x}_k^*, r_k) - f(\mathbf{x}^*) < \varepsilon. \tag{7.15}$$

Thus although $\varepsilon$ can be chosen arbitrarily small we can always find values for $k$ so that

$$f(\mathbf{x}^*) < \phi(\mathbf{x}_k^*, r_k) < f(\mathbf{x}^*) + \varepsilon.$$

Thus as $k \to \infty \, (r_k \to 0)$

$$\underset{r_k \to 0}{\text{Lim}} \, \phi(\mathbf{x}_k^*, r_k) = f(\mathbf{x}^*). \tag{7.16}$$

It follows from the above proof that as $r_k \to 0$

$$f(\mathbf{x}_k^*) \to f(\mathbf{x}^*) \quad \text{and} \quad r_k \sum_{j=1}^{m} \frac{1}{c_j(\mathbf{x}_k^*)} \to 0. \tag{7.17}$$

It can also be shown although the proof is left as an exercise that $f(\mathbf{x}_1^*)$, $f(\mathbf{x}_2^*)$, ..., $f(\mathbf{x}_k^*)$ also form a decreasing sequence so that

$$f(\mathbf{x}_{k+1}^*) < f(\mathbf{x}_k^*). \tag{7.18}$$

Of course if $f(\mathbf{x})$ is convex and the $c_j(\mathbf{x})$ are concave the constrained minimum of $f(\mathbf{x})$ is unique. (Compare with the results of Section 5.3.)

### Example 2

As a second example, where once again an analytical solution is possible, consider the following problem.

Minimise

$$f(x_1, x_2) = \tfrac{1}{3}(x_1 + 1)^3 + x_2$$

where $x_1 - 1 \geqslant 0$, $x_2 \geqslant 0$. In line with equation 7.4

$$\phi(\mathbf{x}, r) = \tfrac{1}{3}(x_1 + 1)^3 + x_2 + r\left(\frac{1}{x_1 - 1} + \frac{1}{x_2}\right).$$

The necessary conditions for the minimum of $\phi$ give

$$(x_1 + 1)^2 - \frac{r}{(x_1 - 1)^2} = 0,$$

$$1 - \frac{r}{x_2^2} = 0,$$

with solutions

$$x_1(r) = (1 + \sqrt{r})^{1/2}, \quad x_2(r) = \sqrt{r}.$$

The minimum value of $\phi(\mathbf{x}, r)$ is then

$$\phi^*(r) = \left\{ \tfrac{1}{3} [ (1 + \sqrt{r})^{1/2} + 1 ]^3 + \sqrt{r} + r \left[ \frac{1}{\sqrt{r}} + \frac{1}{(1 + \sqrt{r})^{1/2} - 1} \right] \right\}$$

$$= \left\{ \tfrac{1}{3} [ (1 + \sqrt{r})^{1/2} + 1 ]^3 + \sqrt{r} + r \left[ \frac{1}{\sqrt{r}} + \frac{(1 + \sqrt{r})^{1/2} + 1}{\sqrt{r}} \right] \right\}$$

$$= \{ \tfrac{1}{3} [ (1 + \sqrt{r})^{1/2} + 1 ]^3 + \sqrt{r} + \sqrt{r} [ 1 + 1 + (1 + \sqrt{r})^{1/2} ] \}$$

Thus we see that as $r \to 0$

$$x_1(r) \to 1, \quad x_2(r) \to 0$$

and

$$\phi^*(r) \to f(1, 0) = \tfrac{8}{3}$$

the results (equations 7.17) being apparent in this particular case.

## 7.2  The SUMT Method of Fiacco and McCormick

The results of the previous section show that we can solve the constrained minimisation problem, minimise $f(\mathbf{x})$ subject to $c_j(\mathbf{x}) \geq 0$, by solving the sequence of unconstrained problems,

$$\text{minimise } \phi(\mathbf{x}, r) = f(\mathbf{x}) + r \sum_{j=1}^{m} \frac{1}{c_j(\mathbf{x})}$$

for a sequence of $r$ values which tend to zero.

This sequential unconstrained minimisation technique (SUMT) was first suggested by Carroll in 1961. His ideas were very thoroughly developed and investigated by Fiacco and McCormick, who not only considered the theory and convergence properties of the method but also developed a practical system for its implementation.

It will seldom be possible to use the method as was done in the two examples of the previous section. It will be rare indeed to be able to find the optimal point of $\phi(\mathbf{x}, r)$ in the form of a function of $r$, $\mathbf{x}^*(r)$, whose limit as $r \to 0$ can be investigated.

Thus in order to be able to exploit the method in a practical manner, we have to turn the theoretical convergence property of the previous section into a computational reality. In theory there is no problem. Given $f(\mathbf{x})$ and the constraint functions $c_j(\mathbf{x})(\geq 0)$ we have to choose an initial value for $r(= r_0)$ (is there a problem there?) to form the function $\phi(\mathbf{x}, r_0)$. This must be minimised and this minimisation can be treated as an unconstrained problem. The Davidon–Fletcher–Powell technique of Chapter 4 should be able to cope with this. Having found the minimum of $\phi(\mathbf{x}, r_0)$ we must reduce the value of $r$. A simple and effective way to do this is to find $r_1 = r_0/c$ where $c$ is a constant greater than 1. In the program given $c$ is chosen to be 10 but this is arbitrary. Values of 12 and 16 etc. will also be successful. We must then minimise $\phi(\mathbf{x}, r_1)$ again using the Davidon–Fletcher–Powell technique. Thus we shall indeed develop an iterative procedure. At stage $k$ we minimise $\phi(\mathbf{x}, r_k)$ with minimum point $\mathbf{x}_k^*$. This can be used, and this is an important computational point, as the first point in the iterative procedure to minimise $\phi(\mathbf{x}, r_{k+1})$ where $r_{k+1} = r_k/c$. Thus it is clear that the $r_k$ form a decreasing sequence tending to zero, and hopefully the sequence of minimum points will converge to the solution of the constrained problem.

The flow chart for the SUMT method follows. There are still however, one or two detailed points to settle.

Flow Chart for SUMT

It is assumed that we have a feasible point at the outset. It is important that in the subsequent computations the points always remain within the feasible region. The Davidon–Fletcher–Powell minimisation procedure is a gradient based method which uses cubic interpolation in its linear searches. Now as $\mathbf{x}$ approaches a constraint from within the feasible region, $\phi(\mathbf{x}, r) \rightarrow \infty$ and as $\mathbf{x}$ approaches a constraint from outside the feasible region, $\phi(\mathbf{x}, r) \rightarrow -\infty$. Thus if the search is made along a line joining two points, one inside and one outside the constrained region, the cubic interpolation will break down since the function has a discontinuity along the line. The minimum will be found outside the region. The method will never be able to re-enter the constrained region and so will fail. These points will need to be considered when using the D.F.P. procedure in the context of this problem.

The initial value to give to $r$ can be important in reducing the number of iterations to minimise $\phi(\mathbf{x}, r)$. It might appear that if $r$ is chosen to be very small at the outset, so that $\phi(\mathbf{x}, r)$ is close to $f(\mathbf{x})$ the method should converge more quickly. However, such a choice can cause serious computational problems. We can see from Fig. 7.1

that for small $r$ the function $\phi(\mathbf{x}, r)$ will change rapidly in the vicinity of its minimum. This rapid change in the function can cause difficulties for a gradient based technique. Of course too large a value of $r$ may mean that the penalty function $P(\mathbf{x})$ in equation 7.4 becomes too dominant. What is required at the outset is a 'reasonable' value.

In many problems the value $r_0 = 1$ is sensible. A more reasoned approach is to realise that if our starting point $\mathbf{x}$ is to be near the minimum of

$$\phi(\mathbf{x}, r) = f(\mathbf{x}) + r \sum_{j=1}^{m} \frac{1}{c_j(\mathbf{x})}$$

$$= f(\mathbf{x}) + rP(\mathbf{x})$$

then the gradient of $\phi(\mathbf{x}, r)$ should be small.

$$\nabla \phi(\mathbf{x}, r) = \nabla f(\mathbf{x}) + r\nabla P(\mathbf{x}). \tag{7.19}$$

The squared magnitude of this vector is

$$\nabla f(\mathbf{x})^T \nabla f(\mathbf{x}) + 2r\nabla f(\mathbf{x})^T \nabla P(\mathbf{x}) + r^2 \nabla P(\mathbf{x})^T \nabla P(\mathbf{x}) \tag{7.20}$$

and this is a minimum when

$$r = \frac{-\nabla f(\mathbf{x})^T \nabla P(\mathbf{x})}{\nabla P(\mathbf{x})^T \nabla P(\mathbf{x})}. \tag{7.21}$$

This initial value for $r$, as suggested by Fiacco and McCormick, appears to give good results in general. The method of reducing $r$ is simple: $r_{k+1} = r_k/c$ where $c = 10$.

The method used to minimise $\phi(\mathbf{x}, r_{k+1})$ is the Davidon–Fletcher–Powell method of Chapter 4. The optimal point of $\phi(\mathbf{x}, r_k)$ is used as the starting value and this appears to be very efficient. The program follows that given in Chapter 4, but care needs to be taken that in doing the linear searches we do not step outside the constrained region. A crude but effective way of doing this is as follows. We have a point $\mathbf{p}$ and a search direction $\mathbf{d} = -\mathbf{Hg}$ (see equation 4.34). A further point $\mathbf{q} = \mathbf{p} + \lambda \mathbf{d}$ is needed in order to set up the cubic interpolation. We start with $\lambda = 2$ (twice the Newton step length) and test if $\mathbf{q}$ is feasible. We thus test $c_j(\mathbf{q})$ to see that it is positive for all $j$. If so we retain $\lambda$, but if a constraint is violated we replace $\lambda$ by $\lambda/a$, form a new point $\mathbf{q}$ and test again. Eventually we find a feasible $\mathbf{q}$ and we can then proceed with the interpolation. The choice of $a$ is not clear. $a = 2$ was successful. By choosing $a = 1 \cdot 05$, our step length becomes close to the distance to the nearest constraint boundary and so is 'safe' for the interpolation process. These steps are carried out by the inner REPEAT loop of the PROCEDURE *cubintmod2*.

The importance of not allowing points to step outside the constrained region during the minimisation process cannot be overemphasised. To this end further precautions have been taken by using the boolean variable *minbracketed* in the PROCEDURE *cubintmod2* to ensure that we find the minimum by interpolation between two trial points. Although the modification to $\mathbf{H}$ when *minbracketed* is false is semi-heuristic it does appear to be successful.

The minimisation of $\phi(\mathbf{x}, r)$ is carried out until two successive function values $f_1$ and $f_2$ are found such that $|(f_1 - f_2)/f_1| < f$ *accuracy*, an input data value. This terminates the REPEAT loop in the body of the PROCEDURE *DFPmod*. In line with equation 7.17 the program terminates when

$$r \sum_{j=1}^{m} \frac{1}{c_j(\mathbf{x}_k^*)} < epsilon$$

where *epsilon* is another input data value. A simpler termination criterion which was also successful was to stop when $r_k$ took on a value less than $10^{-12}$.

A program listing follows. The FUNCTIONs and PROCEDURE as written are appropriate for the solution of the problem:

$$\text{minimise} \quad f(\mathbf{x}) = (x_1 - 1)(x_1 - 2)(x_1 - 3) + x_3$$
$$\text{subject to} \quad x_1, x_2, x_3 \geqslant 0$$
$$x_3^2 - x_1^2 - x_2^2 \geqslant 0, \quad x_1^2 + x_2^2 + x_3^2 - 4 \geqslant 0, \quad x_3 \leqslant 5,$$

so that

$$\phi(\mathbf{x}, r) = f(\mathbf{x}) + r\left(\frac{1}{x_3^2 - x_1^2 - x_2^2} + \frac{1}{x_1^2 + x_2^2 + x_3^2 - 4} + \frac{1}{5 - x_3} + \frac{1}{x_1} + \frac{1}{x_2} + \frac{1}{x_3}\right).$$

We thus have a problem in 3 variables with 6 constraints. The objective function is not convex. The constraint region is not convex but the method is none the less successful. With starting point $(0 \cdot 1, 2, 2 \cdot 1)$ the solution was found after 55 iterations. The true minimum point is at $(0, \sqrt{2}, \sqrt{2})$ with function value $-6 + \sqrt{2}$. The full output is given. The value of using the optimal point of the previous $r$ value as the starting point for the next $r$ value can be seen by the small number of interations required to find the later minima.

```
PROGRAM FiaccoandMcCormick (input,output);
CONST
   n=3;                  { No. of variables in function f }           {**}
   m=6;                  { No. of constraints }                       {**}
   fwx=14; dpx=8;        { Output format constants for x-values }     {**}
   fwf=14; dpf=8;        { Output format constants for function values } {**}
   a=1.05; c=10.0;                                                    {**}
   verysmallvalue=1.0E-30;                                            {**}

TYPE
   vector = ARRAY [1..n] OF real;  convector = ARRAY [1..m] OF real;
   point = RECORD   { To represent values at a single point }
           x, g,              { x-vector and total gradient vector }
           cg : vector;       { gradient vector of penalty function }
           c : convector;     { constraint values }
           phi, g0 : real     { function value and gradient value }
         END;

VAR
   start, minpoint : point;     { Initial and final point in DFP process }
   r : real;                    { Penalty function multiplier }
   faccuracy : real;            { Required accuracy in function values }
   epsilon : real;              { Required accuracy in penalty function }
   it : integer;                { Iteration counter }
   i : integer;  zero : vector;
```

```
FUNCTION f (x:vector): real;
BEGIN  f := (x[1]-1.0)*(x[1]-2.0)*(x[1]-3.0) + x[3]   END; { f }          {**}


FUNCTION penalty (c:convector): real;
VAR  sum : real;  i : integer;
BEGIN  sum:=0.0;  FOR i:=1 TO m DO sum := sum + 1.0/c[i];
  penalty := sum
END; { penalty }


FUNCTION phi (p:point; r:real): real;
BEGIN  phi := f(p.x) + r*penalty(p.c)  END; { phi }


FUNCTION constraints (selector:integer; x:vector): real;
BEGIN  CASE selector OF
        1: constraints := sqr(x[3]) - sqr(x[1]) - sqr(x[2]);         {**}
        2: constraints := sqr(x[1]) + sqr(x[2]) + sqr(x[3]) - 4.0;   {**}
        3: constraints := 5.0 - x[3];                                {**}
        4: constraints := x[1];                                      {**}
        5: constraints := x[2];                                      {**}
        6: constraints := x[3]                                       {**}
      END
END; { constraints }


PROCEDURE gradients (VAR p:point; r:real);
VAR  s1, s2, t1, t2, t3, t12, t23 : real;  i : integer;
BEGIN
  WITH p DO
    BEGIN  t1 := x[1]-1.0;  t2 := x[1]-2.0;  t3 := x[1]-3.0;         {**}
      s1 := 1.0/sqr(c[1]);  s2 := 1.0/sqr(c[2]);                    {**}
      t12 := 2.0*(s1-s2);  t23 := 2.0*(s1+s2);                      {**}
      cg[1] := x[1]*t12 - 1.0/sqr(c[4]);                            {**}
      cg[2] := x[2]*t12 - 1.0/sqr(c[5]);                            {**}
      cg[3] := -x[3]*t23 + 1.0/sqr(c[3]) - 1.0/sqr(c[6]);           {**}
      g[1] := t1*t2 + t2*t3 + t3*t1 + r*cg[1];                      {**}
      g[2] := r*cg[2];  g[3] := 1.0 + r*cg[3];                      {**}
      g0:=0.0;  FOR i:=1 TO n DO g0 := g0 + sqr(g[i]);
      g0 := sqrt(g0)
    END
END; { gradients }


FUNCTION scalarmult (v1,v2:vector): real;
VAR  i : integer;  sum : real;
BEGIN  sum:=0.0;  FOR i:=1 TO n DO sum := sum + v1[i]*v2[i];
  scalarmult := sum
END; { scalarmult }


PROCEDURE inputdata;
VAR  i : integer;
BEGIN  writeln('     NUMBER OF VARIABLES =', n:3);
  writeln('     NUMBER OF CONSTRAINTS =', m:3);
  writeln('     INITIAL POINT');
  FOR i:=1 TO n DO
```

```
    BEGIN write('    X[', i:2, ']'); read(start.x[i]);
      writeln(start.x[i]:fwx:dpx)
    END;
    write('    REQUIRED ACCURACY IN FUNCTION VALUE =');
    read(faccuracy); writeln(faccuracy:fwf:dpf);
    write('    REQUIRED ACCURACY IN PENALTY FUNCTION =');
    read(epsilon); writeln(epsilon:fwf:dpf)
END; { inputdata }


PROCEDURE initialise;
VAR  i : integer;
BEGIN  FOR i:=1 TO m DO start.c[i] := constraints(i,start.x);
    gradients(start,0.0);
    r := -scalarmult(start.g,start.cg)/scalarmult(start.cg,start.cg);
    IF r<0.0 THEN r:=1.0;
    r := c*r;  it:=0;  FOR i:=1 TO n DO zero[i]:=0.0
END; { initialise }


PROCEDURE outputline (it:integer; p:point);
VAR  i : integer;
BEGIN  write(it:6, '    ', p.phi:fwf);
    FOR I:=1 TO n DO write(p.x[i]:fwx:dpx);  writeln
END; { outputline }


PROCEDURE DFPmod (P:point; rr:real; VAR minpoint:point);
TYPE  matrix = ARRAY [1..n] OF vector;
VAR
    Q : point;                          { See program DavidonFletcherPowell    }
    H : matrix;                         { for the definition of these variables }
    d, v, u, mm : vector;
    j, k : integer;    mu, vu : real;


  PROCEDURE initialise;
  VAR  i : integer;
  BEGIN  FOR i:=1 TO n DO BEGIN H[i]:=zero; H[i,i]:=1.0 END;
    P.phi := phi(P,rr);  gradients(P,rr)
  END; { initialise }


  PROCEDURE movepoint (VAR p1:point; p2:point; r:real);
  VAR  i : integer;
  BEGIN  FOR I:=1 TO n DO  p1.x[i] := p2.x[i] + r*d[i]  END; { movepoint }


  PROCEDURE cubintmod2 (VAR p:point; VAR d:vector);
  { A modification of the cubic interpolation routine of the program     }
  { DavidonFletcherPowell. Here a new bracketing routine is included to   }
  { ensure that the points p and q are within the constrained region. If p }
  { and q do not bracket the minimum, the direction of search is altered.  }
  VAR  q, r : point;
    Gp, Gq, Gr : real;  lambda, qx, rx : real;  z, w : real;
    violated, minfound, minbracketed : boolean;  i, j, k : integer;
```

```
    BEGIN
      REPEAT  { Until minimum is bracketed within constrained region }
        Gp := scalarmult(p.g,d);
        IF Gp>0.0 THEN writeln(´WARNING - SEARCH GRADIENT POSITIVE´);
        lambda:=2.0;  movepoint(q,p,lambda);
        REPEAT violated:=false;  { Until no constraints violated }
          FOR k:=1 TO m DO
          BEGIN  q.c[k] := constraints(k,q.x);
          WHILE q.c[k]<0.0 DO  { Constraint violated }
          BEGIN  violated:=true;  lambda:=lambda/a;
            movepoint(q,p,lambda);  q.c[k] := constraints(k,q.x)
          END
          END
        UNTIL  NOT violated;
        q.phi := phi(q,rr);  gradients(q,rr);  Gq := scalarmult(q.g,d);
        minbracketed := (Gq>0.0) OR (q.phi>p.phi);
        IF NOT minbracketed THEN  { Modify H and direction of search }
        BEGIN  FOR i:=1 TO n DO
               FOR j:=1 TO n DO  H[i,j] := H[i,j] - d[i]*d[j]/Gp;
          p:=q;  FOR j:=1 TO n DO d[j] := - scalarmult(H[j],p.g)
        END
      UNTIL minbracketed;  qx := lambda;
      REPEAT { Until r found with function value less than those at p and q }
        z := 3.0*(p.phi-q.phi)/qx + Gp + Gq;  w := sqr(z) - Gp*Gq;
        IF w<0.0 THEN w:=0.0;  w:=sqrt(w);  rx := qx*(z+w-Gp)/(Gq-Gp+2.0*w);
        movepoint(r,p,rx);  FOR k:=1 TO m DO  r.c[k] := constraints(k,r.x);
        r.phi := phi(r,rr);  gradients(r,rr);  Gr := scalarmult(r.g,d);
        minfound := (r.phi<p.phi) AND (r.phi<q.phi);
        IF NOT minfound THEN
          IF Gr>0.0 THEN BEGIN  qx:=rx;  q:=r;  Gq:=Gr  END
          ELSE BEGIN  qx := qx-rx;  p:=r;  Gp:=Gr  END
      UNTIL minfound;
      p:=r  { Return point in p }
    END; { cubintmod2 }



BEGIN  { DFPmod }   initialise;
  REPEAT  { Until minimum found to required accuracy }
    outputline(it,P);  Q:=P;  it:=it+1;
    FOR j:=1 TO n DO  d[j] := -scalarmult(H[j],P.g);
    { Perform cubic interpolation unless minimum found initially }
    IF abs(scalarmult(P.g,d)) > verysmallvalue THEN  cubintmod2(P,d);
    FOR j:=1 TO n DO
    BEGIN  u[j] := P.g[j] - Q.g[j];  v[j] := P.x[j] - Q.x[j]  END;
    FOR j:=1 TO n DO  mm[j] := scalarmult(H[j],u);
    mu := scalarmult(mm,u);  vu := scalarmult(v,u);
    IF (abs(mu)>verysmallvalue) AND (abs(vu)>verysmallvalue) THEN
      FOR k:=1 TO n DO
        FOR j:=1 TO n DO  H[k,j] := H[k,j] - mm[k]*mm[j]/mu + v[k]*v[j]/vu
  UNTIL  abs((Q.phi-P.phi)/Q.phi) < faccuracy;  writeln;
  minpoint:=P
END; { DFPmod }
```

```
BEGIN  { Main Program }
  writeln;  writeln('    FIACCO & MCCORMICK');  writeln;
  inputdata;  writeln;  initialise;
  write('ITERATION', '  ':fwf-4, 'F(X)');
  FOR i:=1 TO n DO write('  ':fwx-5, 'X[', i:2, ']');  writeln;  writeln;
  REPEAT  { Until penalty function is small enough }
    r := r/c;  writeln('DAVIDON-FLETCHER-POWELL WITH R =', r:fwx);  writeln;
    DFPmod(start, r, minpoint);  start := minpoint
  UNTIL  r*penalty(minpoint.c) < epsilon;
  writeln;  writeln('MINIMISATION COMPLETE - FINAL DETAILS ARE :');
  writeln;  outputline(it,minpoint)
END. { Fiacco and McCormick }
```

```
    FIACCO & MCCORMICK

    NUMBER OF VARIABLES =  3
    NUMBER OF CONSTRAINTS =. 6
    INITIAL POINT
    X[ 1]    0.10000000
    X[ 2]    2.00000000
    X[ 3]    2.10000000
    REQUIRED ACCURACY IN FUNCTION VALUE =    0.00000100
    REQUIRED ACCURACY IN PENALTY FUNCTION =   0.00000100
```

| ITERATION | F(X) | X[ 1] | X[ 2] | X[ 3] |
|---|---|---|---|---|
| DAVIDON-FLETCHER-POWELL WITH R = 9.016188E-002 | | | | |
| 0 | -1.592472E+000 | 0.10000000 | 2.00000000 | 2.10000000 |
| 1 | -1.617680E+000 | 0.07556565 | 1.94157862 | 2.13684870 |
| 2 | -1.671175E+000 | 0.09529976 | 1.89345661 | 2.16258122 |
| 3 | -1.980766E+000 | 0.09550912 | 1.50201505 | 1.77302216 |
| 4 | -1.995451E+000 | 0.09558225 | 1.36092436 | 1.63331300 |
| 5 | -2.014784E+000 | 0.09520778 | 1.42040859 | 1.68658989 |
| 6 | -2.015881E+000 | 0.09551950 | 1.41826108 | 1.66903421 |
| DAVIDON-FLETCHER-POWELL WITH R = 9.016188E-003 | | | | |
| 7 | -3.202195E+000 | 0.09550768 | 1.41842182 | 1.66926687 |
| 8 | -3.659067E+000 | 0.03625398 | 1.41842214 | 1.66327007 |
| 9 | -3.787360E+000 | 0.02861214 | 1.41886872 | 1.50255704 |
| 10 | -3.787746E+000 | 0.02969651 | 1.40824606 | 1.49122337 |
| 11 | -3.787920E+000 | 0.02983492 | 1.41176595 | 1.48990067 |
| 12 | -3.788411E+000 | 0.02895900 | 1.41361526 | 1.49349958 |
| 13 | -3.788424E+000 | 0.02909503 | 1.41379939 | 1.49421774 |
| DAVIDON-FLETCHER-POWELL WITH R = 9.016188E-004 | | | | |
| 14 | -4.150635E+000 | 0.02909275 | 1.41410883 | 1.49415281 |
| 15 | -4.295266E+000 | 0.01116913 | 1.41410884 | 1.49247044 |
| 16 | -4.332333E+000 | 0.01059620 | 1.41416109 | 1.44398715 |
| 17 | -4.333235E+000 | 0.00787899 | 1.41469998 | 1.43880103 |
| 18 | -4.333603E+000 | 0.00826374 | 1.41095263 | 1.43712211 |
| 19 | -4.334215E+000 | 0.00894045 | 1.41538254 | 1.43498683 |
| 20 | -4.335283E+000 | 0.00924209 | 1.41441967 | 1.43968110 |
| 21 | -4.335311E+000 | 0.00909729 | 1.41421767 | 1.43946888 |

DAVIDON-FLETCHER-POWELL WITH R = 9.016188E-005

| | | | | |
|---|---|---|---|---|
| 22 | -4.448382E+000 | 0.00909869 | 1.41419042 | 1.43946526 |
| 23 | -4.494551E+000 | 0.00338458 | 1.41419042 | 1.43894061 |
| 24 | -4.505952E+000 | 0.00334628 | 1.41419575 | 1.42285128 |
| 25 | -4.506703E+000 | 0.00289058 | 1.41481659 | 1.42235204 |
| 26 | -4.506749E+000 | 0.00285988 | 1.41421617 | 1.42231935 |

DAVIDON-FLETCHER-POWELL WITH R = 9.016188E-006

| | | | | |
|---|---|---|---|---|
| 27 | -4.542376E+000 | 0.00286557 | 1.41419960 | 1.42219323 |
| 28 | -4.556887E+000 | 0.00108972 | 1.41419965 | 1.42203129 |
| 29 | -4.560428E+000 | 0.00108766 | 1.41420187 | 1.41711614 |
| 30 | -4.560545E+000 | 0.00101789 | 1.41480319 | 1.41697457 |
| 31 | -4.560800E+000 | 0.00087841 | 1.41426171 | 1.41671040 |
| 32 | -4.560807E+000 | 0.00089612 | 1.41420989 | 1.41665098 |

DAVIDON-FLETCHER-POWELL WITH R = 9.016188E-007

| | | | | |
|---|---|---|---|---|
| 33 | -4.572053E+000 | 0.00090583 | 1.41421627 | 1.41673859 |
| 34 | -4.576731E+000 | 0.00031424 | 1.41421625 | 1.41668476 |
| 35 | -4.577861E+000 | 0.00031488 | 1.41421583 | 1.41504235 |

DAVIDON-FLETCHER-POWELL WITH R = 9.016188E-008

| | | | | |
|---|---|---|---|---|
| 36 | -4.581138E+000 | 0.00031426 | 1.41419114 | 1.41504155 |
| 37 | -4.582878E+000 | 0.00010722 | 1.41419125 | 1.41502293 |
| 38 | -4.583249E+000 | 0.00010748 | 1.41419432 | 1.41452217 |

DAVIDON-FLETCHER-POWELL WITH R = 9.016188E-009

| | | | | |
|---|---|---|---|---|
| 39 | -4.584195E+000 | 0.00010745 | 1.41422364 | 1.41451812 |
| 40 | -4.584799E+000 | 0.00004041 | 1.41422361 | 1.41451201 |
| 41 | -4.584949E+000 | 0.00004051 | 1.41422258 | 1.41432603 |

DAVIDON-FLETCHER-POWELL WITH R = 9.016188E-010

| | | | | |
|---|---|---|---|---|
| 42 | -4.585205E+000 | 0.00004050 | 1.41419508 | 1.41432121 |
| 43 | -4.585454E+000 | 0.00001439 | 1.41419513 | 1.41431886 |
| 44 | -4.585503E+000 | 0.00001443 | 1.41419663 | 1.41426004 |
| 45 | -4.585513E+000 | 0.00001443 | 1.41422125 | 1.41424296 |
| 46 | -4.585536E+000 | 0.00000900 | 1.41421802 | 1.41424026 |

DAVIDON-FLETCHER-POWELL WITH R = 9.016188E-011

| | | | | |
|---|---|---|---|---|
| 47 | -4.585650E+000 | 0.00000911 | 1.41421326 | 1.41423704 |
| 48 | -4.585697E+000 | 0.00000347 | 1.41421326 | 1.41423654 |
| 49 | -4.585706E+000 | 0.00000348 | 1.41421331 | 1.41422194 |

DAVIDON-FLETCHER-POWELL WITH R = 9.016188E-012

| | | | | |
|---|---|---|---|---|
| 50 | -4.585736E+000 | 0.00000348 | 1.41421359 | 1.41422192 |
| 51 | -4.585756E+000 | 0.00000126 | 1.41421359 | 1.41422173 |

DAVIDON-FLETCHER-POWELL WITH R = 9.016188E-013

| | | | | |
|---|---|---|---|---|
| 52 | -4.585769E+000 | 0.00000126 | 1.41421359 | 1.41421665 |
| 53 | -4.585776E+000 | 0.00000045 | 1.41421359 | 1.41421658 |

DAVIDON-FLETCHER-POWELL WITH R = 9.016188E-014

| | | | | |
|---|---|---|---|---|
| 54 | -4.585780E+000 | 0.00000045 | 1.41421359 | 1.41421470 |

MINIMISATION COMPLETE - FINAL DETAILS ARE :

| | | | | |
|---|---|---|---|---|
| 55 | -4.585783E+000 | 0.00000016 | 1.41421359 | 1.41421467 |

## 7.3   References

The remarks made in the corresponding section of Chapter 4 are also appropriate here. A great amount of research work has been carried out in this area over the last three decades and much of it is still ongoing. In the last two chapters we have considered in some detail two very important constrained optimisation methods. They are of course two among many. It is hoped that the reader will be stimulated to investigate the references given, and the current literature, for much remains to be done in the search for theoretically sound and computationally practical methods for the constrained optimisation problem.

1   M. J. Box, 'A comparison of several current optimisation methods and the use of transformations in constrained problems', *Comp. Journal*, **9**, 67–77, 1966.
2   C. W. Carroll, 'The created response surface technique for optimising nonlinear restrained systems', *Operations Research*, **9**, 169–184, 1961.
3   A. R. Colville, 'A comparative study on nonlinear programming codes', *IBM Report* No. 320–2949, 1968.
4   A. V. Fiacco and G. P. McCormick, 'The Sequential Unconstrained Minimisation Technique for nonlinear programming, a primal–dual method', *Man. Sc.*, **10**, 360–366, 1964.
5   A. V. Fiacco and G. P. McCormick, 'Computational algorithm for the Sequential Unconstrained Minimisation Technique for nonlinear programming', *Man. Sc.*, **10**, 601–617, 1964.
6   A. V. Fiacco and G. P. McCormick, 'Extensions of SUMT for nonlinear programming: equality constraints and extrapolation', *Man. Sc.*, **12**, 816–828, 1966.
7   D. Goldfarb, 'Extensions of Davidon's variable metric method to maximisation under linear inequality and equality constraints', *SIAM J.Appl. Math.*, **17**, 739–764, 1969.

## Exercises 7

**1**   Use SUMT to minimise $f(x_1, x_2) = 3x_1^2 + 4x_1x_2 + 5x_2^2$ where $x_1, x_2 \geqslant 0$, $x_1 + x_2 \geqslant 4$.

**2**   Minimise $-x_1^2 - x_2^2$ if $x_1, x_2 \geqslant 0$ and $x_1 + 2x_2 \leqslant 3$.

**3** Use SUMT to solve the Post Office Parcel Problem; minimise $V = -x_1 x_2 x_3$ where $0 \leqslant x_i \leqslant 42$, $i = 1, 2, 3$ and

$$x_1 + 2x_2 + 2x_3 \leqslant 72.$$

**4** Minimise, using the SUMT method, the function

$$f(x_1, x_2) = \frac{4}{x_1} + \frac{9}{x_2} + (x_1 + x_2)$$

where $x_1, x_2 \geqslant 0$, $x_1 + x_2 \leqslant S$ if (a) $S = 6$, (b) $S = 4$.

**5** Minimise $f = x_1^2 + x_2^2 + x_3^2$ if $x_1 + x_2 + x_3 \geqslant 3$, $x_1 x_2 x_3 \geqslant 3$

$$x_1, x_2, x_3 \geqslant 0.$$

**6** Experiment with the SUMT program by modification of (a) the initial choice of $r$ (b) changing the constant $a$ (c) changing the constant $c$.

**7** Experiment with the SUMT program by modification of the convergence criteria by (a) using different values of *faccuracy* (b) using different values of *epsilon* (c) trying $r < 1 \cdot 0E - 12$ to terminate the REPEAT loop in the main program.

**8** Show that equation 7.18 is true, viz. $f(x_{k+1}^*) < f(x_k^*)$.

**9** Minimise $(x_1 - 1)^4 + (x_2 - 3)^2$ if $x_1, x_2 \geqslant 0$ and $3x_1^2 + 2x_2^2 \leqslant 21$, $4x_1 + 5x_2 \leqslant 20$.

**10** Minimise $f(x_1, x_2) = x_1^2 + x_2^2$ subject to $x_1 \geqslant 2$, $x_1^2 - x_2^2 \leqslant 1$.

# 8
# Quadratic Programming

## 8.1 Introduction

The term quadratic programming refers to the problem of minimising a quadratic function of $n$ non-negative variables which are also subject to $m$ linear constraints. There is no loss of generality in assuming that these constraints are all of the *less than or equal to* variety. The non-negativity conditions can also be expressed in this way.

Thus our problem is to find $\mathbf{x} = (x_1, x_2, ..., x_n)^T$ such that

$$g_i(\mathbf{x}) = \sum_{j=1}^{n} a_{ij}x_j \leqslant b_i \quad (i = 1, 2, ..., m), \tag{8.1}$$

and
$$-x_j \leqslant 0 \quad (j = 1, 2, ..., n), \tag{8.2}$$

which minimises

$$f(\mathbf{x}) = \mathbf{c}^T\mathbf{x} + \tfrac{1}{2}\mathbf{x}^T\mathbf{G}\mathbf{x}, \tag{8.3}$$

where $\mathbf{c}^T = (c_1, c_2, ..., c_n)$,

and

$$\mathbf{G} = \begin{pmatrix} g_{11} & g_{12} & & g_{1n} \\ g_{21} & & & g_{2n} \\ \cdots\cdots\cdots & & \cdots \\ g_{n1} & & & g_{nn} \end{pmatrix}$$

is a symmetric positive definite matrix.

The restriction of $\mathbf{G}$ to positive definite means that $f(\mathbf{x})$ is a convex function. Thus any local minimum of $f(\mathbf{x})$ subject to the constraints will also be the global minimum subject to the constraints. This global minimum will be determined by finding the solution of the Kuhn–Tucker conditions (5.23) appropriate to this problem.

The Lagrange function (5.16) for this problem will take the form

$$F(\mathbf{x}, \mathbf{q}, \mathbf{u}, \lambda, \mathbf{r}) = f(\mathbf{x}) + \sum_{i=1}^{m} \lambda_i \left( \sum_{j=1}^{n} a_{ij}x_j + q_i^2 - b_i \right) + \sum_{j=1}^{n} u_j(-x_j + r_j^2) \tag{8.4}$$

where we have written the constraints (8.1) and (8.2) as

$$\sum_{j=1}^{n} a_{ij}x_j + q_i^2 - b_i = 0,$$

and
$$- x_j + r_j^2 = 0,$$

with corresponding Lagrange multipliers $\lambda_i$ and $u_j$.

The Kuhn–Tucker conditions are

$$\frac{\partial F}{\partial x_j} = 0, \text{ i.e. } \frac{\partial f}{\partial x_j} + \sum_{i=1}^{m} \lambda_i a_{ij} - u_j = 0 \quad \text{for } j = 1, 2, ..., n; \qquad (8.5)$$

$$\frac{\partial F}{\partial q_i} = 0, \text{ i.e. } \lambda_i q_i = 0 \quad \text{for } i = 1, 2, ..., m; \qquad (8.6)$$

$$\frac{\partial F}{\partial r_j} = 0, \text{ i.e. } r_j u_j = 0 \quad \text{which is equivalent to}$$

$$u_j x_j = 0; \quad j = 1, 2, ..., n, \qquad (8.7)$$

$$\frac{\partial F}{\partial \lambda_i} = 0, \text{ which is equivalent to } \sum_{j=1}^{n} a_{ij} x_j \leqslant b_i; \quad \text{for } i = 1, 2, ..., m; \qquad (8.8)$$

$$\frac{\partial F}{\partial u_j} = 0, \quad \text{which is equivalent to } - x_j + r_j^2 = 0$$

$$\text{i.e. } x_j \geqslant 0 \text{ for } j = 1, ..., n. \quad (8.9)$$

In addition we have from (5.22)

$$\lambda_i \geqslant 0; \quad i = 1, 2, ..., m$$

$$u_j \geqslant 0; \quad j = 1, 2, ..., n. \qquad (8.10)$$

If we put $y_i = q_i^2$ and substitute for $f(\mathbf{x})$ from (8.3) our problem is to find

$$\mathbf{x} \geqslant 0, \quad \mathbf{y} \geqslant 0, \quad \boldsymbol{\lambda} \geqslant 0 \quad \text{and} \quad \mathbf{u} \geqslant 0$$

such that

$$c_j + \sum_{k=1}^{n} g_{kj} x_k + \sum_{i=1}^{m} \lambda_i a_{ij} - u_j = 0; \quad j = 1, 2, ..., n \qquad (8.11)$$

and

$$\sum_{j=1}^{n} a_{ij} x_j + y_i = b_i; \quad i = 1, 2, ..., m \qquad (8.12)$$

where in addition
$$\lambda_i y_i = 0, \quad i = 1, 2, ..., m, \qquad (8.13)$$

$$u_j x_j = 0, \quad j = 1, 2, ..., n. \qquad (8.14)$$

## 8.2 Wolfe's Method of Solution

The conditions (8.11) and (8.12) are linear constraints on the non-negative variables, $x_j$, $y_i$, $\lambda_i$ and $u_j$. Wolfe used the method of linear programming to devise a method to find non-negative values which satisfy these equations along with the conditions (8.13) and (8.14).

Suppose for the moment that all the $c_j$ are negative and the $b_i$ are positive. Then (8.11) and (8.12) can be written

$$\sum_{k=1}^{n} g_{kj}x_k + \sum_{i=1}^{m} \lambda_i a_{ij} - u_j = -c_j \tag{8.15}$$

$$\sum_{j=1}^{n} a_{ij}x_j + y_i = b_i \tag{8.16}$$

where the numerical values on the right hand side are positive. Of course if any of the $c_j$ are positive we can multiply the corresponding equations by $-1$ at this stage so as to obtain a positive value on the right.

But then we can use the technique of linear programming† to find non-negative $\mathbf{x}, \mathbf{y}, \boldsymbol{\lambda}, \mathbf{u}$ which satisfy (8.15) and (8.16).

We introduce a non-negative artificial variable $v_j$ into each of the constraints (8.15) which then become

$$\sum_{k=1}^{n} g_{kj}x_k + \sum_{i=1}^{m} \lambda_i a_{ij} - u_j + v_j = -c_j \tag{8.17}$$

along with (8.16)

$$\sum_{j=1}^{n} a_{ij}x_j + y_i = b_i. \tag{8.18}$$

Subject to (8.17) and (8.18) we try to minimise the linear function

$$z = \sum_{j=1}^{n} v_j. \tag{8.19}$$

Apart from the conditions (8.13) and (8.14) which are imposed on the variables, this is a linear programming problem and $z$ will be minimised when all the $v_j$ are zero in which case (8.17) is equivalent to (8.15).

An initial basic feasible solution to the constraints (8.17) and (8.18) which initiates the simplex method for the minimisation of (8.19) is given by $v_j = -c_j$ and $y_i = b_i$ with all the other variables non-basic. We have of course to express $z$ in terms of these non-basic variables. This is easily done, for from (8.17)

$$z = \sum_{j=1}^{n} v_j = -\sum_{j=1}^{n} c_j - \sum_{j=1}^{n} \left(\sum_{k=1}^{n} g_{kj}x_k\right) - \sum_{j=1}^{n} \left(\sum_{i=1}^{m} \lambda_i a_{ij}\right) + \sum_{j=1}^{n} u_j \tag{8.20}$$

We have also to satisfy the non-linear constraints

$$\lambda_i y_i = 0; \quad i = 1, ..., m$$

$$u_j x_j = 0; \quad j = 1, ..., n.$$

In practice these mean that we have to modify the usual rules for the simplex method, which determine which variable enters and which variable leaves the basis at each iteration. At least one variable of the pair $\lambda_i, y_i$ ($i = 1, ..., m$) and of the pair

---

† Readers who are not familiar with the ideas of linear programming should consult the text *Linear Programming in Pascal* by B. D. Bunday and G. R. Garside before proceeding.

$x_j$, $u_j$ ($j = 1, ..., n$) must remain non-basic at each stage. In theory these extra conditions could cause the simplex procedure to break down and fail to terminate. Wolfe considered this problem in his original paper on the subject, published in Econometrica in 1959, and showed that provided **G** is positive definite, then the modified simplex method will terminate in a finite number of iterations.

We shall illustrate the ideas with a couple of examples which show how the modified simplex method is applied. We might note that there are other procedures for the solution of quadratic programming problems. Beale has devised an elegant simplex based method and Fletcher has constructed a procedure which does not use the simplex method.

**Example 1**

Minimise $f(x_1, x_2) = 8x_1^2 + 4x_1x_2 + x_2^2 - 10x_1 - 15x_2$ where $x_1, x_2 \geq 0$, and are such that

$$x_1 + 3x_2 \leq 9$$
$$x_1 + x_2 \leq 6.$$

In the notation of (8.3), $f(x_1, x_2) =$

$$\tfrac{1}{2}(x_1, x_2)\begin{pmatrix} 16 & 4 \\ 4 & 2 \end{pmatrix}\begin{pmatrix} x_1 \\ x_2 \end{pmatrix} + (-10, -15)\begin{pmatrix} x_1 \\ x_2 \end{pmatrix}$$

Then (8.15) and (8.16) for this problem become

$$
\begin{array}{lllll}
16x_1 + 4x_2 & + \ \lambda_1 + \lambda_2 - u_1 & = 10 \\
4x_1 + 2x_2 & + 3\lambda_1 + \lambda_2 \quad - u_2 & = 15 \\
x_1 + 3x_2 + y_1 & & = 9 \\
x_1 + \ x_2 \quad + y_2 & & = 6
\end{array}
\tag{8.21}
$$

and we have to find non-negative $x_1, x_2, y_1, y_2, \lambda_1, \lambda_2, u_1, u_2$ which also satisfy (8.13) and (8.14)

viz.
$$\lambda_1 y_1 = \lambda_2 y_2 = 0$$
$$u_1 x_1 = u_2 x_2 = 0.$$
$$\tag{8.22}$$

All the values on the right hand side are positive so we introduce non-negative artificial variables $v_1$ and $v_2$ into the first two equations and proceed to minimise

$$z = v_1 + v_2$$

subject to the constraints given. We have

$$
\begin{array}{lllll}
16x_1 + 4x_2 & + \ \lambda_1 + \lambda_2 - u_1 & + v_1 & = 10 \\
4x_1 + 2x_2 & + 3\lambda_1 + \lambda_2 \quad - u_2 & + v_2 & = 15 \\
x_1 + 3x_2 + y_1 & & = 9 \\
x_1 + \ x_2 \quad + y_2 & & = 6 \\
& & v_1 + v_2 & = \ z.
\end{array}
$$

A first basic feasible solution to the constraints is obtained with $v_1 = 10$, $v_2 = 15$, $y_1 = 9$ and $y_2 = 6$ as basis. When $z$ is expressed in terms of the first set of non-basic variables (we simply use the first two equations to eliminate $v_1$ and $v_2$) we obtain

$$z - 25 = -20x_1 - 6x_2 - 4\lambda_1 - 2\lambda_2 + u_1 + u_2$$

The first and subsequent simplex tableaux in the solution are shown below. The so called "complementary slackness" conditions (8.22) which are essentially the conditions (5.20) mean that at each stage at least one of each pair $(\lambda_1, y_1)$, $(\lambda_2, y_2)$, $(x_1, u_1)$, $(x_2, u_2)$ must be non-basic and the rules of the simplex method have to be modified to account for this. (It is assumed that readers are familiar with the Simplex Method for linear programming which is fully described, for example, in *Linear Programming in Pascal* by the authors.) The pivot elements have been asterisked.

| Basis | Value | $x_1$ | $x_2$ | $y_1$ | $y_2$ | $\lambda_1$ | $\lambda_2$ | $u_1$ | $u_2$ | $v_1$ | $v_2$ |
|---|---|---|---|---|---|---|---|---|---|---|---|
| $v_1$ | 10 | $16^*$ | 4 | . | . | 1 | 1 | $-1$ | 0 | 1 | . |
| $v_2$ | 15 | 4 | 2 | . | . | 3 | 1 | 0 | $-1$ | . | 1 |
| $y_1$ | 9 | 1 | 3 | 1 | . | 0 | 0 | 0 | 0 | . | . |
| $y_2$ | 6 | 1 | 1 | . | 1 | 0 | 0 | 0 | 0 | . | . |
| $-z$ | $-25$ | $-20$ | $-6$ | . | . | $-4$ | $-2$ | 1 | 1 | . | . |

The most negative coefficient in the $-z$ row is that of $x_1$ $(-20)$ and the smallest of the ratios $10/16$, $15/4$, $9/1$, $6/1$ is $10/16$. Thus $x_1$ enters and $v_1$ leaves the basis.

| Basis | Value | $x_1$ | $x_2$ | $y_1$ | $y_2$ | $\lambda_1$ | $\lambda_2$ | $u_1$ | $u_2$ | $v_1$ | $v_2$ |
|---|---|---|---|---|---|---|---|---|---|---|---|
| $x_1$ | $\frac{5}{8}$ | 1 | $\frac{1}{4}^*$ | . | . | $\frac{1}{16}$ | $\frac{1}{16}$ | $-\frac{1}{16}$ | 0 | $\frac{1}{16}$ | . |
| $v_2$ | $12\frac{1}{2}$ | . | 1 | . | . | $\frac{11}{4}$ | $\frac{3}{4}$ | $\frac{1}{4}$ | $-1$ | $-\frac{1}{4}$ | 1 |
| $y_1$ | $8\frac{3}{8}$ | . | $\frac{11}{4}$ | 1 | . | $-\frac{1}{16}$ | $-\frac{1}{16}$ | $\frac{1}{16}$ | 0 | $-\frac{1}{16}$ | . |
| $y_2$ | $5\frac{3}{8}$ | . | $\frac{3}{4}$ | . | 1 | $-\frac{1}{16}$ | $-\frac{1}{16}$ | $\frac{1}{16}$ | 0 | $-\frac{1}{16}$ | . |
| $-z$ | $-12\frac{1}{2}$ | . | $-1$ | . | . | $-\frac{11}{4}$ | $-\frac{3}{4}$ | $-\frac{1}{4}$ | 1 | $\frac{5}{4}$ | . |

The most *negative* coefficient in the $-z$ row is that of $\lambda_1$. However, if we applied the simplex rules at this stage $\lambda_1$ would enter the basis and $v_2$ would leave the basis. The result would be a basis containing both $\lambda_1$ and $y_1$ and contradicting (8.22). Thus we look at the next most negative coefficient, which means that $x_2$ enters the basis and $x_1$ leaves the basis and condition (8.22) remains satisfied.

| Basis | Value | $x_1$ | $x_2$ | $y_1$ | $y_2$ | $\lambda_1$ | $\lambda_2$ | $u_1$ | $u_2$ | $v_1$ | $v_2$ |
|---|---|---|---|---|---|---|---|---|---|---|---|
| $x_2$ | $2\frac{1}{2}$ | 4 | 1 | . | . | $\frac{1}{4}$ | $\frac{1}{4}$ | $-\frac{1}{4}$ | 0 | $\frac{1}{4}$ | . |
| $v_2$ | 10 | $-4$ | . | . | . | $\frac{5}{2}$ | $\frac{1}{2}$ | $\frac{1}{2}$ | $-1$ | $-\frac{1}{2}$ | 1 |
| $y_1$ | $1\frac{1}{2}$ | $-11$ | . | 1 | . | $-\frac{3}{4}$ | $-\frac{3}{4}$ | $\frac{3}{4}*$ | 0 | $-\frac{3}{4}$ | . |
| $y_2$ | $3\frac{1}{2}$ | $-3$ | . | . | 1 | $-\frac{1}{4}$ | $-\frac{1}{4}$ | $\frac{1}{4}$ | 0 | $-\frac{1}{4}$ | . |
| $-z$ | $-10$ | 4 | . | . | . | $-\frac{5}{2}$ | $-\frac{1}{2}$ | $-\frac{1}{2}$ | 1 | $\frac{3}{2}$ | . |

$\lambda_1$ cannot enter the basis since $y_1$ is and *would remain* basic.
$\lambda_2$ cannot enter the basis since $y_2$ is and *would remain* basic.
Thus $u_1$ enters the basis and $y_1$ leaves the basis.

| Basis | Value | $x_1$ | $x_2$ | $y_1$ | $y_2$ | $\lambda_1$ | $\lambda_2$ | $u_1$ | $u_2$ | $v_1$ | $v_2$ |
|---|---|---|---|---|---|---|---|---|---|---|---|
| $x_2$ | 3 | $\frac{1}{3}$ | 1 | $\frac{1}{3}$ | . | 0 | 0 | . | 0 | 0 | . |
| $v_2$ | 9 | $\frac{10}{3}$ | . | $-\frac{2}{3}$ | . | $3*$ | 1 | . | $-1$ | 0 | 1 |
| $u_1$ | 2 | $-\frac{44}{3}$ | . | $\frac{4}{3}$ | . | $-1$ | $-1$ | 1 | 0 | $-1$ | . |
| $y_2$ | 3 | $\frac{2}{3}$ | . | $-\frac{1}{3}$ | 1 | 0 | 0 | . | 0 | 0 | . |
| $-z$ | $-9$ | $-\frac{10}{3}$ | . | $\frac{2}{3}$ | . | $-3$ | $-1$ | . | 1 | 1 | . |

$x_1$ cannot enter the basis since $u_1$ is and would remain basic.
Thus $\lambda_1$ enters the basis and $v_2$ leaves the basis.

| Basis | Value | $x_1$ | $x_2$ | $y_1$ | $y_2$ | $\lambda_1$ | $\lambda_2$ | $u_1$ | $u_2$ | $v_1$ | $v_2$ |
|---|---|---|---|---|---|---|---|---|---|---|---|
| $x_2$ | 3 | $\frac{1}{3}$ | 1 | $\frac{1}{3}$ | . | . | 0 | . | 0 | 0 | 0 |
| $\lambda_1$ | 3 | $\frac{10}{9}$ | . | $-\frac{2}{9}$ | . | 1 | $\frac{1}{3}$ | . | $-\frac{1}{3}$ | 0 | $\frac{1}{3}$ |
| $u_1$ | 5 | $-\frac{122}{9}$ | . | $\frac{10}{9}$ | . | . | $-\frac{2}{3}$ | 1 | $-\frac{1}{3}$ | $-1$ | $\frac{1}{3}$ |
| $y_2$ | 3 | $\frac{2}{3}$ | . | $-\frac{1}{3}$ | 1 | . | 0 | . | 0 | 0 | 0 |
| $-z$ | 0 | 0 | . | 0 | . | . | 0 | . | 0 | 1 | 1 |

This gives the optimal solution in which both $v_1$ and $v_2$ are zero and the corresponding values $x_1 = 0$, $x_2 = 3$, $y_1 = 0$, $y_2 = 3$, $\lambda_1 = 3$, $\lambda_2 = 0$, $u_1 = 5$, $u_2 = 0$ satisfy all of the conditions (8.21) and (8.22).

Thus subject to the constraints, $f(x_1, x_2)$ has a minimum value of $-36$ when $x_1 = 0$ and $x_2 = 3$.

**Example 2**
Find $x_1$, $x_2 \geqslant 0$ which minimise

$$f(x_1, x_2) = 6x_1^2 + 5x_1x_2 + 5x_2^2 - 8x_1 + 10x_2$$

when $x_1 + x_2 \geqslant 6$.

We rewrite the constraint in " $\leqslant$ " form. This is a necessary requirement for the corresponding Lagrange multiplier to be non-negative. Thus

$$-x_1 - x_2 \leqslant -6$$

and the Kuhn–Tucker conditions are

$$
\begin{aligned}
12x_1 + 5x_2 &- \lambda_1 - u_1 &&= 8 \\
5x_1 + 10x_2 &- \lambda_1 &- u_2 &= -10 \\
-x_1 - x_2 + y_1 & && = -6
\end{aligned}
$$

(8.23)

where $\quad x_1, x_2, y_1, \lambda_1, u_1, u_2 \geqslant 0 \quad$ and $\quad \lambda_1 y_1 = x_1 u_1 = x_2 u_2 = 0.$   (8.24)

We first multiply the second and third linear constraints by $-1$ so that the right hand side values are all positive. Then we introduce non-negative variables $v_1, v_2, v_3$ and proceed with the minimisation of $z = v_1 + v_2 + v_3$ subject to the modified linear constraints and (8.24). A first basic feasible solution is provided by $v_1 = 8$, $v_2 = 10$ and $v_3 = 6$. The successive tableaux are shown.

| Basis | Value | $x_1$ | $x_2$ | $y_1$ | $\lambda_1$ | $u_1$ | $u_2$ | $v_1$ | $v_2$ | $v_3$ |
|---|---|---|---|---|---|---|---|---|---|---|
| $v_1$ | 8 | $12^*$ | 5 | 0 | $-1$ | $-1$ | 0 | 1 | . | . |
| $v_2$ | 10 | $-5$ | $-10$ | 0 | 1 | 0 | 1 | . | 1 | . |
| $v_3$ | 6 | 1 | 1 | $-1$ | 0 | 0 | 0 | . | . | 1 |
| $-z$ | $-24$ | $-8$ | 4 | 1 | 0 | 1 | $-1$ | . | . | . |

$x_1$ enters the basis and $v_1$ leaves the basis in the usual way.

| | | | | | | | | | | |
|---|---|---|---|---|---|---|---|---|---|---|
| $x_1$ | $\frac{2}{3}$ | 1 | $\frac{5}{12}$ | 0 | $-\frac{1}{12}$ | $-\frac{1}{12}$ | 0 | $\frac{1}{12}$ | . | . |
| $v_2$ | $\frac{40}{3}$ | . | $-\frac{95}{12}$ | 0 | $\frac{7}{12}$ | $-\frac{5}{12}$ | $1^*$ | $\frac{5}{12}$ | 1 | . |
| $v_3$ | $\frac{16}{3}$ | . | $\frac{7}{12}$ | $-1$ | $\frac{1}{12}$ | $\frac{1}{12}$ | 0 | $-\frac{1}{12}$ | . | 1 |
| $-z$ | $-\frac{56}{3}$ | . | $\frac{22}{3}$ | 1 | $-\frac{2}{3}$ | $\frac{1}{3}$ | $-1$ | $\frac{2}{3}$ | . | . |

$u_2$ enters the basis and $v_2$ leaves the basis in the usual way.

| | | | | | | | | | | |
|---|---|---|---|---|---|---|---|---|---|---|
| $x_1$ | $\frac{2}{3}$ | 1 | $\frac{5}{12}$ | 0 | $-\frac{1}{12}$ | $-\frac{1}{12}$ | . | $\frac{1}{12}$ | 0 | . |
| $u_2$ | $\frac{40}{3}$ | . | $-\frac{95}{12}$ | 0 | $\frac{7}{12}^*$ | $-\frac{5}{12}$ | 1 | $\frac{5}{12}$ | 1 | . |
| $v_3$ | $\frac{16}{3}$ | . | $\frac{7}{12}$ | $-1$ | $\frac{1}{12}$ | $\frac{1}{12}$ | . | $-\frac{1}{12}$ | 0 | 1 |
| $-z$ | $-\frac{16}{3}$ | . | $-\frac{7}{12}$ | 1 | $-\frac{1}{12}$ | $-\frac{1}{12}$ | . | $\frac{13}{12}$ | 1 | . |

$x_2$ cannot enter the basis since $u_2$ is and would remain basic. $\lambda_1$ enters the basis and $u_2$ becomes non-basic.

| | | | | | | | | | | |
|---|---|---|---|---|---|---|---|---|---|---|
| $x_1$ | $\frac{18}{7}$ | 1 | $-\frac{5}{7}$ | 0 | . | $-\frac{1}{7}$ | $\frac{1}{7}$ | $\frac{1}{7}$ | $\frac{1}{7}$ | . |
| $\lambda_1$ | $\frac{160}{7}$ | . | $-\frac{95}{7}$ | 0 | 1 | $-\frac{5}{7}$ | $\frac{12}{7}$ | $\frac{5}{7}$ | $\frac{12}{7}$ | . |
| $v_3$ | $\frac{24}{7}$ | . | $\frac{12}{7}^*$ | $-1$ | . | $\frac{1}{7}$ | $-\frac{1}{7}$ | $-\frac{1}{7}$ | $-\frac{1}{7}$ | 1 |
| $-z$ | $-\frac{24}{7}$ | . | $-\frac{12}{7}$ | 1 | . | $-\frac{1}{7}$ | $\frac{1}{7}$ | $\frac{8}{7}$ | $\frac{8}{7}$ | . |

$x_2$ enters the basis and $v_3$ leaves the basis.

| | | | | | | | | | | |
|---|---|---|---|---|---|---|---|---|---|---|
| $x_1$ | 4 | 1 | . | $-\frac{5}{12}$ | . | $-\frac{1}{12}$ | $\frac{1}{12}$ | $\frac{1}{12}$ | $\frac{1}{12}$ | $\frac{5}{12}$ |
| $\lambda_1$ | 50 | . | . | $-\frac{95}{12}$ | 1 | $\frac{5}{12}$ | $\frac{7}{12}$ | $-\frac{5}{12}$ | $\frac{7}{12}$ | $\frac{95}{12}$ |
| $x_2$ | 2 | . | 1 | $\frac{7}{12}$ | . | $\frac{1}{12}$ | $-\frac{1}{12}$ | $-\frac{1}{12}$ | $-\frac{1}{12}$ | $\frac{7}{12}$ |
| $-z$ | 0 | . | . | 0 | . | 0 | 0 | 1 | 1 | 1 |

This gives the optimal solution and the values $x_1 = 4$, $x_2 = 2$, $\lambda_1 = 50$ satisfy all the Kuhn–Tucker conditions. The constrained minimum of $f(x_1, x_2)$ is 144.

## 8.3 A Computer Program for Wolfe's Method

The program which follows implements Wolfe's method. The first data value is an integer which indicates whether or not all the intermediate working will be output as illustrated in the examples. A non-positive value suppresses this output. Otherwise the output is very similar to the working we obtain when solving the problem by hand. For large problems the output may overflow one line of a VDU screen or printer.

The appropriate values of $n$ and $m$ together with the value of $n + m$ and $3(n + m)$ will have been set in the program CONST declaration before compilation.

For the first $n$ constraints, the elements in each successive row of the upper triangle of the matrix **G** are input, followed by the corresponding element of the vector **c**. Next come the further $m$ constraints, row by row, with elements $a_{ij}$ preceding $b_i$. All input is handled by the PROCEDURE *inputdata*.

The initial tableau is completed by the PROCEDURE *completetableau*. If the objective function is $\frac{1}{2}\mathbf{x}^T\mathbf{G}\mathbf{x} - \mathbf{c}^T\mathbf{x}$ and the linear constraints are $\mathbf{A}\mathbf{x} \leqslant \mathbf{b}$ where **b** and **c** are non-negative we construct the tableau below:

| Column No. | | $1 \dots n$ | $n + 1 \dots n + m$ | $n + m + 1 \dots n + 2m$ | $\dots 2(n + m)$ | $\dots 3n + 2m$ |
|---|---|---|---|---|---|---|
| Constraint | Value | $x[1] \dots x[n]$ | $y[1] \dots y[m]$ | $\lambda[1] \dots \lambda[m]$ | $u[1] \dots u[n]$ | $v[1] \dots v[n]$ |
| 1 | | | | | | |
| 2 | | | | | | |
| $\vdots$ | **c** | **G** | **0** | $\mathbf{A}^T$ | $-\mathbf{I}_n$ | $\mathbf{I}_n$ |
| $n$ | | | | | | |
| $n + 1$ | | | | | | |
| $\vdots$ | **b** | **A** | $\mathbf{I}_m$ | **0** | **0** | **0** |
| $n + m$ | | | | | | |
| $-z$ | Negative sum for each column over rows containing artificial basic variables $v_i$ | | | | | 0 |

For any negative $c_i$ the value is negated, as is the $-1$ in each of the $u$-columns. Otherwise the $i$th row of the matrix **G** is negated together with the $i$th row of **A** in the $\lambda$-columns. For any negative $b_i$, the value is negated as is the $i$th row of **A** in the $x$-columns. In this case an additional artificial variable becoming the base variable for the $i$th row is added and the artificial objective function modified accordingly. Otherwise the base variable is $y_i$.

The boolean array *nonbasic* contains the status of each variable, the vector *basic* contains the column numbers of the basic variables in each row and the vectors $x$, $y$, *lambda,* $u$ and $v$ contain the column numbers in the tableau for the respective variables. The FUNCTION *varchar* and the FUNCTION *varindex* convert from column number to actual variable type and index respectively.

The procedure *nextbasicvariable* finds the variables to enter and leave the basis by the usual simplex rules. However, we check that the conditions (8.13) and (8.14) are satisfied and if not make a different choice of variable to enter the basis. The elements of the boolean array *prohibited* prevent repetition of a previously excluded variable. The value of *pindex* identifies the variable complementary to that chosen for entry to the basis. Not more than one of this pair is allowed to be basic. The chosen variable cannot be admitted to the basis if the complementary variable is already basic and is not the one to be replaced.

Following the program listing the output of the program when used to solve examples 1 and 2 is given. As can be seen it virtually reproduces the earlier calculations.

```
PROGRAM Wolfe (input,output);
CONST
   n=2;   m=2;          { No. of original variables and constraints }    {**}
   nplusm=4;            { n+m }                                          {**}
   threenplusm=12;  { 3*(n+m) }                                         {**}
   fwt=6; dpt=2;        { Output format constants for tableau values }   {**}
   fwi=1;               { Output format constant for variable indices }  {**}

TYPE  nrange = 1..n;  mrange = 1..m;  nplusmrange = 1..nplusm;
   vector = ARRAY [nrange] OF real;  matrix = ARRAY [nrange] OF vector;
   row = ARRAY [1..threenplusm] OF real;
   tableau = ARRAY [nplusmrange] OF row;
   column = ARRAY [nplusmrange] OF real;
   baseindex = ARRAY [nplusmrange] OF integer;
   rowboolean = ARRAY [1..threenplusm] OF boolean;
   nindex = ARRAY [nrange] OF integer;  mindex = ARRAY [mrange] OF integer;
VAR
   t : tableau;                   { Tableau of values }
   rhs : column;                  { Right hand side of constraints }
   basic : baseindex;             { Indices of basic variables }
   nonbasic : rowboolean;         { Basic/non-basic status of variables }
   c : vector;                    { Vector c in Equation (8.3) }
   G : matrix;                    { Matrix G in Equation (8.3) }
   zminus : row;                  { Column sums over artificial variables }
   x, u, v : nindex;              { Indices of the columns in the tableau }
   y, lambda, vextra : mindex;    { corresponding to the variables        }
   it, rowlength,                 { No. of iterations and effective row }
                                  { length of tableau                   }
   new, old : integer;            { Indices of new and old basic variable }
   rhsneg : real;                 { Sum of rhs over artificial variables }
   solution,                      { Indicates when solution has been found }
   printon : boolean;             { Output suppression indicator }
   i, j : integer;  obj : real;  xvec : vector;
```

```
PROCEDURE initialise;
VAR  i, k : integer;  zero : row;
BEGIN  rowlength := 3*n+2*m;
  { Set modifying index, i.e. column number, for each variable }
  FOR i:=1 TO n DO x[i]:=i;  k:=n;  FOR i:=1 TO m DO y[i]:=k+i;  k:=k+m;
  FOR i:=1 TO m DO lambda[i]:=k+i;  k:=k+m;  FOR i:=1 TO n DO u[i]:=k+i;
  k:=k+n;  FOR i:=1 TO n DO v[i]:=k+i;  k:=k+n;
  FOR i:=1 TO m DO vextra[i]:=k+i;
  { Zeroise tableau }
  FOR i:=1 TO threenplusm DO zero[i]:=0.0;
  FOR i:=1 TO nplusm DO t[i]:=zero;  zminus:=zero;
  { Set unit matrices within tableau }
  FOR i:=1 TO n DO
  BEGIN  t[i,u[i]]:=1.0;  t[i,v[i]]:=1.0 END;
  FOR i:=1 TO m DO t[y[i],y[i]]:=1.0;  it:=0;  solution:=false
END;  { initialise }



PROCEDURE inputdata;
VAR  i, j, p : integer;  val : real;
BEGIN  read(p);  printon := p>0;  { p<=0 suppresses intermediate output }
  FOR i:=1 TO n DO  { Input coefficients of matrix G and vector c }
  BEGIN
    FOR j:=x[i] TO x[n] DO
      BEGIN read(val); t[i,j]:=val; t[j,i]:=val;
            G[i,j]:=val; G[j,i]:=val
      END;  read(rhs[i]);  c[i]:=rhs[i]
  END;
  FOR i:=1 TO m DO  { Input coefficients of matrix A and vector b }
  BEGIN FOR j:=1 TO n DO
        BEGIN read(val); t[n+i,j]:=val; t[j,lambda[i]]:=val END;
    read(rhs[n+i])
  END
END;  { inputdata }



PROCEDURE completetableau;
VAR  i, j, vindex : integer; sum : real;
  PROCEDURE negate (VAR x:real);
  BEGIN  x:=-x END;  { negate }
BEGIN
  { Ensure all right hand sides are positive and set initial base variables }
  FOR i:=1 TO n DO
  BEGIN IF rhs[i] < 0.0 THEN BEGIN negate(rhs[i]); negate(t[i,u[i]]) END
        ELSE
        BEGIN FOR j:=x[1] TO x[n] DO negate(t[i,j]);
              FOR j:=lambda[1] TO lambda[m] DO negate(t[i,j])
        END;
    basic[i] := v[i]
  END;  vindex := vextra[1]-1;
  FOR i:=n+1 TO nplusm DO
    IF rhs[i] < 0.0 THEN
```

```
    BEGIN negate(rhs[i]);   FOR j:=1 TO nplusm DO negate(t[i,j]);
      vindex := vindex+1;   basic[i] := vindex;
      t[i,vindex] :=1.0;   rowlength := vindex
    END
    ELSE   basic[i] := y[i-n];
  { Compute column sums over artificial variables }
  FOR j:=1 TO 2*nplusm DO
  BEGIN   sum:=0.0;
    FOR i:=1 TO nplusm DO IF basic[i]>=v[1] THEN sum := sum + t[i,j];
    zminus[j] := -sum
  END;   sum := 0.0;
  FOR i:=1 TO nplusm DO IF basic[i]>=v[1] THEN sum := sum + rhs[i];
  rhsneg := -sum;
  FOR j:=1 TO rowlength DO nonbasic[j]:=true; { Set status of variables }
  FOR i:=1 TO nplusm DO nonbasic[basic[i]]:=false
END;   { completetableau }


FUNCTION varchar (k:integer): char;
{ Returns the character of the variable in column k }
BEGIN   IF k<=n THEN varchar:='X'
        ELSE IF k<=nplusm THEN varchar:='Y'
             ELSE IF k<=n+2*m THEN varchar:='L'
                  ELSE IF k<=2*nplusm THEN varchar:='U' ELSE varchar:='V'
END;   { varchar }


FUNCTION varindex (k:integer): integer;
{ Returns the index of the variable in column k }
BEGIN   IF k > 2*nplusm THEN k := k - 2*nplusm
        ELSE IF k > nplusm THEN IF k > nplusm+m THEN k := k - nplusm - m
                                                ELSE k := k - nplusm
                     ELSE IF k > n THEN k := k - n;
  varindex := k
END;   { varindex }



PROCEDURE nextbasicvariable (VAR next, last : integer);
{ Computes the values of next and last, the indices, respectively, of }
{ the next variable to enter the basis and the variable it replaces.  }
CONST   smallvalue = 1.0E-6;   largevalue = 1.0E20;
VAR   i, j, minindex, maxindex, pindex : integer;   min, max, ratio : real;
      found : boolean;   prohibited : rowboolean;
BEGIN   min := -smallvalue;   found := false;
  FOR j:=1 TO rowlength DO prohibited[j] := false;
  WHILE NOT found DO
  BEGIN   minindex:=0;   maxindex:=0;
    FOR j:=1 TO rowlength DO { Find most -ve coefficient in '-z' row }
      IF nonbasic[j] AND NOT prohibited[j] THEN
       'IF zminus[j] < min THEN BEGIN min:=zminus[j]; minindex:=j END;
    IF minindex=0 THEN
      IF abs(rhsneg) < smallvalue THEN   { Solution found }
      BEGIN   found:=true;   solution:=true   END
      ELSE BEGIN IF min<0.0 THEN min:=smallvalue END
    ELSE
```

```
  BEGIN  { Find ´paired´ variable from Equations (8.13) and (8.14) }
    pindex := varindex(minindex);
    CASE varchar(minindex) OF
       ´X´: pindex:=u[pindex];  ´Y´: pindex:=lambda[pindex];
       ´L´: pindex:=y[pindex];  ´U´: pindex:=x[pindex];
       ´V´: pindex:=v[pindex]
    END;
    { Find basic variable to be replaced }
    max:=largevalue;
    FOR i:=1 TO nplusm DO
      IF t[i,minindex] > smallvalue THEN
      BEGIN  ratio := rhs[i]/t[i,minindex];
        IF ratio < max THEN BEGIN max:=ratio; maxindex:=i END
      END;
    { Attempt to replace old basic variable with new basic variable }
    IF maxindex=0 THEN  { No replacement found }
    BEGIN  prohibited[minindex]:=true;  min := -smallvalue  END
    ELSE
      IF nonbasic[pindex] OR (pindex=basic[maxindex]) THEN
      BEGIN  { Basic variable can be replaced }
        IF printon THEN
           writeln(´      ´, varchar(minindex), varindex(minindex):fwi,
                    ´ ENTERS´BASIS, ´, varchar(basic[maxindex]),
                    varindex(basic[maxindex]):fwi,
                    ´ BECOMES A NON-BASIC VARIABLE´);
        nonbasic[basic[maxindex]] := true;  basic[maxindex] := minindex;
        nonbasic[minindex] := false;  found := true
      END
      ELSE  { Variable cannot enter basis }
      BEGIN
        IF printon THEN
           writeln(´      ´, varchar(minindex), varindex(minindex):fwi,
                    ´ CANNOT ENTER BASIS SINCE ´, varchar(pindex),
                    varindex(pindex):fwi, ´ IS A BASIC VARIABLE´);
        prohibited[minindex] := true;  min := -smallvalue
      END
    END
  END;
  next := minindex;  last := maxindex
END;  { nextbasicvariable }



PROCEDURE outputtableau;
VAR  i, j : integer;
  PROCEDURE varheading (ch:char; k:integer);
  VAR  i : integer;
  BEGIN FOR i:=1 TO k DO write(´ ´:fwt-fwi-1,ch,i:fwi) END; { varheading }
BEGIN writeln; writeln(´     ITERATION ´, it:2);
  write(´     BASIC VAR.    VALUE´, ´ ´:fwt-5);  varheading(´X´,n);
  varheading(´Y´,m);  varheading(´L´,m);  varheading(´U´,n);
  varheading(´V´, rowlength-2*nplusm);  writeln;
  FOR i:=1 TO nplusm DO
```

```
    BEGIN  write(´ ´:8, varchar(basic[i]), varindex(basic[i]):fwi,
                 ´ ´:6, rhs[i]:fwt:dpt, ´ ´);
      FOR j:=1 TO rowlength DO write(t[i,j]:fwt:dpt);  writeln
    END;  write(´ ´:8, ´-Z´, ´ ´:6, rhsneg:fwt:dpt, ´ ´);
      FOR j:=1 TO rowlength DO write(zminus[j]:fwt:dpt);  writeln;  writeln
END;  { outputtableau }



PROCEDURE transformtableau (next, last : integer);
{ Compute new tableau values to reflect change of basis }
VAR  i, j : integer;  pivot, savez : real;  savecol : column;
BEGIN
    pivot := t[last,next];  rhs[last] := rhs[last]/pivot;
    FOR j:=1 TO rowlength DO t[last,j] := t[last,j]/pivot;
    FOR i:=1 TO nplusm DO savecol[i]:=t[i,next];  savez:=zminus[next];
    FOR i:=1 TO nplusm DO
      IF i<>last THEN
      BEGIN  rhs[i] := rhs[i] - savecol[i]*rhs[last];
        FOR j:=1 TO rowlength DO
            t[i,j] := t[i,j] - savecol[i]*t[last,j];
      END;
    FOR j:=1 TO rowlength DO zminus[j] := zminus[j] - savez*t[last,j];
    rhsneg := rhsneg - savez*rhs[last];  it := it+1
END;  { transformtableau }



BEGIN  { Main Program }
    writeln;  writeln(´     QUADRATIC PROGRAMMING - WOLFE´´S METHOD´);
    writeln;  initialise;  inputdata;  completetableau;
    REPEAT
      IF printon THEN outputtableau;
      nextbasicvariable(new,old);
      IF NOT solution THEN transformtableau(new,old)
    UNTIL solution;
    { Output final solution }
    writeln;  writeln(´     FINAL SOLUTION´);  writeln;
    writeln(´     BASIC VAR.    VALUE´);  writeln;
    FOR j:=1 TO nplusm DO
    BEGIN  writeln(´ ´:8, varchar(basic[j]), varindex(basic[j]):fwi,
                   ´ ´:6, rhs[j]:fwt:dpt)
    END;  writeln;
    writeln(´     MINIMUM OF Z = ´, rhsneg:fwt:dpt);  writeln;
    FOR i:=1 TO n DO xvec[i]:=0.0;
    FOR i:=1 TO nplusm do { Search for x´s in basic variables }
      IF varchar(basic[i]) = ´X´ THEN xvec[varindex(basic[i])] := rhs[i];
    obj:=0.0;  { Compute value of objective function }
    FOR i:=1 TO n DO
      FOR j:=1 TO n DO obj := obj + xvec[i]*G[i,j]*xvec[j];
    obj := 0.5*obj;    FOR i:=1 TO n DO obj := obj + xvec[i]*c[i];
    writeln(´     MINIMUM OF OBJECTIVE FUNCTION = ´, obj:fwt:dpt)
END.  { Wolfe }
```

QUADRATIC PROGRAMMING - WOLFE'S METHOD

ITERATION   0

| BASIC VAR. | VALUE | X1 | X2 | Y1 | Y2 | L1 | L2 | U1 | U2 | V1 | V2 |
|---|---|---|---|---|---|---|---|---|---|---|---|
| V1 | 10.00 | 16.00 | 4.00 | 0.00 | 0.00 | 1.00 | 1.00 | -1.00 | 0.00 | 1.00 | 0.00 |
| V2 | 15.00 | 4.00 | 2.00 | 0.00 | 0.00 | 3.00 | 1.00 | 0.00 | -1.00 | 0.00 | 1.00 |
| Y1 | 9.00 | 1.00 | 3.00 | 1.00 | 0.00 | 0.00 | 0.00 | 0.00 | 0.00 | 0.00 | 0.00 |
| Y2 | 6.00 | 1.00 | 1.00 | 0.00 | 1.00 | 0.00 | 0.00 | 0.00 | 0.00 | 0.00 | 0.00 |
| -Z | -25.00 | -20.00 | -6.00 | 0.00 | 0.00 | -4.00 | -2.00 | 1.00 | 1.00 | 0.00 | 0.00 |

X1 ENTERS BASIS, V1 BECOMES A NON-BASIC VARIABLE

ITERATION   1

| BASIC VAR. | VALUE | X1 | X2 | Y1 | Y2 | L1 | L2 | U1 | U2 | V1 | V2 |
|---|---|---|---|---|---|---|---|---|---|---|---|
| X1 | 0.62 | 1.00 | 0.25 | 0.00 | 0.00 | 0.06 | 0.06 | -0.06 | 0.00 | 0.06 | 0.00 |
| V2 | 12.50 | 0.00 | 1.00 | 0.00 | 0.00 | 2.75 | 0.75 | 0.25 | -1.00 | -0.25 | 1.00 |
| Y1 | 8.37 | 0.00 | 2.75 | 1.00 | 0.00 | -0.06 | -0.06 | 0.06 | 0.00 | -0.06 | 0.00 |
| Y2 | 5.37 | 0.00 | 0.75 | 0.00 | 1.00 | -0.06 | -0.06 | 0.06 | 0.00 | -0.06 | 0.00 |
| -Z | -12.50 | 0.00 | -1.00 | 0.00 | 0.00 | -2.75 | -0.75 | -0.25 | 1.00 | 1.25 | 0.00 |

L1 CANNOT ENTER BASIS SINCE Y1 IS A BASIC VARIABLE
X2 ENTERS BASIS, X1 BECOMES A NON-BASIC VARIABLE

ITERATION   2

| BASIC VAR. | VALUE | X1 | X2 | Y1 | Y2 | L1 | L2 | U1 | U2 | V1 | V2 |
|---|---|---|---|---|---|---|---|---|---|---|---|
| X2 | 2.50 | 4.00 | 1.00 | 0.00 | 0.00 | 0.25 | 0.25 | -0.25 | 0.00 | 0.25 | 0.00 |
| V2 | 10.00 | -4.00 | 0.00 | 0.00 | 0.00 | 2.50 | 0.50 | 0.50 | -1.00 | -0.50 | 1.00 |
| Y1 | 1.50 | -11.00 | 0.00 | 1.00 | 0.00 | -0.75 | -0.75 | 0.75 | 0.00 | -0.75 | 0.00 |
| Y2 | 3.50 | -3.00 | 0.00 | 0.00 | 1.00 | -0.25 | -0.25 | 0.25 | 0.00 | -0.25 | 0.00 |
| -Z | -10.00 | 4.00 | 0.00 | 0.00 | 0.00 | -2.50 | -0.50 | -0.50 | 1.00 | 1.50 | 0.00 |

L1 CANNOT ENTER BASIS SINCE Y1 IS A BASIC VARIABLE
L2 CANNOT ENTER BASIS SINCE Y2 IS A BASIC VARIABLE
U1 ENTERS BASIS, Y1 BECOMES A NON-BASIC VARIABLE

ITERATION   3

| BASIC VAR. | VALUE | X1 | X2 | Y1 | Y2 | L1 | L2 | U1 | U2 | V1 | V2 |
|---|---|---|---|---|---|---|---|---|---|---|---|
| X2 | 3.00 | 0.33 | 1.00 | 0.33 | 0.00 | 0.00 | 0.00 | 0.00 | 0.00 | 0.00 | 0.00 |
| V2 | -9.00 | 3.33 | 0.00 | -0.67 | 0.00 | 3.00 | 1.00 | 0.00 | -1.00 | 0.00 | 1.00 |
| U1 | 2.00 | -14.67 | 0.00 | 1.33 | 0.00 | -1.00 | -1.00 | 1.00 | 0.00 | -1.00 | 0.00 |
| Y2 | 3.00 | 0.67 | 0.00 | -0.33 | 1.00 | 0.00 | 0.00 | 0.00 | 0.00 | 0.00 | 0.00 |
| -Z | -9.00 | -3.33 | 0.00 | 0.67 | 0.00 | -3.00 | -1.00 | 0.00 | 1.00 | 1.00 | 0.00 |

X1 CANNOT ENTER BASIS SINCE U1 IS A BASIC VARIABLE
L1 ENTERS BASIS, V2 BECOMES A NON-BASIC VARIABLE

ITERATION   4

| BASIC VAR. | VALUE | X1 | X2 | Y1 | Y2 | L1 | L2 | U1 | U2 | V1 | V2 |
|---|---|---|---|---|---|---|---|---|---|---|---|
| X2 | 3.00 | 0.33 | 1.00 | 0.33 | 0.00 | 0.00 | 0.00 | 0.00 | 0.00 | 0.00 | 0.00 |
| L1 | 3.00 | 1.11 | 0.00 | -0.22 | 0.00 | 1.00 | 0.33 | 0.00 | -0.33 | 0.00 | 0.33 |
| U1 | 5.00 | -13.56 | 0.00 | 1.11 | 0.00 | 0.00 | -0.67 | 1.00 | -0.33 | -1.00 | 0.33 |
| Y2 | 3.00 | 0.67 | 0.00 | -0.33 | 1.00 | 0.00 | 0.00 | 0.00 | 0.00 | 0.00 | 0.00 |
| -Z | 0.00 | 0.00 | 0.00 | 0.00 | 0.00 | 0.00 | 0.00 | 0.00 | 0.00 | 1.00 | 1.00 |

FINAL SOLUTION

BASIC VAR.    VALUE

| BASIC VAR. | VALUE |
|---|---|
| X2 | 3.00 |
| L1 | 3.00 |
| U1 | 5.00 |
| Y2 | 3.00 |

MINIMUM OF Z =   0.00

MINIMUM OF OBJECTIVE FUNCTION = −36.00

QUADRATIC PROGRAMMING − WOLFE'S METHOD

ITERATION   0

| BASIC VAR. | VALUE | X1 | X2 | Y1 | L1 | U1 | U2 | V1 | V2 | V3 |
|---|---|---|---|---|---|---|---|---|---|---|
| V1 | 8.00 | 12.00 | 5.00 | 0.00 | −1.00 | −1.00 | 0.00 | 1.00 | 0.00 | 0.00 |
| V2 | 10.00 | −5.00 | −10.00 | 0.00 | 1.00 | 0.00 | 1.00 | 0.00 | 1.00 | 0.00 |
| V3 | 6.00 | 1.00 | 1.00 | −1.00 | 0.00 | 0.00 | 0.00 | 0.00 | 0.00 | 1.00 |
| −Z | −24.00 | −8.00 | 4.00 | 1.00 | 0.00 | 1.00 | −1.00 | 0.00 | 0.00 | 0.00 |

X1 ENTERS BASIS, V1 BECOMES A NON−BASIC VARIABLE

ITERATION   1

| BASIC VAR. | VALUE | X1 | X2 | Y1 | L1 | U1 | U2 | V1 | V2 | V3 |
|---|---|---|---|---|---|---|---|---|---|---|
| X1 | 0.67 | 1.00 | 0.42 | 0.00 | −0.08 | −0.08 | 0.00 | 0.08 | 0.00 | 0.00 |
| V2 | 13.33 | 0.00 | −7.92 | 0.00 | 0.58 | −0.42 | 1.00 | 0.42 | 1.00 | 0.00 |
| V3 | 5.33 | 0.00 | 0.58 | −1.00 | 0.08 | 0.08 | 0.00 | −0.08 | 0.00 | 1.00 |
| −Z | −18.67 | 0.00 | 7.33 | 1.00 | −0.67 | 0.33 | −1.00 | 0.67 | 0.00 | 0.00 |

U2 ENTERS BASIS, V2 BECOMES A NON−BASIC VARIABLE

ITERATION   2

| BASIC VAR. | VALUE | X1 | X2 | Y1 | L1 | U1 | U2 | V1 | V2 | V3 |
|---|---|---|---|---|---|---|---|---|---|---|
| X1 | 0.67 | 1.00 | 0.42 | 0.00 | −0.08 | −0.08 | 0.00 | 0.08 | 0.00 | 0.00 |
| U2 | 13.33 | 0.00 | −7.92 | 0.00 | 0.58 | −0.42 | 1.00 | 0.42 | 1.00 | 0.00 |
| V3 | 5.33 | 0.00 | 0.58 | −1.00 | 0.08 | 0.08 | 0.00 | −0.08 | 0.00 | 1.00 |
| −Z | −5.33 | 0.00 | −0.58 | 1.00 | −0.08 | −0.08 | 0.00 | 1.08 | 1.00 | 0.00 |

X2 CANNOT ENTER BASIS SINCE U2 IS A BASIC VARIABLE
L1 ENTERS BASIS, U2 BECOMES A NON−BASIC VARIABLE

ITERATION   3

| BASIC VAR. | VALUE | X1 | X2 | Y1 | L1 | U1 | U2 | V1 | V2 | V3 |
|---|---|---|---|---|---|---|---|---|---|---|
| X1 | 2.57 | 1.00 | −0.71 | 0.00 | 0.00 | −0.14 | 0.14 | 0.14 | 0.14 | 0.00 |
| L1 | 22.86 | 0.00 | −13.57 | 0.00 | 1.00 | −0.71 | 1.71 | 0.71 | 1.71 | 0.00 |
| V3 | 3.43 | 0.00 | 1.71 | −1.00 | 0.00 | 0.14 | −0.14 | −0.14 | −0.14 | 1.00 |
| −Z | −3.43 | 0.00 | −1.71 | 1.00 | 0.00 | −0.14 | 0.14 | 1.14 | 1.14 | 0.00 |

X2 ENTERS BASIS, V3 BECOMES A NON-BASIC VARIABLE

ITERATION 4

| BASIC VAR. | VALUE | X1 | X2 | Y1 | L1 | U1 | U2 | V1 | V2 | V3 |
|---|---|---|---|---|---|---|---|---|---|---|
| X1 | 4.00 | 1.00 | 0.00 | -0.42 | 0.00 | -0.08 | 0.08 | 0.08 | 0.08 | 0.42 |
| L1 | 50.00 | 0.00 | 0.00 | -7.92 | 1.00 | 0.42 | 0.58 | -0.42 | 0.58 | 7.92 |
| X2 | 2.00 | 0.00 | 1.00 | -0.58 | 0.00 | 0.08 | -0.08 | -0.08 | -0.08 | 0.58 |
| -Z | 0.00 | 0.00 | 0.00 | 0.00 | 0.00 | 0.00 | 0.00 | 1.00 | 1.00 | 1.00 |

FINAL SOLUTION

| BASIC VAR. | VALUE |
|---|---|
| X1 | 4.00 |
| L1 | 50.00 |
| X2 | 2.00 |

MINIMUM OF Z = 0.00

MINIMUM OF OBJECTIVE FUNCTION = 144.00

## 8.4  References

1  E.M.L. Beale, *Numerical methods,* in Nonlinear Programming (Ed. J. Abadie), Chapt. VII, North-Holland, 1967.
2  R. Fletcher, *A general quadratic programming algorithm*, J. Inst. Maths., **7**, 76–91, 1971.
3  P. Wolfe, *The simplex method for quadratic programming*, Econometrica, **27**, 382–398, 1959.

## Exercises 8

1  Minimise $10x_1^2 + 6x_1x_2 + 3x_2^2 - 40x_1 - 27x_2$ for $x_1, x_2 \geqslant 0$ and

$$x_1 + x_2 \leqslant 6$$
$$2x_1 + 3x_2 \leqslant 11$$

2  Minimise $3x_1^2 + x_2^2 + 8x_3^2 + 2x_1x_2 + 4x_1x_3 - 16x_1 + 10x_2 + 2x_3$ for $x_1, x_2, x_3 \geqslant 0$ and

$$x_1 + 2x_2 + 3x_3 \geqslant 10$$
$$x_1 + x_2 \leqslant 6$$

3  (a) Use Wolfe's method to minimise $x^2 + y^2$ if $x \geqslant 0, y \geqslant 0$ and $x + y \geqslant 5$.
    Compare your result and working with Exercises 6, Question 1.
  (b) Use Wolfe's method to minimise

$$3x_1^2 + 4x_1x_2 + 5x_2^2 \quad \text{for} \quad x_1, x_2 \geqslant 0$$

and $x_1 + x_2 \geqslant 4$.
Compare the result and the working with Exercises 6, Question 3 and Exercises 7, Question 1.

**4** Two different products $X$ and $Y$ are made from the same raw material and processed on the same machines. Each week 350 kg of material are available for processing. Each unit of $X$ requires 4 kg and each unit of $Y$, 5 kg of material. Each unit of $X$ requires 30 minutes of processing and each unit of $Y$ requires 20 minutes of processing and each week 200 hours of machine time are available. Manufacturing costs are $\$3x^2$ for $x$ units of $X$ and $\$4y^2$ for $y$ units of $Y$. If the net revenue excluding production costs per unit of $X$ and $Y$ is $\$340$ and $\$290$ find how many units of each should be made each week.

**5** Consult Wolfe's paper in Econometrica and study his proof that his method will terminate under certain conditions (unfortunately his notation differs from ours).

# Suggestions for Further Reading

Research on optimisation is still progressing at a rapid pace. We hope that readers will have had their appetites whetted and now be ready to move on to some more recent theoretical and computational advances in the area. The list given is a small selection from many possible books and journal papers.

P. R. Adby and M. A. H. Dempster, *Introduction to Optimisation Methods*, Chapman and Hall, 1974.

D. P. Bertsekas, 'Combined primal–dual and penalty function methods', *SIAM Journal on Control*, 13, 521–545, 1975.

D. P. Bertsekas, *Constrained Optimisation and Lagrange Multiplier Methods*, Academic Press, 1982.

B. D. Craven, *Mathematical Programming and Control Theory*, Chapman and Hall, 1978.

J. E. Dennis and J. J. Moré, 'Quasi-Newton methods, motivation and theory', *SIAM Review*, 19 46–89, 1977.

R. Fletcher, 'An ideal penalty function for constrained optimisation', *J. Inst. Maths. App.*, 15, 319–342, 1975.

P. E. Gill, W. Murray and M. H. Wainwright, *Practical Optimization*, Academic Press, 1982.

S-P. Han, 'A globally convergent method for nonlinear programming', *J. Opt. Theory App.*, 22, 297–309, 1977.

M. R. Hestenes, *Conjugate Direction Methods in Optimization*, Springer-Verlag, 1980.

D. Q. Mayne and N. Maratos, 'A first order exact penalty function algorithm for equality constrained optimisation problems', *Math. Prog.*, 16 303–324, 1979.

M. J. D. Powell, 'Some convergence properties of the conjugate gradient method', *Math. Prog.*, 11, 42–49, 1976.

M. J. D. Powell, 'Algorithms for nonlinear constraints that use Lagrangian functions', *Math. Prog.*, 14, 224–248, 1978.

M. J. D. Powell, 'A fast algorithm for nonlinearly constrained optimisation calculations', (in *Numerical Analysis*, Edited by G. A. Watson), 144–157, Springer-Verlag, 1978.

M. J. D. Powell (Editor), *Nonlinear Optimization*, Academic Press, 1982.

D. Shanno, 'Conjugate gradient methods with inexact searches', *Maths. of Op. Res.*, 3, 244–256, 1978.

# Solutions to Exercises

## Exercises 1

**1** Local max. of $\frac{4}{27}$ when $x = \frac{1}{3}$; local min. of 0 when $x = 1$.

**2** Max of $\frac{1}{2}$ when $x = 1$; min. of $-\frac{1}{2}$ when $x = -1$.

**3** Note $a \cos \theta + b \sin \theta \equiv \sqrt{(a^2 + b^2)}\cos(\theta - \alpha)$ where $\tan \alpha = b/a$.

**4** $A = r^2 \sin 2\theta(1 + \cos 2\theta)$.

**5** $f'(x)$ changes sign from $-$ve to $+$ve but $f'(0)$ is not defined.

**6** 0 when $x = 0$. $f'(x)$ changes sign from $-$ve to $+$ve but $f'(0)$ is not defined.

**7** $-1/(3\sqrt{3})$.

**9** Global min. of $-24 \cdot 3696$ at $0 \cdot 7808$, local max. of $40 \cdot 7245$ at $3 \cdot 7619$, local min. of $11 \cdot 9576$ at $5 \cdot 9572$.

**10** Min. 0 at $(0, 0)$.

**11** Max. 0 at $(0, 0, 0)$.

**15** $-2b_1 p_1 + (a_1 + a_2)p_2 + c_1 b_1 - c_2 a_2 = 0$
$(a_1 + a_2)p_1 - 2b_2 p_2 + c_2 b_2 - c_1 a_1 = 0$.

**16** $-0 \cdot 2766$ when $x = 0 \cdot 5885$.

## Exercises 2

**4** 198.

**5** $x = 0 \cdot 47$.

**6** $5 \cdot 96$; 12.

**7** $x = 0 \cdot 47$; $f(x) = 2 \cdot 32$; 11.

**9** $x = 1 \cdot 763$, $f(x) = -0 \cdot 0973$.

**10** Min. of $0 \cdot 0465$ at $(0 \cdot 2558, -0 \cdot 1163)$.

**15** $0 \cdot 5885$.

## Exercises 3

**2** (i) 0 at $(1, 2, 3)$ (ii) 0 at $(1, 1)$.

**6** (i) 0 at $(1, 1)$ (ii) 0 at $(0, 0, 0)$ (iii) 0 at $(1, 10)$.

**10** 0 at $(1, 0)$.

**11** 0 at $(3, 2)$.

**12** $(3, 2)$, $(3 \cdot 5844, -1 \cdot 8481)$, $(-3 \cdot 7793, -3 \cdot 2832)$, $(-2 \cdot 80511, 3 \cdot 1313)$.

**13** $x = 1$, $y = 2$, $z = 3$ or any permutation.

**14** $a = 31 \cdot 87$, $b = 1 \cdot 79$.

**15** (i) $\ln(a) = 3 \cdot 0296$; $(a = 20 \cdot 68)$; $n = 2 \cdot 48$. (ii) $a = 22 \cdot 3$, $n = 2 \cdot 45$.

## Exercises 4

**6** Min. 0 at $(4, -3, -0 \cdot 5)$.

**7** Min. 0 at $(0 \cdot 25, 0 \cdot 75)$.

**8** Min. 0 at $(1, 0)$.

**9** Min. 0 at $(3, 2)$. See also Exercises 3, question 12.

**10** Min. $-1$ at $(1, 1)$.

## Exercises 5

**3** $x = \dfrac{kbc}{A}$, $y = \dfrac{kac}{A}$, $z = \dfrac{kab}{A}$ where $A = ab + bc + ca$.

**5** Max. of 108 at $(1, 2, 3)$.

**7** Min. of $12 \cdot 5$ when $x = y = 2 \cdot 5$.

**8** $x = \frac{9}{14}$, $y = \frac{2}{14}$, Min. $f = -\frac{371}{196}$.

**13** Max. 70; min. 20.

**14** If $\sqrt{\alpha} + \sqrt{\beta} \leqslant S\sqrt{\gamma}$, $x_1 = \sqrt{\dfrac{\alpha}{\gamma}}$, $x_2 = \sqrt{\dfrac{\beta}{\gamma}}$.

Otherwise $x_1 = \dfrac{S\sqrt{\alpha}}{\sqrt{\alpha} + \sqrt{\beta}}$, $x_2 = \dfrac{S\sqrt{\beta}}{\sqrt{\alpha} + \sqrt{\beta}}$.

**15** $x_1 = 20$, $x_2 = 11$, $x_3 = 15$; Vol. $= 3300$.

**16** $x_1 = 24$, $x_2 = 12$, $x_3 = 12$; Vol. $= 3456$.

## Exercises 6

**1** Min. $12 \cdot 5$ when $x = y = 2 \cdot 5$.

**2** Min. $-\frac{371}{196}$ when $x = \frac{9}{14}$, $y = \frac{2}{14}$.

**3**   Min. 44 when $x_1 = 3$, $x_2 = 1$.

**5**   (a) $x_1 = 2$, $x_2 = 3$; (b) $x_1 = \frac{8}{5}$, $x_2 = \frac{12}{5}$,

**6**   Min. $-1$ when $x_1 = 3$, $x_2 = \sqrt{3}$.

**7**   $30 \cdot 24$; $x_1 = 1 \cdot 7818$, $x_2 = 4 \cdot 4898$.

**8**   $6 \cdot 2403$; $x_1 = x_2 = x_3 = 1 \cdot 4422$.

**9**   $0$; $x_1 = 3$, $x_2 = 4$.

**10**   $-28 \cdot 6153$; $x_1 = 2 \cdot 9155$, $x_2 = 4 \cdot 1231$, $x_3 = 2 \cdot 3805$.

## Exercises 7

**1**   44 when $x_1 = 3$, $x_2 = 1$.

**2**   $-9$ when $x_1 = 3$, $x_2 = 0$.

**3**   $-3456$ when $x_1 = 24$, $x_2 = 12$, $x_3 = 12$.

**4**   (a) $x_1 = 2$, $x_2 = 3$; $f = 10$ (b) $x_1 = \frac{8}{5}$, $x_2 = \frac{12}{5}$, $f = \frac{41}{4}$.

**5**   $f = 6 \cdot 2403$; $x_1 = x_2 = x_3 = 1 \cdot 4422$.

**9**   0 when $x_1 = 1$, $x_2 = 3$.

**10**   7 when $x_1 = 2$, $x_2 = \sqrt{3}$.

## Exercises 8

**1**   $x_1 = 1$, $x_2 = 3$. Min of $f(x_1, x_2) = -66$.

**2**   $x_1 = 3$, $x_2 = 2$, $x_3 = 1$. Min. of $f(x_1, x_2, x_3) = 37$.

**3**   (a) $x = y = 2 \cdot 5$. Min. is $12 \cdot 5$.
       (b) $x_1 = 3$, $x_2 = 1$. Min. is 44.

**4**   $x = 50$, $y = 30$.

# Index